DAVID O. MCKAY LIBRARY

3 1404 00778 8562

D0583894

APR 1 4 2005

WITHDRAWN

DEC 2 0 2023

DAVID O. MCKAY LIBRARY
DAVID BYU-IDAHO
REXBURG ID 83460-0405

THE COLLECTED WORKS OF

ERIC VOEGELIN

VOLUME 24

HISTORY OF POLITICAL IDEAS

VOLUME VI

REVOLUTION AND THE
NEW SCIENCE

PROJECTED VOLUMES IN THE COLLECTED WORKS

HISTORY OF POLITICAL IDEAS
Series Editor, Ellis Sandoz

EDITORIAL BOARD

Paul Caringella

Jürgen Gebhardt

Thomas A. Hollweck

Ellis Sandoz

The Editorial Board offers grateful acknowledgment to the Earhart Foundation, Liberty Fund, Robert J. Cihak, M.D., John C. Jacobs, Jr., and Hermann Moyse, Jr., for support provided at various stages in the preparation of this book for publication. A special thanks for support goes to the Charlotte and Walter Kohler Charitable Trust.

The University of Missouri Press offers its grateful acknowledgment for a generous contribution from the R. C. Kemper Charitable Trust and Foundation in support of the publication of this volume. A special thanks for support goes to the Charlotte and Walter Kohler Charitable Trust.

THE COLLECTED WORKS OF

ERIC VOEGELIN

VOLUME 24

HISTORY OF POLITICAL IDEAS

VOLUME VI

REVOLUTION AND THE
NEW SCIENCE

EDITED WITH AN INTRODUCTION BY
BARRY COOPER

UNIVERSITY OF MISSOURI PRESS

COLUMBIA AND LONDON

Copyright © 1998 by
The Curators of the University of Missouri
University of Missouri Press, Columbia, Missouri 65201
Printed and bound in the United States of America
All rights reserved

5   4   3   2   1   02   01   00   99   98

Library of Congress Cataloging-in-Publication Data
(Revised for volume VI)

Voegelin, Eric, 1901–
    [Selections, 1997]
    History of political ideas / edited with an introduction by Barry
Cooper
        p. cm. — (The collected works of Eric Voegelin ; v. 24)
    Includes index.
    Contents: v. VI. Revolution and the New Science.
    ISBN 0-8262-1126-7 (vol. I : alk. paper)
    ISBN 0-8262-1142-9 (vol. II : alk. paper)
    ISBN 0-8262-1154-2 (vol. III : alk. paper)
    ISBN 0-8262-1155-0 (vol. IV : alk. paper)
    ISBN 0-8262-1194-1 (vol. V : alk. paper)
    ISBN 0-8262-1200-X (vol. VI : alk. paper)
    ISBN 0-8262-1174-7 (set)
        1. Philosophy. 2. History—Philosophy. 3. Political science—
Philosophy. I. Cooper, Barry. II. Title. III. Series: Voegelin, Eric,
1901–   Works. 1989 ; v. 24.
    B3354.V88   1989 v. 24
    320'.09—dc21   97–13266
                                                              CIP

∞ ™ This paper meets the requirements of the
American National Standard for Permanence of Paper
for Printed Library Materials, Z39.48, 1984.

Designer: Albert Crochet
Typesetter: Bookcomp, Inc.
Printer and binder: Thomson-Shore, Inc.
Typeface: Trump Mediaeval

Grateful acknowledgment is given for permission to reprint herein an
excerpt from Eric Voegelin, *From Enlightenment to Revolution*,
ed. John H. Hallowell, Copyright © 1975 Duke University Press.

Contents

REVOLUTION AND THE NEW SCIENCE

Editor's Introduction

In writing this volume of his *History of Political Ideas*, Voegelin confronted several "methodological" questions that had been skirted, avoided, or dealt with indirectly in his treatment of the political events and the political ideas of earlier historical periods. On the basis of his systematic analysis of "the materials," *Revolution and the New Science* brought directly into focus what we now call the question of historicity. The occasion was Voegelin's discussion of Vico's *New Science* in Chapter 3 of this volume, which was substantially completed by the summer of 1941.[1] Voegelin's reflections on Vico, along with his analysis of Toynbee's *Study of History*, led eventually to his developing the concept of "historiogenesis," the final version of which was not published until 1974, in Volume IV of *Order and History*.[2] The position Voegelin reached at the end of the Vico chapter justified the opening words of his best-known book, *The New Science of Politics*: "The existence of man in political society is historical existence; and a theory of politics, if it penetrates to principles, must at the same time be a theory of history."[3] *The New Science of Politics* may well be read as an *hommage à Vico*, and in any event, the themes first brought into focus in this volume of *History of Political Ideas* were the subject matter of extended analysis over the next three decades.

As early as 1943, Voegelin had publicly indicated the proper procedural or methodological context within which *History of*

1. Voegelin to Friedrich Engel-Janosi, September 24, 1941, Voegelin Papers, Hoover Institution Archives, Stanford, box 11, file 7.
2. *The Ecumenic Age* (Baton Rouge: Louisiana State University Press, 1974), chap. 1.
3. *The New Science of Politics: An Introduction* (Chicago: University of Chicago Press, 1952), 1.

I

Political Ideas was to be situated.[4] In November of that year, the political theory panel of the Research Committee of the American Political Science Association met in Washington to discuss current research needs and achievements. Voegelin presented a report, subsequently published in the *American Political Science Review* under the title "Political Theory and the Pattern of General History."[5] Voegelin discussed "the general history of political ideas" as this topic had been presented in the existing texts by William Archibald Dunning, Charles Howard McIlwain, George H. Sabine, and Thomas Ira Cook.[6] By "general history," Voegelin meant to distinguish this category of writing from specialized monographic treatments of individual thinkers and time periods and from analyses of traditional political problems such as sovereignty, authority, constitutional government, and so on. The topics covered by a "general history," he said, were international in scope, but the literary form "is almost an American monopoly."[7] Moreover, the "general history of political ideas" was a "young science," dating, in fact, from Dunning's differentiation of his own enterprise from the work of Pierre Janet, whose standard work, *Histoire de la science politique dans ses rapports avec la morale*,[8] Dunning considered too restrictive and too parochial.

As with many such innovations, Dunning's new science was clearer about its own subject matter than about its structure. In 1944, when Voegelin's report was first published, there was even

---

4. Voegelin associated the term *methodology* with the half century of debates in Germany between the several "schools" of social science that ended in the 1920s (see *The New Science of Politics*, 10ff.). The term, therefore, must be used with caution.

5. *American Political Science Review* 38 (1944): 746–54. Voegelin's report was reprinted in Ernest S. Griffith, ed., *Research in Political Science* (Chapel Hill: University of North Carolina Press, 1948), 190–201. Citations in the text are from the *APSR* version.

6. Dunning, *A History of Political Theories, Ancient and Medieval* (New York: Macmillan, 1902), *A History of Political Theories from Luther to Montesquieu* (New York: Macmillan, 1905), and *A History of Political Theories from Rousseau to Spencer* (New York: Macmillan, 1920); McIlwain, *The Growth of Political Thought in the West: From the Greeks to the End of the Middle Ages* (New York: Macmillan, 1932); Sabine, *A History of Political Theory* (New York: Holt, Rinehart and Winston, 1937); Cook, *A History of Political Philosophy from Plato to Burke* (New York: Prentice-Hall, 1936).

7. Voegelin did not explicitly discuss why this was so, though it is clear from his analyses of American jurisprudence in *On the Form of the American Mind* that he would have found a practical and prudential motivation. See the analysis of this question in David M. Ricci, *The Tragedy of Political Science: Politics, Scholarship, and Democracy* (New Haven: Yale University Press, 1984), 67–69.

8. 3d ed., 2 vols. (Paris: Lacan, 1887).

less agreement on these matters than there had been in Dunning's day, a generation earlier. There were two reasons for this: first, there had been an enormous increase in the sheer historical evidence that a scholar was obliged to master; second, there had been a substantial revision in the understanding of the conventional structure of history. Accordingly, Voegelin wrote, it was advisable to outline "the ways in which the development of historical science has affected the more special problems of a general history of political ideas."

Historians of political ideas, as did other intellectual historians and other historians in general, conventionally considered history to be analogous to a straight line along which "mankind," the phenomenon containing and expressing the ideas, moves "in continuity through the ancient, modern and medieval phases." The theological origin of the straight-line "idea," as Voegelin explains in Chapter 1 of this book, was empirically adequate so long as one remained within the spiritual horizon and identified Christian spiritual universalism with the historical horizon of the Western world. In other words, the straight-line "idea" was persuasive only if in good conscience one might ignore parallel non-Western histories or remain ignorant of the history of the preclassical civilizations. For Voegelin, however, this position had been untenable for three hundred years, though it had not generally been questioned until, in the generation after Hegel, the problem of parallel non-Western history and historical activity became a central topic of pragmatic as well as theoretical concern to Europeans.[9] The pragmatic importance of the non-European power of Russia in European affairs was clearly evident after the Congress of Vienna. The work of Orientalists brought new knowledge of parallel Near and Far Eastern civilizations into the public realm once again. Following the First World War, the work of Spengler and Toynbee on the internal cycles of a plurality of civilizations severely qualified the conventional linear pattern.

Voegelin reflected on the significance of these changes in the pattern of political history and raised the question of the relationship between political history and political ideas. One possibility,

---

9. Voegelin's own concern with "parallel histories" was initially indicated in the prefatory note to his article "Das Timurbild der Humanisten: Eine Studie zur politischen Mythenbildung," *Zeitschrift für Öffentliches Recht* 17 (1937): 544–45. The article, without the prefatory note, was reprinted in *Anamnesis: Zur Theorie der Geschichte und Politik* (Munich: Piper, 1966), 153–78.

he said, is that the history of political ideas is without form and structure of its own. If so, a so-called history of political ideas is properly identified as a chronological encyclopedia of successive opinions. A minimum understanding of history, namely that it is "the unfolding of a pattern of meaning in time," would be violated by such a compendium. On the other hand, the view of Janet, that only highly integrated doctrines and "systems" deserve to be considered because only the great thinkers achieve results that can properly be called "scientific," leads to the conclusion that the pattern of general history has little bearing on the pattern of a history of political ideas.[10] The first option would have made the entire enterprise of a general history futile and so may be dismissed out of hand. Voegelin's own work on the impact of Timur (or Tamerlane) on Western political ideas, including Machiavelli's evocation of a savior-prince, indicated as well that the second conclusion is erroneous.[11] The real problem was, and is, to specify the relationship between the history of political ideas and political history in a philosophically defensible way.

In this context, Dunning's advance over Janet, that is, his superior penetration of the problem, was clear: he distinguished "political theory," by which he meant opinions, sentiments, and ideas "whether integrated into a scientific system or not, which tends to explain the origin, nature, and scope of the authority of rulership," from Janet's more narrow and systematic "political science." Dunning proceeded upon the methodological assumption that a "theory" mattered not because it was systematic or scientific but because it was "in touch" with actual political history and existing political institutions. On this basis, the pattern of the history of political ideas is to be subordinated to the structure of political history. Dunning, however, was a progressive (as was Janet) and understood the direction of history as tending toward the separation of politics "from ethical, theological, legal and other contexts." The most serious consequence of this position in Voegelin's opinion

10. In contemporary political science, the first assumption is made by some members of the so-called Cambridge school, while the second assumption seems to guide the work of some "Straussians."

11. In addition to the article "Das Timurbild," just cited, for details see also Voegelin's chapter on Machiavelli in *The Collected Works of Eric Voegelin*, vol. 22, *History of Political Ideas*, vol. IV, *Renaissance and Reformation*, ed. David L. Morse and William M. Thompson (Columbia: University of Missouri Press, 1998), 31–87.

was that it eliminated from consideration Mesopotamian, Persian, and Israelite history even though "a good deal of Western political thought is deeply rooted" in this pre-Hellenic context.

The most important problem with his approach, however, was that, apart from the late medieval question of the separation of church and state, Dunning was compelled by his principles of interpretation to exclude a large amount of medieval material on the grounds that no "political history" took place. In Voegelin's view, "the elimination as irrelevant of a phase of history, which is in direct and broad continuity with our own, because its structure of political ideas differs from ours, cannot be justified by any standard of scientific method." By the simple expedient of abandoning any commitment to historical progress, George Sabine, with whose well-known textbook Voegelin's original *History of Political Ideas* was intended to compete, had made a major advance. He was able to describe the structure of political ideas as they were revealed in history, whether in the form of science or of "an undifferentiated complex of community order" that includes such things as ethics, law, and religion. By so doing, Sabine organized the historical materials into three major parts. The first was on the polis, the second on the universal community, and the last on the national state. "With the elaboration of this methodological position," Voegelin said, "the problem of principles has come to a rest." Commitment to a linear progressive "ancient-medieval-modern" model had finally been abandoned and the "structure of a history of political theory is unconditionally subordinated to the structure of political history."[12] On this basis, which in Voegelin's view was provisionally adequate, he enumerated the chief problems with which "the historian of political theory" is currently concerned. According to Voegelin, three questions were involved: (1) the choice of a pattern on the basis of which the materials may be organized; (2) the classification and integration of new materials on the basis of the pattern adopted; (3) revision of the pattern on the basis of interpreting new materials that do not conform to the categories of the original organization.

---

12. Sabine's "historicism" has been criticized by Leo Strauss on just these grounds. See Sabine, "What Is a Political Theory?" *Journal of Politics* 1 (1939): 2, and Strauss, *What Is Political Philosophy? And Other Studies* (Glencoe, Ill.: Free Press, 1959), chap. 1 and 223–28.

With respect to the first question, what mattered was less the fidelity to the position developed, for example by Toynbee or by the editors of the *Cambridge Ancient* or *Cambridge Medieval History,* than the need to be aware that some such choice of a pattern was needed in order to organize the materials at all. Second, however, is the actual development of the historical sciences through the publication of specialized studies in the areas of political theory and political history. In consequence, "the historian of political theory . . . has the fascinating opportunity of trying his hand at bringing the two complexes of knowledge together." *History of Political Ideas* was, among other things, Voegelin's sustained attempt at bringing together these two "complexes of knowledge."

In his report to the APSA, he indicated several problem areas where scholars were directing their energies. Two were particularly pertinent for the materials covered in this volume. First, the interpretation of existing governmental authority is not the most important question in political science. The importance of government during periods of relative stability might remain undiminished, but "in the initial phases of civilizational cycles, the problems of community-substance, of its creation, its delimitation, and its articulation," were at least of equal significance, and likewise during periods of crisis, dissolution, and regeneration of the "community-creating political myth," questions of community substance or meaning came to the fore. Accordingly, the integration of a history of political ideas to the process of political history would entail an account "of the ideas concerned with the mythical creation of communities, and of the far-reaching theological ramifications of those ideas." On the side of "ideas" therefore, the political scientist had to consider a great deal more than what Janet or even Dunning considered relevant to their respective disciplines. In arriving at this conclusion, Voegelin's study of Vico was central.

In addition, any concern with the evocation of new political communities would influence the interpretation of established political communities. Thus, for example, the call for spiritual renovation to be found in Plato's political philosophy was not a theory of the polis but a theory of "the lethal crisis of the *polis.*" Likewise, the appearance of Christianity involved less the reception of Stoic ethical theory and an accommodation with temporal authority than the creation of a new mystical body centered on the experience of the *pneuma* of Christ. "Precisely," wrote Voegelin, "the so-called non-political ideas, as for instance the eschatological sentiments and ideas, are the great source of political fermentation and revolution throughout Western history to this day." The same problem reappeared in connection with the disintegration of medieval political order. Concerning the medieval sources themselves, Voegelin observed that, on the one hand, there is considerable new knowledge of the migration period, much of which was in fact digested and presented in the prewar volumes of Toynbee's *History*. It was possible, therefore, to consider Teutonic political ideas in a way that could not be conceived either by Dunning or by the Carlyles in their standard multivolume study. Furthermore, the organization of medieval political thought in light of the spiritual movements associated with the Franciscans and Joachim of Fiore, which mark the beginning of a new evocation, had become possible in light of Alois Dempf's great study, *Sacrum Imperium*.[13] Voegelin provided his detailed analyses of these questions in earlier volumes of *History of Political Ideas*. In a period covered by the present volume, the creation of the mystical political bodies that sought to replace the mystical spiritual body of Christ was well underway.

This process of substitution of one mystical body for another was akin to the discovery of "parallel" histories. Alongside the well-known and amply documented crystallization of the institutions of the national state, there developed a complex array of sectarian—or as Voegelin calls them in this volume—apostatic communities that vivify the more familiar institutions. With respect to the history of political ideas as ordinarily or conventionally understood, the debate across the centuries between Voltaire and Bossuet ended, as it were, with Enlightened opinion triumphant. Voegelin's presentation of the issue between Voltaire and Bossuet in Chapter 1 is, in the first place, a model of economy and controlled scholarly exegesis. In addition to these conventional virtues, however, Voegelin pointed to the important spiritual consequences that followed from the adoption of Voltaire's position on a socially significant scale. First, the "idea" of transcendental spiritual universalism was replaced by the "idea" of an intramundane universalism of reason. As Voegelin

13. R. W. and A. J. Carlyle, *A History of Medieval Political Theory in the West,* 6 vols. (London and Edinburgh: Blackwood, 1903–1936); Dempf, *Sacrum Imperium: Geschichts- und Staatsphilosophie des Mittelalters und der politischen Renaissance* (Munich: Oldenbourg, 1929; 4th ed., 1973).

7

indicated, the new "idea" was justified in terms of a secular com-monsense morality motivated by the sentiment of compassion for humanity and directed by social utility. It was, however, based on an assumption, derived from the impressive achievements of Newton in the field of celestial mechanics, that knowledge had to be based on the methods of physics if it was to count as science. In order for Voltaire to sustain such an opinion, he had to reject the experience, still present in Bossuet, of the cognition of faith. He did so by attacking the linguistic expression of that experience in the form of Christian doctrine and, in particular, in the Christian the-ology of history that Bossuet had accepted along with its doctrinal form. Voltaire did not simply reject Bossuet's doctrine, however, and substitute his own, but turned the experience of the cognition of faith into a psychological accident. This position Voegelin called "spiritual obscurantism."

Because it was based upon a denial of the cognitive value of the experiences of faith, the development from spiritual obscurantism to dogmatic atheism was predictable in the sense that it followed an obvious *logique du coeur*. First, if faith was not an act of cognition, then it was necessarily an act of imagination. In contrast to Voltaire, who was forced to confront the doctrine of Bossuet, the intellectuals who followed Voltaire's lead assumed the validity of his spiritual obscurantism and took it as a starting point for further speculation. For such persons, the conclusion to be drawn was clear: the alleged spiritual experiences really had no valid content to them, which is to say they were not, properly speaking, experiences of anything. Thus did the assertive materialism of Holbach and Helvétius follow the tentativeness of Voltaire, an account of which is to be presented in detail in Volume VIII of *History of Political Ideas*.[14] Likewise, the sentiment of Newtonian usefulness could be elaborated into a Benthamic moral calculus. The importance of this development of political ideas, however, was that it constituted the generalization or popularization of a new philosophical anthropology rather than a penetrating theoretical insight or discovery.

On the other hand, by ignoring a great deal of what would now be called world history in order to conform to an essentially Augus-tinian pattern, Bossuet left himself exposed to Voltaire's criticism.

---

14. Several chapters have already been published in Voegelin, *From Enlighten-ment to Revolution*, ed. John H. Hallowell (Durham: Duke University Press, 1975).

Thus Bossuet's *Discourse on Universal History,* which had nothing to say of China or India, was hardly living up to its title. Notwithstanding Voltaire's spiritual shortcomings, his empirical and commonsensical as well as witty criticism of Bossuet had the undoubted merit of drawing attention to the inadequacies of the doctrinal form in which the putatively universal spiritual insights were cast. What was required to meet Voltaire's objections was a philosophy of history that combined the spiritual insights of Bossuet with the empirical breadth of Voltaire. In Voegelin's argument, as developed in Chapter 3 of this volume, Vico provided a giant step in the right direction.

In the short intervening chapter Voegelin provides a brief account of a major symptom of the spiritual as well as intellectual disintegration of the Western body politic into a collection of mutually schismatic politico-religious bodies. Voegelin focused in particular on the growth of a new set of conventions by which Europeans expressed their disdain for one another's national particularities. To the English, for example, the German spirit was obscure, whereas the French spirit typically substituted logic for common sense; to the French, the German spirit was without civilization and the English was opportunistic; to the Germans, the French were superficial and the English were uncultured. The significance of such "amenities," he said, lay not in their accuracy regarding the several national characteristics but in their being symptoms of a newly respectable spiritual parochialism and a growing mutual unintelligibility.

The respectability of this parochial recrimination, in turn, was a reflection of the political history of Europe. By the eighteenth century, the several national communities had developed more or less comprehensive "ideas" of themselves as replacements for the no longer meaningful medieval Christian and imperial "ideas." Voegelin termed the process by which the new mystical bodies of the nations gained respectability "apostatic revolt." Voltaire's was the most articulate voice of apostasy; that he was heard is evident from the changes in the history of Western political ideas but also from the course of political history. Not only did the several parochial national bodies politic substitute themselves for the mystical body of Christ, they also began to insulate themselves against one another, as the litany of uncomplimentary epithets indicated above clearly shows. In place of the parochial religious tensions and cycle of wars of the sixteenth century, one finds parochial national tensions and wars that have still not come to an end four centuries later.

Regarding the actual configuration of so-called national characteristics, the chief determinant was the constellation of ideas and sentiments, which varied from nation to nation, *at the time* of the particular apostatic revolt. In the French example, the apostasy of Voltaire took the form of a revolt in the name of universal reason against Catholic Christian universalism. In England, as Voegelin shows in detail in Chapter 4, the anti-Catholic attitude had long been settled by the Anglican schism and the Puritan revolution. Because there was no institutional guardian of the Western spiritual tradition in existence, there could be no intellectual expression of it as one finds in Bossuet. Instead the English conflict was between a Protestant, personal, and idiosyncratic interpretation of Scripture and secularized individualism. The conflict was muted or "understated" because the established Church of England was without significant spiritual force in the first place. In England there was neither the enthusiasm nor the spiritual zest needed to produce a "counterreligion" of Reason, Positivism, or Humanitarianism as there was in France. Between the solidity and resiliency of English social forms, including the Church of England, and the personal freedom of the individual within those forms, the life of the spirit, Voegelin said, "moves in an even twilight of preservation and euthanasia." That few English persons were sensitive to the spiritual issues is further evidence of the strength of their conventions of respectability, civility, and "gentlemanliness."[15]

In contrast, the German apostasy was complicated by three interrelated tensions. First, the ongoing Catholic-Protestant conflict overlapped with regionally dominant principalities in such a way that neither could form the new body politic to the exclusion of the other. Second was the tension between a waning imperial tradition and a plurality of minor territorial principalities, on the one hand, with the trend toward national unification and closure analogous to the Atlantic nations of France and England, on the other. Third, social differences remained between the colonized territories of the east and old settlement areas of the south and west that was

---

15. Voegelin also explored this issue in "The Oxford Political Philosophers," *Philosophical Quarterly* 3 (1953): 97–114.

ended only precariously by the nineteenth-century Prussian-led wars of national unification. These social differences have recently reemerged after the "reunification" of Germany.

Differences in the political history of the European political societies made uniform apostatic developments unlikely in the extreme. In Germany, for example, the absence in the nineteenth century of both national political institutions and uniform religious commitments precluded a national revolution in the name of reason as had taken place earlier in France. Likewise, German Protestantism was not characterized by idiosyncratic scriptural interpretation and so never developed into the corresponding secular forms of individualism that, in turn, helped shape English parliamentary political institutions. Whereas in England Parliament became, in Toynbee's language, "idolized," in Germany it was never more than a technique of rule without deep attachments of sentiment. There was, accordingly, in Germany no parallel to the French relationship between reason and revelation or to the English one between parliamentary government and secular individualism. Instead, Voegelin said, one finds a plurality of political institutions juxtaposed to a long sweep of metaphysical and mystical speculation moving from Kant and Herder through Fichte, Hegel, Schelling, and Marx. The speculative efforts of the German thinkers, unlike those of their counterparts in France and England, could not penetrate or inform the institutions of a national polity because none existed.[16]

The German relationship of "juxtaposition" between the events of political history and the history of political ideas meant that one might simply accept or reject existing political institutions rather than give internal coherence to the national body politic. Hegel and Marx are conventionally identified as typifying the two alternatives. The gap between events and ideas was bridged by the wars of national unification, but Bismark's *Realpolitik* was not, in Voegelin's view, equivalent to the English or French revolutions and consequently did not solidify and articulate the national substance as a body politic either. Voegelin believed that an opportunity for a national revolution was missed in 1918 because Marxism paralyzed

16. See John H. Hallowell, *The Decline of Liberalism as an Ideology, with Particular Reference to German Politico-Legal Thought* (Berkeley: University of California Press, 1943), and Voegelin's review in *Journal of Politics* 6 (1944): 107–9.

the workers' parties, which alone might have supplied the necessary strength to carry such a revolution through. "The overdue revolution was finally realized, in 1933, borne by the middle-class of an industrialized society and resulting in a national as well as an international catastrophe." That the Nazi revolution was a disaster must not obscure the fact that it was part of a pattern common to the division of the West into national states of which the English and French revolutions were simply prior instances.

The term *closure,* which Voegelin associated with the English, French, and German revolutions, contained both a spiritual and a legal or institutional dimension. The former, which is conventionally related to the history of political ideas, referred to the complex of problems relating the new schismatic and apostatic meanings of the preschismatic past. The latter, which conventionally belongs to political history and resulted in the political form of the sovereign state, referred to the complex of problems concerning the political relations among the several new sovereign entities issuing in the disintegration of Western society in the great wars of the twentieth century.

On the basis of these distinctions between spiritual and legal closure, Voegelin summarized the differences between the French, English, and German examples. In the first two, the institutional establishment of a unified national state preceded the spiritual closure, whereas in Germany the sequence was reversed. Accordingly, in France and England the process of spiritual closure could take for granted the existence of the political state, whereas in Germany the simultaneous development of both phases introduced additional disturbances. For example, the wisdom of Bismark's policy in forcing Germany in the direction of a national state remained a live issue long after the actual political unification had been attained. So far as the central European areas are concerned, it is far from clear, even in the last decade of the twentieth century, that an imperial-federal construction would not be a more appropriate political form.

To this account of the English, French, and German responses to the problem of disintegrating Western Christian society and the differentiation of distinctive national characteristics, Voegelin added in Chapter 3 an analysis of the Italian. The structure of Italian political ideas no less than Italian political institutions presented a strong contrast to transalpine developments. The territorial states of the north, even in Germany, had long superseded the city-state, whereas in Italy the culture of the city-state remained the dominant political form until late in the nineteenth century.

The difference in political culture between the north and Italy led to a number of intricate complexities. On the one hand, the political and economic revolutions of thirteenth- and fourteenth-century Italy anticipated developments on the scale of the transalpine national state, sometimes by centuries. The balance of power as a means of limiting political disorder among the several small Italian states, for instance, was well developed long before the technique was used among the larger northern territorial states. Italian political thinkers, therefore, had good reason to consider their fellows the most sophisticated practitioners of the political arts.[17] On the other hand, the superior military force of the French and Spanish national states, especially after the appeal by Milan to Charles VII in 1494, meant an end to an independent Italian political culture. Notwithstanding their great skill in the practice of politics on the Italian peninsula, it was also clear that the city-states were no match for the territorial states in more serious conflicts.

Accordingly, the conventional term for the period between the French invasion of 1494 and the Risorgimento of the nineteenth century is *decadence*. The term is justified, but only with respect to the weakness of Italy as a military and political power as compared to other European nations. Certainly the existence of political thinkers of the stature of Machiavelli, Guicciardini, Campanella, and Vico means that the term is inadequate as a general description of the consequences of the French invasion. One must, for instance, take account of Machiavelli's characterization of the French as barbarians. Only if one makes the equally conventional but also unjustified assumption that the national state is necessarily the goal toward which all peoples aspire can one conclude that the Italian failure to achieve that goal was a genuine failure and a symptom of weakness.

Granted that the conflict of political cultures is not settled simply in terms of who commands the larger battalions—in this case,

---

17. The importance of Machiavelli, for example, in setting the agenda for the conduct of modern politics has long been recognized. Simply in terms of vocabulary, he was the first to use the word *state* as an analytically precise term in political science.

the barbaric foreigners—it is also true that, within Italy, the trend toward a national culture during the fourteenth century was effectively reversed and a period of what has been termed "municipalization" began. Regional differences accordingly were stressed rather than merely acknowledged, and, under the pressure of the Counter-Reformation, many sensitive and energetic individuals emigrated to more congenial places. The political and intellectual contexts, Voegelin said, must both be borne in mind when considering the work of Giambattista Vico.

"The work of Vico," Voegelin wrote, "is recognized today as the magnificent beginning of a modern philosophy of history and politics."[18] His lasting achievement was to establish a "new foundation of a science of politics and ideas." Nevertheless, Vico's work "remained almost unknown in its own time and exerted little immediate influence." There were three reasons for this. First, Vico's Italian is difficult to read, even for native speakers, which was one of the consequences of the "municipalization" of literary discourse.[19] Second, the actual subject matter was complex. The substance of his work was a philosophy of history, but it was presented by way of erudite philological studies, theories of language and aesthetics,

18. Voegelin, review of the translation of *The New Science* by Thomas Goddard Bergin and Max Harold Fisch, in *Catholic Historical Review* 35 (1949–1950): 75. Thirty years later, however, B. A. Hadock was still of the opinion that "Vico's position in the history of political thought has yet to be established. . . . This lacuna is perfectly intelligible. Vico did not write a 'classic' of political philosophy" ("Vico on Political Wisdom," *European Studies Review* 8 [1978]: 165). On the other hand, consider Isaiah Berlin, *Against the Current: Essays in the History of Ideas* (Oxford: Clarendon, 1991), 4. Adrienne Fulco claimed more defensibly that "what is lacking is an overview of Vico's political ideas and an evaluation of his role as a political theorist" ("Vico and Political Science," in Giorgio Tagliacozzo, ed., *Vico: Past and Present* [Atlantic Highlands: Humanities Press, 1981], 175).

19. "Vico's Italian," wrote Leon Pompa, "is undeniably very difficult indeed. His works were invariably written at great speed; he used sentences of great length, which are often tortuous, chaotic and incorrect in construction; he expressed himself frequently with grim irony, which can sometimes confuse the sense of what he says; his works are illuminated by brilliant aphorisms together with a deliberate play upon words, while interlaced to the point of incomprehensibility by obscure and condensed intellectual allusions; he used ordinary language in an idiosyncratic and technical way without offering the help of many definitions" (preface to *Vico: Selected Writings* [Cambridge: Cambridge University Press, 1982], xiii). Isaiah Berlin made a similar remark: "Vico's elaborate, convoluted, 'baroque' prose, archaic even in its own time, with its constant digressions, occult references, esoteric allusions, and lack of any apparent order or easily intelligible structure, faced the reader with a huge and impassable jungle, which discouraged even the intellectually enterprising" ("Corsi e Ricorsi," *Journal of Modern History* 50 [1978]: 481). See also Paul Hazard, *The European Mind (1680–1715)* (London: Hollis and Carter, 1953), 414.

and analyses of Roman law and political institutions. Because he was anxious to avoid the attention of the Inquisition, there were also present in his work a host of spurious authorities and silences regarding his real sources.[20] Moreover, the style of historiography to which Vico conformed was one that found merit in collecting materials rather than in presenting a systematic, discursive exposition of methods or interpretative results. The task of distinguishing the principles of Vico's method from the materials to which he applied it is accordingly both subtle and complex. Perhaps for these reasons alone, Vico has received comparatively little attention from political scientists.

The greatest obstacle to understanding Vico, however, is the intimate and meditative character of the *New Science*, particularly when it is read in conjunction with his *Autobiography*. In this respect Vico found a worthy successor in Voegelin. Just as Voegelin argued that his own consciousness was the instrument by which he and political scientists generally undertook the task of analysis, so Vico's story of his own life turned into a verification of the principles of the *New Science*. The book published by that name is not a single, systematic treatise. Rather it is a compendium of Vico's thought, begun in 1708, when the author was forty, and continued until his death in 1744, when the "third" *New Science* was published. In fact, there were so many revisions that the "third" edition is sometimes called the ninth version. So far as Vico's

20. See Max H. Fisch, "The Academy of the Investigators," in *Science, Medicine and History: Essays on the Evolution of Scientific Thought and Medical Practice Written in Honour of Charles Singer*, ed. E. Ashworth Underwood (London: Oxford University Press, 1953), 521–63. The most complete examination of the presence and activities of the Inquisition in Vico's Naples is Gino Bedani, *Vico Revisited: Orthodoxy, Naturalism, and Science in the "Scienza nuova"* (Oxford: Berg, 1989), chap. 1. Bedani also drew attention to class-based opposition to Vico from ecclesiastical landowners who were not above seeking assistance from the Inquisition against upstarts in the *ceto civile*, the civil or administrative class (153–54, 278). The consequences for Vico's "art of writing" have been accordingly emphasized by Straussian readers. See Frederick Vaughan, *The Political Philosophy of Giambattista Vico* (The Hague: Martinus Nijhoff, 1972), and Theodore A. Sumberg, "Reading Vico Three Times," *Interpretation* 17 (1990): 347–54, both of whom are highly skeptical of Vico's claim to be a faithful son of the church. On the other hand, as Thomas Berry observed, "an accusation of this kind," regarding Vico's skeptical attitude toward Christianity, "is so insidious that any proofs offered to the contrary might be taken by some as a manifestation of the perfection with which he accomplished this deception, which, it is suggested, was partially conscious and partially subconscious on his part" (*The Historical Theory of Giambattista Vico* [Washington, D.C.: Catholic University of America Press, 1949], 12).

language is concerned, the later texts, based upon even more years of meditation, were written in an increasingly personal style, so that the entire thirty-six-year enterprise may be seen as a complex series of interrelated reports, not unlike Voegelin's own work, stretching from the early 1940s until his death in January 1985.

Voegelin, as other Vico scholars, divided the development of his thought into three phases. The first was the criticism of Descartes's scientism, marked by the publication of the *Metaphysics* in 1710. The second phase may be dated from 1720–1721 and the publication of a treatise that Vico referred to as his *Diritto universale.*[21] The *Diritto universale* continued Vico's critical reflections on the basis of the metaphysical insights he had developed in his polemic against Descartes. The subject matter of his analysis on this occasion was the theory of natural law expounded by Grotius, Selden, and Pufendorf—all northerners, all Protestants. He deployed an enormous philological knowledge to show that the origins of Roman political institutions were far different than the natural law theorists imagined. The natural law advocates, along with Descartes, made the error of assuming that because a law is given in the context of one set of institutions, namely their own, it must be equally "objective" in any context whatsoever. According to Vico this was an error because it overlooked the inherent connection between historical institutions and the putatively universal and unconditioned content of natural law. One of the strangest consequences, in Vico's opinion, was the notion that society and civilization began on the basis of a contract that presupposed the attributes of eighteenth-century bourgeois civility.

21. The full title of the metaphysics is *De antiquissima italorum sapentia ex linguae latinae originibus eruenda: Liber primus: Metaphysicus,* in *Opere di G. B. Vico,* ed. Fausto Nicolini, Giovanni Gentile, and Benedetto Croce, 6 vols. (Bari: Laterza, 1911–1914), 1:127. A partial translation is available in Pompa, ed., *Vico: Selected Writings,* 47ff. See also the translation of L. M. Palmer, *On the Most Ancient Wisdom of the Italians* (Ithaca: Cornell University Press, 1988). To summarize Vico's criticism boldly, he argued that Descartes's was an "insane method" because it applied geometry to the "caprice, rashness, occasion and fortune" of human life and so produced rational lunatics (*On the Most Ancient Wisdom,* 99). The *Diritto universale* is not available in English. Three major texts are involved: the *Synopsi del Diritto universale,* 1720; the *De uno universi juris principio et fine uno,* 1720; and the two-part *De Constantia Juris Prudentis,* 1721. They have been republished in a three-volume modern edition in *Opere* II:1–3 (1936). The *Diritto universale* has largely been ignored by contemporary commentators. See, however, Mark Lilla, *G. B. Vico: The Making of an Anti-Modern* (Cambridge: Harvard University Press, 1993), 70ff.

This "conceit of scholars" is more than just a minor flaw. It is an "impious conceit," because it is based upon the premise that humans can attain wisdom, or even insights, unassisted by God. In fact, contractarians become skeptics, not wise, because their rationality is directed toward the prerational foundations of social life. But this approach, said Vico, was futile, because it cut human beings off from participation in divine truth, and dangerously corrupting as well, because the young in particular would follow it and grow contemptuous of prudence and common sense. They would turn into smug skeptics, keen only to apply their "insane method" mechanically.

The second part of the *De constantia* uses the term *New Science* for the first time, in reference to philology. Philology was understood as the science that explores the origins of things by exploring the origins of their names, for the "things" of society, namely religious and legal institutions, are signified by names and flow from the mind of man, which brings us to the third phase of Vico's thought, marked by the publication of the first version of the *New Science,* in 1725. In this work, the course of Roman history, discussed in *De constantia*, was typified as a course to which the histories of all peoples conform, an "ideal eternal history," Vico called it. The second and third editions of the *New Science* enlarged and modified the position of 1725.

During the 1940s, when Voegelin was writing this chapter, the secondary literature was still quite modest.[22] The most important study was Croce's 1911 book, *The Philosophy of Giambattista Vico.*[23] Voegelin expressed misgivings about Croce's interpretation, which he characterized as secularist and progressive, and argued that Vico's greatness lay in his Christian awareness of the problems of the spirit, not in his efforts at constructing a secular philosophy

22. In the decades since, the secondary literature on Vico has grown enormously. As one observer said, "Vico has become not only a relic but an icon, not only a classic but a commodity," and, as happens to all commodities, Vico has been industrialized as well. See Donald R. Kelley, "Giovanni Battista Vico," in *European Writers: The Age of Reason and Enlightenment,* ed. George Stade (New York: Charles Scribner's Sons, 1984), 3:312. Much of this secondary material (and I make no claim to having read more than a large sample) is either useful enough scholarly exegesis of a historical kind or an appropriation of Vico's texts or themes. At its best, the second type of appropriation can result in *Finnegans Wake*, but mostly it results in papers by various *dotti* on "Vico and the Hermeneutics of Critical Sociology" and the like.

23. Trans. R. G. Collingwood (London: Macmillan, 1913; rpt. New York: Russell and Russell, 1964).

of history along the lines of Voltaire.[24] Vico was aware, Voegelin said, that "the great irruptions of transcendental reality do not fall into the patterns that can be constructed regarding the historical courses of human civilizations." Accordingly, Vico avoided the error of attempting to find the meaning of history in the humanly intelligible structures of profane history.

Voegelin summarized his own understanding of Vico with the remark that his was a "well-constructed theory of politics and history," having at its core a strongly argued philosophical anthropology on the basis of which history is interpreted as the temporal unfolding of the potentiality of the human mind. The details of any particular Vichian interpretation, since it was based upon the actual collection and mastery of existing materials, were bound to be superseded by advances in historical knowledge, refinements of philological techniques, and so on. The "ideas" of Vico's philosophical anthropology and his philosophy of history as the intelligible unfolding of the human mind, no less than its meditative form, are what attracted Voegelin's attention. His focus, however, remained Vico's position "in a general history of political ideas."

To begin with, the name *new science* echoed both Bacon's *Novum Organum* (1620) and Galileo's Dialogues on *Two New Sciences* (1638). For Vico, however, the *Scienza nuova* was a "true science of substance in opposition to a science of physical phenomena, while, at the same time, it is a science of politics in emulation of the imposing science of nature." In his *Autobiography*, for example, Vico said of his book: "By this work, to the glory of the Catholic religion, the principles of all gentile wisdom human and divine have been discovered in this our age and in the bosom of the true Church, and Vico has thereby procured for our Italy the advantage of not envying Protestant Holland, England or Germany their three princes of this science."[25] Such a claim raised the obvious question: what had Vico accomplished that outweighed both the achievements of natural science and the northerners' new theories of natural law?

Voegelin's brief answer was: "the insight into, and reversal of, the Western apostatic movement." The *New Science*, therefore, offered

24. This division between Vico scholars who emphasize the Christian spirituality at the core of Vico's work and those who emphasize his heterodoxy and historicism has persisted to the present.

25. Vico, *Autobiography*, 173, in *Opere*, V:53.

both an analysis of "the hubris of disoriented man who is obsessed by his *amor sui*" and an antidote to it. Vico's position within an unbroken Catholic tradition, combined with his Italian sentiment of resistance to the pretensions of northerners, provided him with the necessary strength to undertake his massive and isolated act of resistance. Vico was not, for that reason, "anachronistic" or "antimodern." Voegelin's reasoning was akin to that deployed earlier when he indicated that Italy could not properly be called decadent for failing to have formed itself into a territorial state. In the same way, philosophers are not obliged to move through the penumbra of Voltairean spiritual obscurantism to the darkness of progressivism, utilitarianism, romanticism, materialism, and all the rest in order to discover something is amiss. Vico's "genius" was to be able to anticipate fruits of apostasy without having to begin the *voyage au bout de la nuit*. Voegelin would have agreed with the words of A. Robert Caponigri, who said that Vico "diagnosed the crisis of the modern spirit even before it had arisen."[26]

The details of Voegelin's exegesis of Vico's forty-year meditation are beautifully expressed in his own words. What is striking, however, is that, as in Voegelin's interpretation of Bodin, one finds the interpreter presenting his own philosophy of history and consciousness by way of the texts written by his predecessors.[27] One might, for example, summarize the position of both Vico and Voegelin with the observation that the course of a civilization resulted from the cooperation between, or the partnership of, the providential and the human, the architect and the artificer. Voegelin adopted as his own Vico's dictum that it is wrong for philosophers to meditate solely upon a civilized human nature—that is, a human nature conditioned and made articulate by religion and law—because, in Voegelin's words, religions and legal institutions "are precisely the medium within which the function of philosophy grows as a rational penetration of the initial mythical substance." What the philosophers heretofore have not done is meditate on the human nature that produced the religion and law that in turn produced

---

26. A. Robert Caponigri, "Vico and the Theory of History," *Giornale di Metafisica* 9 (1954): 184.

27. A comparison of Voegelin's remarks regarding the *verum-factum* argument of the *Metaphysics* of 1710 with his comments on the famous paragraph 331 of *The New Science* published thirty years later clarifies not only Vico's philosophy of consciousness but Voegelin's as well.

philosophers. By this argument, philosophy had no autonomous authority but rather derived what authority it had from the civilizational substance on which it reflected. The task of the philosopher of history, therefore, includes the understanding of his or her own historicity, which entails bringing the mythical meaning or substance of one's own civilization within one's rational grasp. The philosopher of history cannot, therefore, transcend the myth by a feat of personal creativity because the myth is a transpersonal reality to begin with. But, added Voegelin, "he can transcend it speculatively by exploring the origin and the course of the myth and by accepting the myth consciously as the transpersonal substance by which his personal meditation lives." This observation applied to Vico's personal situation as an interpreter of Western civilization, and also to Voegelin's, and anyone else's.

The chapter on Vico is, in many respects, the centerpiece of this volume. In the context of a growing legal and spiritual "closure" in the self-understanding of Western humanity, Voegelin found in Vico a recovery and a rearticulation of the tension between world-immanent pragmatic—or, as Vico called it, "gentilician"—history and the world-transcendent divine source or ground of all being, including history. Vico's recovery of the Augustinian evocation of the tension between the two cities, the two loves, of sacred and profane history, was itself a major intellectual and spiritual achievement. In addition, however, by casting his insight in the form of a philosophy of history, Vico could account for Augustine's place in a civilizational cycle, for his understanding of the epoch after Christ as the *saeculum senescens,* and for the rejection of the sentiments expressed in Augustine's understanding by later individuals. Vico added to Augustine's magnificent evocation or self-interpretation the dimension of a critical interpretation, which Voegelin was able to appropriate and, with minimal changes, integrate into his own political science.

"The English Quest for the Concrete," with which this volume closes, is something of a portmanteau chapter. As Voegelin explains in the introduction to it, the details of the period are well known, though the gestalt is elusive. English thinkers, especially Bishop Berkeley, from whom the term *concrete* was taken, were looking for it because it had escaped them, partly in consequence of the disorientation that followed the upheavals associated with the events between the Puritan and the Glorious Revolutions. Partly as well, the extrapolation of Newton's celestial mechanics into the ordinary realm of terrestrial mechanics helped to complete the process of detachment and abstraction from the concrete realities of existence.

Considered simply as a discussion of the contours of the English apostatic revolt, this chapter belongs with the analyses of "The New Order" presented in Volume VII of *History of Political Ideas*. The thematic treatment of Newton continues the analysis of Voltaire's vulgarizations of the great natural philosopher set out in Chapter 1 of this volume, but it also continues the theme of "phenomenalism" that was first introduced in Chapter 5 of Volume V, "Man in History and Nature," and then further discussed in Chapter 1 of Part Eight in Volume VII. To make the philological matters surrounding this text even more complex, large sections of "The English Quest for the Concrete" were published as an independent article, "The Origins of Scientism."[28] The reason for the somewhat disjointed organization of the materials lies in the order in which the several chapters were written, rewritten, and then reorganized as the manuscript of the *History* expanded. Because the manuscript was never prepared for publication by the author, the exact sequence of topics and chapters remains fragmented.

Even so, "The English Quest for the Concrete" contains an inner logic, also borrowed from Bishop Berkeley, whose "search for the concrete," Voegelin said, "ranged through the realms of being from matter to God and through the varieties of experience from sense perception to faith." Following a brief description of the social and political disorder of eighteenth-century England, Voegelin presented his analysis of the eclipse of God and the transformation of the cognition of faith into a psychological attitude. Thus one finds clearly explained reasons for Voegelin's severe judgments regarding Locke.[29] In addition, the discussion of sense perception of material phenomena within the context of hypothesis, abstractions, and mathematical models also conforms to Berkeley's procedure. The

---

28. "The Origins of Scientism," *Social Research* 15 (1948): 462–94.
29. See, for example, Voegelin's letters of April 15 and 20, 1953, in *Faith and Political Philosophy: The Correspondence between Leo Strauss and Eric Voegelin*, trans. and ed. Peter Emberley and Barry Cooper (University Park: Penn State University Press, 1993), 92–97. See below, 171–79, and *The Collected Works of Eric Voegelin*, Vol. 25, *History of Political Ideas*, Vol. VII, *The New Order and Last Orientation*, ed. Jürgen Gebhardt and Thomas A. Hollweck (Columbia: University of Missouri Press, 1999), Part 7, chap. 6.

significance of Newtonian "scientism" and the reductionist arguments of Locke is that they contributed to the impoverishment of human experience and thereby added to, and reinforced, the prevailing spiritual disorder.

I have tried to maintain a light editorial hand in preparing the manuscript for publication. Voegelin's English grew more polished with practice, and his characteristic infelicities of style, many of which concerned idiomatic use of prepositions, grew less frequent. I have also checked his translations with the original texts and, where available, with published English versions. In all cases I have left Voegelin's translations in place on the grounds that he knew what he wished the English versions to say.

I would like to thank the Earhart Foundation and the Social Sciences and Humanities Research Council of Canada for continuing financial support of my research on Voegelin's political science. Ellis Sandoz has been an unfailing source of inspiration and exhortation, and Jane Lago of the Press has done a splendid job of copyediting. I am very grateful as well to Carolyn Andres for having so diligently processed so many thousands of words, all in the cause of science.

Barry Cooper

REVOLUTION AND THE NEW SCIENCE

CONTENTS

PART SIX
REVOLUTION

1

Apostasy

The eighteenth century is traditionally called the century of Enlightenment and Revolution. The two categories have their merit insofar as they focus attention on obviously important intellectual and political complexes. Their merit in this respect is beyond doubt, as is the merit of the alternative designation, the Age of Reason. However, they have little value as systematic categories that aim adequately to characterize the substance of the sentiments and ideas that crystallize in the various complexes of Reason, Enlightenment, and Revolution. For this substance we shall use the term *consciousness of epoch*. The eighteenth century is characterized fundamentally by a new consciousness of epoch, by the sentiment that an age has come to its close and that a new age of Western civilization is being inaugurated. Before entering into the analysis of ideas itself, we shall attempt a brief characterization of the new historical sentiment and of the problems of periodization raised by it.

§1. The Rearticulation of the Christian Era

Consciousness of epoch is not in itself a new phenomenon in Western history. It did not make itself felt all of a sudden after 1700. We encountered it for the first time at the height of imperial Christianity, in the thirteenth century. Under the title "The Structure of the *Saeculum*,"[1] we dealt with the first stirring of intramundane forces and with their tendency to rearticulate the structure of the Christian era. The movement that, in the eighteenth century,

1. *The Collected Works of Eric Voegelin*, vol. 20, *History of Political Ideas*, vol. II, *The Middle Ages to Aquinas*, ed. Peter von Sivers (Columbia: University of Missouri Press, 1997), 105 ff.

took the form of Enlightenment, and is still with us today in the forms of Communist and National Socialist millennial ideas, is a continuation of the movement that started in the thirteenth century. It is distinguished, however, from the earlier phases of this process by its increased intensity, by its comprehensiveness, which embraced all aspects of human existence, and above all by its broad social effectiveness, which resulted in the final disruption of the medieval sentiments of a Western community and paved the way for new types of schismatic political movements. Only if we realize the continuity of the process in which the consciousness of epoch evolves from its first individual and sectarian stirrings to the intensity and effectiveness of national and supranational mass movements can we gain the proper perspective for a periodization of Western intellectual history and can we penetrate to the categories that have to be employed in an adequate analysis of modern political ideas. Hence we shall summarize briefly the principal phases of this process.

The central problem of the thirteenth century, to be continued in the eighteenth, was the rearticulation of the Christian era. We surveyed the stirring of intramundane forces in the characterology of John of Salisbury, in the spiritualism of Saint Francis, in the pathos of rulership of Frederick II, in the intellectual faith of Siger de Brabant, in the idea of an intramundane order of action developed by the Lombard lawyers, and in the climactic self-interpretation of these forces as the symptoms of a new era in the speculation of Joachim of Fiore. The consciousness of epoch was vivid enough in Joachim to crystallize in the idea of a Third Realm of the Spirit that would follow the Realms of the Father and the Son. This idea tended to disrupt the Augustinian conception of the *saeculum* as a time of waiting for the second coming of Christ insofar as it envisaged a new era of meaning in sacred history. The idea was strong enough even to engender in the circle of Franciscan Spirituals the belief in a *corpus mysticum Francisci*, but ultimately it remained ineffectual and did not break through to the level of a mass movement that might lead to the transformation of institutions.

After 1300 the new intramundane forces revealed their strength in a host of minor sectarian movements: in the English and Bohemian pre-Reformation, in the movement of German mysticism, in the reorganization of the church, and in the trend toward sovereign, absolute state organization. A world of sentiments, institutions, and ideas was growing and hollowing out the structure of imperial Christianity. But the shell of church and empire did not break for another two centuries, when during the sixteenth and seventeenth centuries the church split under the impact of the Reformation, and when, after the Thirty Years War, the constitution of the empire became the appendix to an international treaty.

The time from Joachim of Fiore to Luther, that is, the time from the first stirrings of the consciousness of epoch to the outbreak of mass movements on a European scale, we may characterize as a period of social incubation. The actual disruption of medieval institutions, which occurred with the Reformation, created the new social facts of a plurality of churches as well as of a plurality of sovereign states. This new field of social facts then became the material with which the movement of ideas had to cope. In the two preceding parts of this study, we dealt with the period of confusion and settlement following the great outbreak. We analyzed the rhythm of this period from the formation of the fighting fronts in Reformation and Counter-Reformation, through the wars of intervention, to the stabilization of the religious issue in the idea of tolerance and of the temporal issue in the idea of the closed sovereign state. The net result of this period we may express as the growing realization that the institutional unity of Christian mankind had broken down irrevocably and that the plurality of parochial institutions that expressed the diversified field of intramundane social forces had become an established fact. With the Peace of Utrecht of 1713, the balance of power had become accepted as the political constitution of Western mankind; the afterglow of the medieval tension between the empire and the states separating from it died with the great renunciation by the Habsburgs and by France of the desire to dominate Europe by controlling Spain.

The elimination of church and empire as public powers was accompanied by a growth of new community substances that functionally tended to become substitutes for the dissolving substance of Christian mankind. Within the sovereign national states, the intensity of national consciousness was noticeably increasing. The English Revolution of the seventeenth century revealed for the first time the strength of the new demonic parochialism. It revealed both faith in the nation as the chosen people as well as the universalist claim that the parochial national civilization represents Civilization writ large. On the international scale we could observe

33

a variety of ideas that attempted to cope with the new situation: an idea of mankind that assumed a nature of man equal for all, an idea of the *Christianitas* as the Western civilizational unit, in opposition to non-Western civilizations, ideas concerning the relations among Christian republics, and ideas concerning intercivilizational relations. Last, the search for a nature of man beyond the strife of the confessions expressed itself in the attempt to use the Stoic idea of nature as the basis for speculations on natural law. The idea of nature developed in the mathematized sciences of the external world influenced the interpretation of man, and the new psychology of passions was used to determine the generic nature of man.

The trend toward a new order of substances, thus, had a considerable breadth and momentum. Nevertheless, we do not find before 1700 a comprehensive interpretation of man in society and history that would take into account the constituent factors of the new situation. These factors include: the breakdown of the church as the universal institution of Christian mankind, the plurality of sovereign states as ultimate political units, the discovery of the New World and the more intimate acquaintance with Asiatic civilizations, the idea of a non-Christian nature of man as the foundation for speculation on law and ethics, the demonism of parochial, national communities, and the idea of the passions as motivating forces of man. Only after 1700 did the cumulative effect of these several factors make itself felt in the acute consciousness that, in the aggregate, an epoch had come to its end and that the new situation required a gigantic effort of interpretation in order to recover, for the existence of man in society and history, a meaning that could substitute for the lost meaning of Christian existence.

This problem is, indeed, of such a magnitude that even today all its dimensions are not often recognized. But in the eighteenth century we find at least the first clear consciousness of its outlines and the first efforts at formulation of a new understanding. We can approach it perhaps best by studying the reasons that induced Voltaire to write his *Essai sur les moeurs* for his hostess and friend, the Marquise du Châtelet-Lorraine.

§2. Bossuet and Voltaire

The Marquise du Châtelet was a woman whose charms were equaled by her intellectual powers. She had enjoyed the pleasures of life under the Regency and now, in her riper years, was participating actively in the development of mathematics and of the sciences of her age. This Venus Newtonia, as Frederick the Great named her, experienced the urge to enlarge her horizon beyond the arts and the natural sciences into the field of history, and for that purpose she studied Bossuet's *Discours sur l'histoire universelle.* The illustrious lady was not amused by the *Discours.* Voltaire reports two of her marginal notes. On a page of Bossuet's chapter on Israel she wrote: "One may talk much of this people in theology, but it merits little space in history." And in the section on the Roman empire she wrote: "Why does the author say that Rome engulfed all the empires of the universe? Russia alone is bigger than all the Roman empire."

a. Bossuet's Universal History

The two notes touch the crucial problems of the *Discours.* Bossuet's treatise consists of a chronological survey of events from Adam to Charlemagne (part I), followed by two discursive parts on the unfolding of religion and on the empires. The conception of history and the organization of materials is still that of Saint Augustine. The unfolding of religion, presented in part II, corresponds to the sacred history of Saint Augustine's *Civitas Dei;* the revolution of the empires, presented in part III, to the profane history of Orosius. For Bossuet in the seventeenth, as for Saint Augustine in the fifth century, the universality of history lies in the providential guidance of mankind toward the true religion. The history of Israel, the appearance of Christ, and the history of the church are the meaningful history of mankind, whereas profane history and the rise and fall of empire have only the function of providing the educative tribulations for Israel and the church, preparatory to the ultimate triumph.[2] The *Discours,* published in 1681, showed that even at this late date a universal interpretation of history still had

2. "Ainsi tous les grands empires que nous avons vu sur la terre ont concouru par divers moyens au bien de la religion et à la gloire de Dieu, comme Dieu même l'a déclaré par ses prophètes." Bossuet, *Discours sur l'Histoire universelle,* in *Oeuvres complètes de Bossuet* (London: Regley, 1862), 4:232. Hereafter abbreviated as *O.C.* with volume and page number. The passage is translated by Elborg Forster in Bossuet, *Discourse on Universal History,* ed. Orest Ranum (Chicago: University of Chicago Press, 1976), 302: "Thus all the great empires we have seen on this earth have contributed in various ways to the welfare of religion and to the glory of God, as God himself has told us through his prophets."

to use the patristic pattern, although the monographic accounts of profane history had developed richly following the example of the humanists of the sixteenth century. In spite of the inroads of profane history on the traditional historical accounts, however, no historian would have dared to challenge the Christian idea of universality in the face of the reawakened religious sentiments of Reformation and Counter-Reformation.[3]

b. Secularized History

The notes of the Marquise du Châtelet challenged the Christian universality frankly by the appeal to a profane principle of universality. The note on the relative importance of Israel opposed history to theology. "History" is in this remark a realm independent of the providential plan; its meaning and order, if any, cannot be derived from the drama of fall and salvation. The people of Israel may have had a unique importance in the sacred drama, but they have little importance in a field whose structure is determined by the rise and fall of political powers. This aspect of the note, however, would not yet be revolutionary; Bossuet might even agree with the Marquise on this point and insist that precisely for this reason he had dealt with Israel in the *Suite de la religion* and not in part III on the history of empires. The note became revolutionary by its implication that the sacred history, the "theology," was unimportant, and that profane history had a monopoly on determining the relevance of peoples and events. The center of universality had been shifted from the sacred to the profane level, and this shift implied a turning of the tables: that the construction of history would, in the future, not be subordinated to the religious drama, but that Christianity would be understood as an event in history. Through this shift in the center of interpretation the dualism of sacred and profane history disappeared. Profane history is profane only so long as sacred history is accepted as the absolute frame of reference; when this position

3. The only major attempt at a world history before 1700 from a humanistic point of view is the *History of the World to the Year of Human Salvation 1504* of Sabellicus (1435–1506). An incipient humanistic universalism makes itself felt, however, only in the extension of Bruni's methods to a subject matter that usually was dealt with in sacred history. Otherwise no constructive ideas are introduced. See on this question Eduard Fueter, *Geschichte der neueren Historiographie*, 3d ed. (Munich and Berlin: Druck and Oldenbourg, 1936), 33 ff.; on the absence of any nontheological approach to the problem of universal history before the eighteenth century, see 288 ff.

is abandoned, the two histories merge on the level of secularized history. By secularization we intend to signify the attitude whereby history, including Christian religious phenomena, is conceived as an intramundane chain of human events, while, at the same time, there is retained the Christian belief in a universal, meaningful order of human history.

c. The Relevance of Rome

The second note, on the relative importance of Russia and Rome, was quite as revolutionary as the first, because it introduced the category of quantity as a standard, which in turn challenged the function of Rome as a constituent factor of Western universality. The relevance of Rome has never been a question of its size. Western civilization, as it emerged from the Middle Ages, rested on the unique and precarious balance between the elements of ancient civilizations that were merged in it: Hellenic rationalism, Israelitic subjective spiritualism, and the Roman jurisdictional order governing private wills and public offices. The *koine* of Hellenistic civilization, the universality of the Roman *imperium,* and the catholicity of the church were continued on a new ethnical basis in the Christian imperial merger of the Middle Ages. We recognize them in their transformations of scholastic intellectualism and of the temporal and spiritual orders of Western mankind. The link between the two worlds, ancient and medieval, was the church: in the Roman period the church grew into the empire with its Hellenistic civilization, while in the Middle Ages the temporal order of the barbarian kingdoms grew into the spiritual and civilizational tradition of the church. And the church could achieve this linkage between the two worlds because it continued not only its own spiritual catholicity into the Middle Ages, but transmitted as well the universal claim of the Roman imperial order by adopting the emperor of the West into the double headship of Christian mankind.

An attack on the relevance of Rome was, therefore, an attack on the joint strength of the three civilizational voices of antiquity that was achieved in medieval Western civilization. This astounding counterpoint of three civilizations with a recipient fourth is the characteristic trait by which Western civilization is distinguished from all the other civilizations of mankind. It is the source of the richness and amplitude by which it is objectively superior to

other civilizations. The combination of spiritualism and rationalism is the source of its dynamism, and the merger of the three
universalisms of antiquity is the source of the imperial pathos of
Europeanism. But it is also the source of a danger to which no
other civilization is exposed in the same manner. The danger is
that the component forces will follow their own momentum if the
miracle of their balance is disturbed at any point. Such disturbances
may be initiated externally by historical changes in power relations.
The closure of the civilizational, spiritual, and political cosmion,
as well as of the myth of its universality, can dominate public
sentiments so long as the plurality of other worlds does not impress
itself too strongly on the mind. In the Roman period the sentiment
of universality apparently could be maintained by a magnificent
forgetfulness about the Sassanian empire, and even greater forgetfulness about the remoter parts of the Eurasian continent and of
Africa. Throughout the Middle Ages the sentiment could continue
to be held against Islam by the crusading expansiveness that put
the Muslims into the position of a temporary infidel nuisance
that ultimately would be overcome. However, with the Turkish
and Mongol advances, with the discovery of America, with the
increased knowledge of China and India, and with the emergence of
Russia, an uneasiness inevitably beset the sentiment of medieval
universality. If the existence of mankind in history had a universal
meaning at all, it would have to rest on something different from the
myth provided by the dissolving institutions of church and empire.
The remark of the Marquise du Châtelet, of course, did not start
a revolution; it rather acknowledged the existence of a revolution
that had in fact taken place. An intelligent woman could state with
the innocence of the child who saw the emperor without clothes
what the foremost thinkers of the seventeenth century would still
have shuddered to admit.

d. Voltaire's Universal History

Voltaire was receptive to the criticisms of the Marquise. She complained that in his universal history Bossuet had forgotten nothing but the universe, and Voltaire undertook by his *Essai* to supplement the missing parts. He recognized the value of Bossuet's
Discours for the history of antiquity, though not without voicing

severe strictures for inaccuracies and the favoritism shown to Israel. He restricted his task to the addition of studies on China, India, Persia, and Islam, and to a continuation of the *Discours* from the time of Charlemagne to Louis XIII. The supplementary character of the *Essai* implies that universality in historiography can be achieved by completeness, and insofar as the *Essai* implies this identification it rather opens than solves the problem of universality. By completeness one can compose an encyclopedia, but that does not automatically achieve a unity of meaning. It is true that Voltaire's *Essai* in its final form has the distinction of being the first universal history,[4] in the sense that it embraces the whole of mankind, as it was known at the time, in his survey. But it is also true that it reveals the weakness of all universal histories and *Weltgeschichten* since Voltaire: the impossibility of finding a meaning that could substitute, on the larger scene, for the providential meaning of Western history under the Christian interpretation. The meaning, of course, cannot be found because a meaningful construction of history from a secular, intramundane position presupposes that history is known as a whole; since history

---

4. On the history of publication, extending from 1745 to 1753, and on the relations of the *Essai sur les moeurs et l'esprit des nations, et sur les principaux faits de l'histoire, depuis Charlemagne jusqu'à Louis XIII* to the other historical works of Voltaire, the *Siècle de Louis XIV* and the *Siècle de Louis XV*, see the bibliographical note in Fueter's *Geschichte der neueren Historiographie*, 349 ff. The *Essai* was published in 1753 under the title *Abrégé de l'Histoire universelle*. The edition used by Voegelin is that of *Oeuvres complètes de Voltaire* (1785), vols. 16–21. For the motivation of Voltaire and the criticisms of the Marquise du Châtelet see the *Remarques pour servir de Supplément à l'Essai*, in *Oeuvres*, vol. 21, particularly the *Première remarque*. On Voltaire's view of Bossuet see furthermore the *Avant-propos* to the *Essai*, in *Oeuvres*, vol. 16, 300 f.; and *Le pyrrhonisme de l'Histoire*, chap. 2, in *Oeuvres*, vol. 31, 13 ff. Voltaire lived at Cirey, as the guest of the Marquise du Châtelet, from 1734 to 1749.

There have been several editions of Voltaire's *Works* since the 1753 edition that Voegelin used. New material is regularly surfacing and is continually being printed in *Studies on Voltaire and the Eighteenth Century*. The philosophical problems are both fascinating and formidable. See, for example, Theodore Besterman, "Twenty Thousand Voltaire Letters," in his *Editing Eighteenth-Century Texts* (Toronto: University of Toronto Press, 1968). The most recent English translation is cited where available along with the critical French edition. Voegelin's translations are retained except for minor corrections where words have been omitted. The 1753 edition was not available to the editor. Instead we used the *Oeuvres complètes de Voltaire, Nouvelle édition*, 50 vols. (Paris: Garnier, 1880–1882) or the *Complete Works of Voltaire*, 135 vols. (Geneva: Institut et Musée Voltaire; Oxford: Voltaire Foundation, 1970–1977). The references Voegelin provided are clear enough that the text can be determined in the later editions.

is known only for the past, all secular constructions can but result in a perspective from the present of the author. Even the limitation of a finite perspective, however, would presuppose the empirical existence of a recognizable structure of human history, but no such structure, comprising the major civilizations of mankind beyond the Western, is recognizable. The Christian construction of the Augustinian type could be truly universal because it embraced the "whole" of history in the anticipation of the second coming of Christ as the end of history. When this transcendental universalism disintegrates under the impact of profane materials that cannot be related, however tenuously, to the course of sacred history, the universality of meaning has to degenerate into the ideal of empirical completeness.

§3. The Reconstruction of Historical Meaning

The ideal of empirical completeness, however, cannot occupy more than a transitory position in the movement of ideas. As soon as the question is raised as to why one should know with any degree of completeness whatever has happened in the existence of mankind in time, the curiosity shop is revealed as senseless. Encyclopedic knowledge, collected in handbooks, has to be moved into the functional position of a collection of materials that ultimately might become of importance for a *relevant* interpretation of history. And when historians do not entertain the idea of such ultimate use of their inquiries, historical research develops into a practice of vocational asceticism. Then, it ceases to have a meaning for history altogether and becomes a discipline for the personal life of the historian.

a. The Esprit Humain *as the Object of History*

The ideal of completeness is, in fact, no more than an incidental factor in the *Essai sur les moeurs*. Voltaire embarks on a reconstruction of historical meaning, and the pattern resulting from his efforts became the standard of secularist reconstruction for more than a century. The object of the *Essai* is "the history of the human spirit and not the detail of facts, which are usually distorted anyway." There is no sense in exploring the family history of some medieval feudatory who made war against the king of France: "we rather have to see by what steps we have advanced from the barbarian rusticity of his time to the politeness of ours."[5] The struggle between the spiritual and temporal powers is the guiding principle for the understanding of Western Christian history. But these powers are powers of "opinion." When the "opinions" are purified, that is, when people cease to believe in the claims of popes and emperors, we enter a new period of increasing truth and reason. The evolution of "opinion" is the principle that enables the historian to order and select the events that are illustrative of this meaningful development.

What is the cause of this fortunate change of opinion? On this point the argument is somewhat hazy, as so frequently with Voltaire when a serious question has to be answered. When history, says Voltaire, is conceived in the terms just indicated, we can observe the spectacle of errors and prejudices following each other and defeating truth and reason. By and by men will enlighten themselves by this picture of their misfortunes and stupidities; societies will rectify their ideas and man will begin to think. Obviously Voltaire is begging the question. The picture of errors and prejudices is the picture that he is painting in the *Essai* for the first time. The enlightening, however, must have begun at some earlier time, for now we are already well on the way of progress. To be precise, we have been on this way since the time of Henry IV. With Voltaire, we have to glide gracefully over this century and a half and over its problem of causation in order to arrive at the conclusion that now, in the *Essai*, the purpose is not to assemble a mass of facts but to make a selection that will enable the reader to judge "the extinction, the renaissance, and the progress of the human spirit *(l'esprit humain)*," for this is the only method appropriate for a general history.[6]

These remarks of Voltaire touch on the principal categories that have to be used in the secular construction of history, and they contain by implication the rules that have to be observed for their successful use. The *esprit humain* and its changes have become the object of general history. The transcendental *pneuma* of Christ is replaced by the intramundane spirit of man, and the change of

---

5. Voltaire, "Remarques pour servir de supplément à l'essai sur les moeurs et l'esprit des nations," in *Oeuvres*, vol. 24, *Mélanges*, III (Paris: Garnier, 1879), 547.
6. Ibid., 548.

heart by the change of opinion. The *corpus mysticum Christi* has given way to the *corpus mysticum humanitatis*. The meaning of history on this intramundane level is constructed as an analogue to the Christian meaning so closely that we can trace the parallelism step by step. In any construction of a meaningful universal history, the presumption is that the object studied shows a meaningful structure that is constituted as a whole. In the Christian account, the whole is constituted through the idea of the Creation and the descent of mankind from Adam; in the secular construction, the whole is evoked as a totality of empirical knowledge. The ideal of empirical completeness, which appeared as a degenerative substitute for Christian universality, of no more than transitory importance, becomes the secular analogue of the divine creation of mankind if it is coupled to a new construction of historical meaning.

b. Intramundane Sacred History

As we have indicated above, since human history has no recognizable structure of meaning, the construction has to resort to a deceptive interpretative device. Here Voltaire has set the standard: the historian selects a partial structure of meaning, declares it to be total, and arranges the rest of the historical materials more or less elegantly around this preferred center of meaning. The construction is a derivative of the Christian division into sacred and profane history, with the difference, however, that the new sacred history has no transcendental implications. The partial history selected as sacred gains its preferential status because it serves as the expression of a new inner-worldly religiousness. The operation is rationally untenable, and the constructions are short-lived because they have to follow closely the rapidly changing inner-worldly sentiments of the eighteenth and nineteenth centuries. Nevertheless, they are of decisive importance in the history of political ideas because they are genuine evocations of new communities that tend to replace the Christian *corpus mysticum*.

In the analysis of the construction we have to distinguish between the categories of meaning and the historical materials to which they are applied. The categories of meaning are again Christian analogues. Voltaire spoke of extinction, renaissance, and progress of the human spirit. The extinction corresponds to the Fall, the renaissance to the Redemption, the progress to a Third Realm of spiritual perfection. The materials entering into the system were the Middle Ages (extinction), the era of toleration beginning with Henry IV (renaissance), and Voltaire's own age (progress). The categorization was not analogous to the Augustinian, with its *saeculum senescens*, but rather to the trinitarian speculation of Joachim of Fiore. Voltaire resumed the rearticulation of history at the point where the thinkers of the thirteenth century had to abandon it in face of the orthodox resistance—with the fundamental change of substance, however, that the spirit of the new Third Realm was not the spirit of the autonomous Christian personality but the spirit of the autonomous intellectual. While Voltaire's construction was not thoroughly elaborated, it clearly foreshadowed the later constructions of Saint-Simon and Comte with their "laws" of the three phases: the religious, the metaphysical, and the positive-scientific. Since the content that enters the categories is an independent variable, it foreshadows as well the possibility that new materials may enter the categorical pattern, as has actually happened in the Marxian and National Socialist constructions.

c. The Structure of Intramundane History

Insight into the type of secular construction created by Voltaire permits the formulation of a few rules for the interpretation of the historico-political conceptions that have arisen in its wake. A historical conception like the Voltairean, Comtian, or Marxian is unacceptable at its face value. Its claim to offer a valid interpretation of universal history, or—in the nineteenth century—of a sociological "law," is untenable. In our analysis of these conceptions we shall have to distinguish between the following levels of construction. First, they contain a "thesis of generality," namely that the sequence of evolutionary phases, selected as "sacred history," is the general pattern of the history of mankind into which all empirical materials can be fitted in a satisfactory manner. While this "thesis of generality" inevitably is false for the reasons given above, it retains its importance as a clue to the particular "model" that has been "generalized." The particular "model" marks the second level in the construction to which we have to penetrate. Comte's law of the three phases is no more a law of universal history than the Marxian scientific conception of an evolution

43

tending toward ultimate communism or Voltaire's three phases of enlightenment. The general thesis, however, is based on a particular but nevertheless meaningful structure of history that may have been observed correctly. Voltaire, for example, has correctly seen that the struggle between the spiritual and temporal powers was decisive for the Middle Ages, and Comte's analysis of the Middle Ages was a great achievement for its time. Both thinkers have seen correctly that with the rise of the autonomous critical intellect an epoch is marked in Western history. Hence the model construction can rank very high as an empirical analysis of a particular phase of history in spite of the fact that the model is used as a secular "sacred history." Third and last, we have to penetrate beyond the model into the sentiments that cause its imaginative transformation into a general pattern of history. On this level we have to observe the shift from the transcendental faith in the spirit of Christ to Voltaire's intramundane faith in the *esprit humain*. We must then follow additional shifts of intramundane faith from Voltaire's *esprit*, to Comte's faith in the organizing and engineering intellect, to the Marxian faith in the proletarian as the true man and the proletariat as the chosen people, and further on to the various beliefs in chosen nations and a chosen race. Of the various strata of the historical construction, the upper levels that contain the "model" and the "thesis of generality" are no more than an ephemeral dogmatic surface beneath which lie the basic movements of intramundane religious sentiments that descend from the deification of reason and intellect to the deification of the animal basis of existence. If we may use Schelling's term somewhat freely, we may designate this basic movement of religious sentiments as a theogonic process.

§4. The Continuity of Christian with Intramundane Problems

The trinitarian conception of secular history is closely related to the Joachitic. This relation, however, has hardly ever become overtly conscious because the creators of the various secular, historical constructions have in most instances interpreted their own ideas as constituting a break with Christianity. They supposed that the continuity was interrupted and that a new beginning was made when Reason and Science (always capitalized) defeated the dogmatism of the churches. The preceding analysis has shown, however,

44

that the trinitarian pattern of the secular construction evolves in close analogy with the Christian Trinitarian pattern of history. The selected "models" of Voltaire's or Comte's histories have, by virtue of the "thesis of generality," the same function in the secular context that the "sacred history" does in the Christian conception. We have now to show that the parallelism is not accidental, but that a continuity of problems leads from the earlier conception to the later. We have to inquire particularly into the intellectual operations and the changes of sentiment that result in the "break" of continuity.

a. The Variations of Intramundane History

A key to the problem of continuity is offered by the development of secular history after Voltaire. Below the surface of dogmatic symbols we observed the movement of intramundane religious sentiments, pressing the interpretation of history and politics downward from the spirit to the animal basis of existence. Neither the "model" of the secular "sacred history" nor the dogmatic symbols on the level of the "thesis of generality" remain constant. They change continuously in accordance with the stratum of human nature that commands the attention of the time and thereby becomes the object of the process of deification. The rapid descent from reason, through the technical and planning intellect, to the economic, psychological, and biological levels of human nature as the dominant elements in the constitution of an image of man is a strong contrast to the imposing stability of Christian anthropology through eighteen centuries. Once the transcendental anchorage is surrendered, the descent from rational to animal nature, so it seems, becomes inevitable. The instability of the intramundane "sacred histories" becomes the characteristic trait of the new age. The great dogmatic constructions after Voltaire hardly outlasted the generation during which they were created. Where does this curious instability of sentiment originate? What are the antecedents of the religious disorientation that expresses itself in the frantic creation of new gods?

b. Bossuet's Histoire des variations des Églises protestantes

The answers to these questions were given by Bossuet. The instability of the secular historical constructions continues an instability

45

that begins with the schisms of the Reformation in the sixteenth century. Bossuet observed the phenomena of religious disorientation and of the consequent instability of sentiment and dogma at a time when this rapid variation still took place within the general framework of Christian doctrine. In the *Histoire des variations des Églises protestantes* (1688), he surveyed the Protestant variations of Lutheranism, Zwinglianism, and Calvinism. In the preface to the *Histoire* he furnished some suggestions concerning the dynamics of heresies. The succession of Protestant variations seemed to him comparable to the succession of heresies in the early Christian period, and he therefore based his own view of the problem on a remark by Tertullian concerning the early variations: "The heretics, says Tertullian, change their rules, that is their *confessions of faith*; every one of them believes himself entitled to change and modify the tradition by his own light *(esprit)*, for it is by his own light that the author of the sect has formed the tradition; heresy remains true to its nature when it does not cease to innovate, and its progress is similar to its origin. What is permitted to Valentinus, is permitted to the Valentinians; the Marcionites have the same right as Marcion; and the authors of a heresy have no more right to innovate than their sectarian followers."[7] Instability, thus, is the consequence of the initial break. Once the authority of tradition is broken by the individual innovator, the style of individual innovation determines the further course of variations. Or, in the words of Chrysostom: "Avoid the novelties in your discourse, for matters will not rest there: one novelty produces another; and we deviate without end, once we have begun to deviate."[8]

Bossuet's own attitude was that of the ecclesiastical statesman. The unstable course of heresies, and their tendency to beget new heresies, is caused by the nature of the *esprit humain*, which cannot cease to crave for the sweetness of novelty once it has tasted it. And it is, furthermore, caused by the difference between a perfect truth revealed by God and the weak production of the human mind. This second argument, however, has a peculiar sociological flavor in Bossuet's context, for Bossuet did not rely so much on the contrast between the truth of faith and the false-

7. Bossuet, preface to *Histoire des variations des Églises protestantes,* in *O.C.,* 4:410.
8. Quoted by Bossuet, ibid.

hood of heresy as on the circumstance that the truth of faith is to be found in the collective wisdom of the church and of the fathers, whereas innovation is a source of falsehood because it is the product of an individual. The individual will not be capable of anticipating clearly all the implications of an innovation, and the inconveniences appearing on second thought will compel corrections and thereby further deviation from the truth. The intellectual powers of the individual cannot substitute for the accumulated wisdom of the collectivity.[9] In these reflections Bossuet touched upon a fundamental problem of the function of ideas in modern history: the impossibility of creating a spiritual substance and an intellectual style for a community under the condition of free competition between individual intellectuals. The problem still appeared to him under the special form of the tension between the authority of the church and the individualism of the reformers. This special form, however, was but the first instance of a general phenomenon: that established community substances, or incipient communities, have been continuously dissolved and broken by the competition of new foundations until the chaotic multiplicity of sects, schools, parties, factions, movements, groupings, associations, and *Bünde* is reached that characterized the European social situation before the outbreak of violence in our time.[10] The continuity of the problem will appear more clearly if we compare Bossuet's remarks to a passage from a modern ecclesiastical statesman who also had to deal with the problem of heresy. He found the following features characteristic of the heretics: "a disdainful attitude toward theory and an inclination toward eclecticism; disrespect for the tradition of their own organization; anxiety for personal 'independence' at the expense of anxiety for objective truth; nervousness instead of consistency; readiness to jump from one position to another; lack of understanding of revolutionary centralism and hostility toward it; and finally

9. Bossuet, ibid., 4:413. For a modern formulation of this problem see the volume *Foi et "mystiques" humaines* in *Études carmélitaines* 22:1 (April 1937). See in this volume particularly Étienne de Greeff, "Le Drame humain et la psychologie des 'mystiques' humaines," 105–55. A copy of this journal is in Voegelin's library at the University of Erlangen.

10. See Karl Mannheim, *Man and Society in an Age of Reconstruction*, trans. E. Shils (New York: Harcourt Brace and World, 1940), 40 and pt. II, "Social Causes of the Contemporary Crisis in Culture," 79–114.

inclination to substitute clique ties and personal relationships for party discipline."[11]

c. *The* Libre Examen

It has been said of Bossuet that he was a Gallican in order to be a Catholic, and a Catholic in order to be a Christian.[12] Christianity outside the one, visible church was inconceivable to him. This attitude would not be noteworthy if it were simply a manifestation of Catholic adherence to Symbolon and dogma. It becomes of importance in a history of political ideas because it expressed Bossuet's concern about Christianity as a historical phenomenon. The church preserves and develops the Christian tradition; if the authority of the church is questioned, the living continuity of Christianity is broken. One must not question the tradition in any one point, for such questioning inevitably will lead to the ultimate questioning of Christianity as a whole: what guaranty do we have of the sacredness of Scripture unless we receive it on the authority of the church? This was Bossuet's decisive argument. His concern was not the content of heresies but the fact of schism and its origin in the *libre examen*. The critical inquiry into tradition and Scripture must lead to the disintegration of Christianity. That the Christian sources can be interpreted in more than one way, Bossuet did not deny. On the contrary, he stressed the point in order to show where the variations of interpretation have led the Protestant reform. Hence he was inclined to accentuate the claims of the majority against the rebellious individual. "What pride is it to believe that an individual can understand the word of God better than all the rest of the church; in that event there will be as many religions as there are heads."[13] He had a very clear conception of the consequences of independence based on the authority of critical reason. He is not so much afraid of Protestantism as a new religion as of the principle of historical criticism introduced by the reversion to an original meaning of Christianity. The Catholic historians of his time, Ellies Dupin and Richard Simon, who organized critical editions of, and

11. Leon Trotsky, *A Petty-Bourgeois Opposition in the Socialist Workers Party*, rpt. in Trotsky, *In Defence of Marxism* (New York: Pioneer, 1942), 43.

12. G. Lanson, *Bossuet* (Paris: Lecène et Oudin, 1891), 365.

13. Bossuet, *Conférence avec M. Claude, Ministre de Charenton, sur la Matière de l'Église*, in *O.C.*, 5:347.

commentaries on, the patristic literature and the Old and New Testaments, induced him no less to controversies and countermeasures than the Protestants. Worse than a Protestant heresy, which at least still takes Christianity seriously, was the indifferentism of historical and philological investigation, because Christianity as a divine evocation in history would be exposed to atrophy and destruction if it were submitted to rational criticism and psychological investigation as a myth. "Under the pretext that we should admit only what we can understand clearly—a proposition that is very true within certain limits—everybody grants himself the freedom to say: I understand this, and I don't understand that; and on this basis he approves or rejects whatever he wants; . . . Under this pretext a freedom of judgment is introduced that encourages one to advance whatever one thinks, without regard to tradition."[14] In Protestantism and historical critique Bossuet saw primarily not a danger to the Catholic Church but a danger to Christianity. In the free judgment and independent interpretation he saw foreshadowed the rational dissolution of the Christian mystery, which occurred with the eighteenth-century movement toward deism and atheism.[15]

d. *Bossuet's* Conférence avec M. Claude

The decisive point of transition from schismatic Protestantism to the historicization of Christianity was touched on by Bossuet incidentally in his religious colloquy with M. Claude, the Huguenot minister of Charenton.[16] Bossuet pressed the question of the authority of the church, and Claude maintained the necessity of independent judgment. Finally, Claude introduced the instance of the synagogue who condemned Christ and declared that he was not the

14. Bossuet, *Lettres*, in *Oeuvres complètes*, 31 vols. (Paris: Vivès, 1863–1867), 27:221, quoted in Lanson, *Bossuet*, 369.

15. See on this question Lanson, *Bossuet*, chap. 7, particularly 353–78. For an account of Bossuet's controversies with Catholic historians see Paul Hazard, *The European Mind, 1680–1715*, trans. J. Lewis Day (London: Hollis and Carter, 1953), 202–9.

16. The occasion for the conference was furnished by the desire of Mlle de Durras, the niece of Turenne, to have herself informed on the Catholic and Protestant positions, preparatory to her conversion to Catholicism. The conference took place in Paris, in 1678. See Bossuet, *O.C.*, 5, "Avertissement," 331–33. Marshal Turenne had been converted by Bossuet to Catholicism. See *O.C.*, 1:30. See also E. E. Raynolds, *Bossuet* (Garden City: Doubleday, 1963), 64, and W. J. Sparrow Simpson, *A Study of Bossuet* (London: S.R.C.K., 1937), chap. 4, "Bossuet's Conference with Claude."

Messiah promised by the prophets. Would Bossuet maintain in this case that the individual who followed Christ against the decision of the synagogue had acted wrongly? In this case obviously the individual, acting independently, had rightly done what Bossuet wished to deny the Christians of the future. Bossuet rose to the occasion. He pointed out to his opponent that Claude denied by implication that God had no other external means *(moyen extérieur)* to dissipate the doubts of the ignorant but the authority of the church. In order to support this argument, one would have to assume that at the time no authority existed on which the faithful could rely. "But, sir, who would say that, when Jesus Christ himself was on earth, that is, the Truth itself, who appeared visibly among mankind?" His authority certainly was contested, as it happens in these days to the church; still, his authority was infallible.[17]

According to Bossuet's account, Claude was at a loss for an answer. On the level of this argument, he obviously was faced by a dilemma: either he would have to deny the convincingly visible presence of the Truth in Christ, or he would have to attribute to the founders of the reformed churches a visible presence of the Truth. The first assumption would have made of the Incarnation a historical human opinion about the nature of Christ with which other men might disagree. The second assumption would have perverted the meaning of the Reform and erected the Reformers into paracletical figures. Claude was not willing to make either one of these assumptions. He remained in the peculiar suspense of early Protestantism: of interpreting a step, which like every historical step is a step forward, as a step backward to the origins. The forward character of the step, as sensed by Bossuet, revealed itself fully only in the following centuries when, under the pressure of historical critique and liberal theology, Protestantism evolved forms that were "progressive" to the point that Christianity was thinned out to a code of social ethics and Christ became one of the great teachers of mankind together with Confucius, Einstein, and other gentlemen. The active religious forces, on the other hand, expressed sentiments that led to the evocation of explicit new realms and new leaders. We observed the hesitation of Voltaire in this respect: he was an advocate of Enlightenment, but he did not declare himself the Light.

17. Bossuet, *O.C.*, 5:348.

Comte and Marx were less restrained in this respect. The later mass movements have evolved into new *corpora mystica*—a fact that is veiled only thinly by their heritage of antireligious ideology.[18]

§5. The Dynamics of Secularization

a. The Dissociation of the Western Universalisms

The preceding analysis has shown the continuity of the process by which Christianity became historicized and history secularized. We have a sufficient foundation now for a few general remarks concerning the dynamics of the process. The eighteenth century has to be characterized as the age in which the dissociation of the three European universalisms reached the stage of critical consciousness. The harmonious balance of spirit, reason, and *imperium* could be maintained as an idea only so long as the actual dissociation did not pass beyond a certain limit. The first of the three component factors to break loose from the combination was the *imperium*. With the fragmentation and particularization of the *imperium* through the national realms, a substitute order had to be found for the world of Western political units, and we saw it in formation with the rise of international law during the time of Grotius. The establishment of a secularized, autonomous sphere of politics outside the spiritual-temporal unity of Christian mankind moved the spiritual order into the position of the church in the modern sense, namely a religious organization distinct from the autonomous political organization of the state. The second component factor to move away from the combination was reason. The tendency became noticeable in the nominalism and Averroism of the Middle Ages. It received its social support from the increasing numbers of lawyers, royal administrators, philosophers, and scientists outside the ecclesiastical order,

---

18. I have analyzed the conflict of, and the continuity between, Christian and inner-worldly problems on the occasion of the French development because in France the conflict between Catholicism on the one side and Protestantism and Enlightenment on the other has compelled a clearer consciousness of the issues than the parallel development in England where the Catholic position had practically no function in the movement of ideas. The transition from Protestant rationalism to secular deism in England was gradual and compromising. Neither the Christian nor the secular positions had protagonists like Bossuet and Voltaire. For the English history see Sir Leslie Stephen, *History of English Thought in the Eighteenth Century* (1876), 3d ed. (1902; rpt. New York: Harcourt, Brace and World, 1962), with a preface by Crane Brinton, 2 vols. See particularly vol. 1, chap. 2, "The Starting-Point of Deism."

and it reached the stage of autonomous secular reason in the natural science and natural law of the seventeenth century.

These changes brought the church face to face with the problem of its own spirituality. The ascendancy of the spiritual power in the Middle Ages was not dependent on its spirituality alone but was based to an equal degree on its strength as the superior civilizing force of Christian mankind. It could exert this civilizing function by virtue of the inheritance it had acquired through the compromise with Roman-Hellenistic civilization. By the twelfth century both the civilizing function and the inheritance that made it possible had become sources of the friction that inevitably accompanies any process of dissociation. When, first, the civilizing work of the church had been successful to the point that the growing Western communities in the cities and the realms could continue it on their own, the new situation required a voluntary withdrawal of the church from its material position as the paramount economic power—a position that could be justified earlier by its actual civilizing performance. The church, however, did not liquidate its economic and political position voluntarily. When, second, an independent, secular civilization began to grow, a conflict between the contents of this new civilization and the ecclesiastical inheritance from antiquity was bound to ensue. This new situation required a voluntary surrender on the part of the church of the ancient civilizational elements that proved incompatible with the new Western civilization, as well as a new civilizational compromise similar to that which the early church concluded with Roman-Hellenistic civilization. And again the church proved hesitant in adjusting adequately or in time.

b. The Phases of Dissociation

These necessities and failures of adjustment caused frictions in the process of dissociation. The principal phases of the process, determined by the character of the predominant friction, are roughly three—making allowances for overlapping.

The first phase extended from 1300 to 1500. During this time the dissociation of the *imperium* reached its acute stage. The refusal of the church to reduce its economic and financial power in the particularized *imperia* led to the Anglicanism of the fourteenth century, to the Gallicanism of the fifteenth, and finally to the Reformation and the general confiscation of church property. As far as hypothetical propositions can be entertained in history at all, those scholars are probably right who believe that the schism of the Reformation could have been avoided by the church if it had judiciously reduced the property holdings that later were taken away by force.

The second phase extended from 1500 to 1700. Astronomy and physics developed, and the heliocentric conception of the universe clashed with the Babylonian cosmology of the Old Testament. It was the time of the causes célèbres of Giordano Bruno and of Galileo. The aftermath of this type of friction reached into the nineteenth century with the issue of evolution.

The third phase extends from 1700 to the present. It is the age of historical science and of higher criticism along with the clash of a critical treatment of sacred texts—of church history and the history of dogma—with the ecclesiastical interpretation of the truth of faith.

c. First and Second Phases: Spiritual Destruction and Respiritualization

The sequence of these frictions, which invariably culminated in the victory of the forces dissociating from the medieval compound, has left deep scars in the spiritual and intellectual structure of the West. The adventures of political and rational autonomy have not simply left a spiritual church as the residue. The frictions and maladjustments have worked a profound spiritual destruction in the autonomous secular sphere and have severely impaired the civilizational position of the church. The first type of friction resulted in a far-reaching expropriation of the church. Nevertheless, the confiscation of church property alone would not have endangered the spiritual substance. The decisive consequences of the struggle between the spiritual and temporal powers over this question, going as far back as the Investiture Struggle, was the political tension between the church and the state in the course of which the spiritual institution was finally relegated to the private sphere, while the autonomous political institutions achieved a monopoly of the public sphere. As we have seen in an earlier part of this study,[19] this privatization of the spirit left the field open for a respiritualization

19. Voegelin, *The Middle Ages to Aquinas*, chaps. 4–11.

of the public sphere from other sources, in the forms of nationalism, humanitarianism, liberal and socialist economism, and biologism. The growth of a plurality of counterspirits and counterchurches in opposition to the traditional spiritual institutions is the most fateful consequence of the failure of the church to find a compromise with the new pluralistic world of politics.

The tension originating in the problems of the first phase was aggravated by the friction caused by the advancement of science. This second failure of adjustment left the church with the stigma of obscurantism, and that of a force opposed to freedom of scientific inquiry attaches to it in popular opinion today, even after the church has made its peace with science. Again, the clash did not simply drive science into an autonomous development, which in itself would not have constituted a danger to the spiritual substance of Christianity. More fateful was the spiritual devastation wrought by the widespread conviction that the rational-scientific approach could be a substitute for the spiritual integration of the personality. Accepting the scientistic creed had a result similar to the establishment of autonomy in the political sphere, namely the openness of the individual to respiritualization from non-Christian sources. So far as the church was concerned the problem of leadership that was present, though less seriously, even in the first phase, came to dominate the third phase. The church was losing its leadership, not only the leadership of the civilizational process itself, but spiritual leadership as well. The futile opposition of the church to the civilizational process engendered an increasing opposition among the bearers of that new process against the claim of the church to be the institution that preserves authoritatively the Western spiritual tradition. Hence the inadequacy and belatedness of the civilizational compromise came to be of growing importance as a cause of de-Christianization and non-Christian respiritualization.

d. Third Phase: The Authority of the Church and the Christian Symbols

The gravest problem for the spiritual substance of Christianity arose in the third phase, from the conflict between Christian symbolism and the rational, historical critique of it. The symbolic language in which the truth of Christianity is expressed stems from Hebrew and Hellenistic sources. The mythical language was, at the time of its original employment, a precise instrument for expressing the irruption of transcendental reality, its incarnation, and its operation in man. In the age of Christ and the centuries of early Christianity, this language was not a "myth" but the exact terminology for the designation of religious phenomena. It became a "myth" as a consequence of the penetration of the world by a rationalism that destroys the transcendental meanings of symbols taken from the world of the senses. In the course of this "de-divinization" *(Entgötterung)* of the world, sensual symbols ceased to be transparent for transcendental reality; they became opaque and were no longer revelatory of the immersion of the finite world in the transcendent. Christianity became historicized in the sense that a universe of symbols that belonged to the age of the myth was seen in the perspective of categories that belong to an age of rationalism. In this perspective, when symbols and dogmas are seen in a "literal," disenchanted opaqueness from the outside, they acquire the "irrationality" that brings them into conflict with logic, with rational biology, critical history, and so on. For a modern man who has grown up outside the Christian traditions and institutions, it is extremely difficult to regain the original meaning of ancient symbolisms, be they Hellenic or Christian. It is possible, however, to gain an understanding of the problem by observing the symbolisms of modern spiritual perversions, which are quite as far beyond the sphere of rational critique as the ancient symbolisms. Anybody who has ever tried to explain to a convinced Marxist that the idea of a communist stateless society is a derivative eschatology, and that Marxism is not a "scientific" socialism—or who has tried to explain to a fanatic of world organization that terms such as *world peace, peace-loving nations,* or *aggressors* are not concepts of empirical politics but symbols of an intramundane eschatology—can gauge by the reaction of his victim how senseless it must have appeared to an early Christian if somebody had argued against Incarnation by offering biological reasons.

In this historical situation the church has shown admirable wisdom as far as the defensive attitude is concerned. It has resisted steadfastly all tampering with the symbols through modernistic, rational interpretations that would reduce the mystery of the transcendental drama to a psychology of intramundane human experiences. Nothing could have been gained by concessions to such a psychology, and the spiritual substance preserved in the symbols would have been endangered. Less admirable, however, has been the church's helplessness in dealing actively with the problem. A problem undeniably exists, and it cannot be solved, like the problems of the first and second phases could be solved, namely, by a belated acceptance of the new situation. It is not for us to offer a solution. But certainly a part of it would have to be a new Christian philosophy of history and of mythical symbols that would, first, make intelligible the new dimension of meaning that has accrued to the historical existence of Christianity through the fact that the church has survived two civilizations. Second, it would make intelligible the categories of myth as an objective language for the expression of a transcendental irruption. It would show myth to be a more adequate and exact instrument of expression than any rational system of symbols. Myth, therefore, must not be misunderstood by being taken literally, which would result in opacity, nor reduced to an experiential level of psychology. Obviously it is a task that would require a new Thomas rather than a neo-Thomist. The master stroke of ecclesiastical statesmanship, Saint Paul's identification of the three community forces of his time (the Pagan, the Hebrew, and the Christian) with the three laws (natural law, Hebrew external law, Christian law of the heart) has not been duplicated in our time. The Pauline translation of the triad of forces into progressively higher levels of spirituality made the historical situation meaningful and intelligible for his contemporaries. If we formulate somewhat drastically the deepest sentiment that causes the postmedieval spiritual tensions of the West, we might say: the bearers of Western civilization do not want to be a senseless appendix to the history of antiquity. On the contrary, they want to understand their civilizational existence as meaningful. If the church is not able to see the hand of God in the history of mankind, men will not remain peaceable and satisfied but will go out in search of gods who take some interest in their civilizational efforts. The church has abandoned its spiritual leadership insofar as it has left postmedieval man without guidance in his endeavors to find meaning in a complex civilization that differs profoundly in its horizons of reason, nature, and history from the ancient civilization that was absorbed and penetrated by the early church. In the face of this abandonment of the *magisterium* it is futile for Christian thinkers to accuse modern man who will not submit to the authority of the church of *superbia*. There is always enough *superbia* in man to make the accusation plausible, but the complaint dodges the real issue: that man in search of authority cannot find it in the church, through no fault of his own. From dissatisfaction at being engaged in a civilizational process without meaning stem the attempts at a reconstruction of meaning through the evocation of a new "sacred history" that began with Voltaire. And with Voltaire began as well the concerted attack on Christian symbols and the attempt at evoking an image of man in the cosmos under the guidance of inner-worldly reason. We have to turn now to this highly effective attack, which advanced the apostatic movement within a generation from the deism of Descartes and Locke to the atheism of Holbach and La Mettrie.

§6. Voltaire's Attack

Voltaire was not a systematic thinker. He did not elaborate a system of concepts and axioms that would have served as the basis for an attack on Christian symbols and particularly on the concepts of a Christian anthropology. He was completely up to date with the trends of his age, and his attacks took the form of pamphlets on persecution affairs, of aphoristic articles, aperçus, malicious witticisms, sallies à propos, sarcasms, and satires. The principles of the attack were implied in the critical and publicistic work, but they must be disengaged from a wealth of literary pieces, and a comprehensive presentation of Voltaire's position would have to take into account practically the whole of his production. In spite of interesting variations and nuances, a good deal of this work is repetitious. For most of the questions relevant in our context, we can penetrate to the core of the position by means of the articles in the *Dictionnaire philosophique*.

The form of the attack is intimately related to its content. A systematic elaboration of problems was unnecessary for Voltaire because he was sufficiently equipped with convictions. He inaugurated the type of man who is at the height of an age that is at the height of human civilization. He surveyed the horizon of mankind historically and geographically. He possessed as well a surprisingly solid smattering of knowledge with regard to physics, philosophy, public affairs, and even religious questions. He developed his intellectual and moral faculties to the point where they could become the standard for others: if Voltaire did not understand

Leibniz, the philosopher obviously had written something that he did not understand himself. From the apex of his reason and humanity he could see the evil in the world that has been caused by obscurantism and malice. With the fire of tolerance he would attack superstition and persecution, frequently with great courage and at a personal risk. The full consciousness of his superiority, however, did not impair his humility: faced with the mysteries of religion he would frankly admit that he did not understand them and that, therefore, they had to be eliminated from the public scene. The light of reason should fall into every corner of the human mind; and if it falls on a substance that is solid enough not to be dissolved by its rays, the obstacle should be destroyed because it is a scandal to enlightened man.

a. The Éléments de philosophie de Newton

What is reason? And when is man enlightened? The answer to these questions cannot be simple. The reason of Voltaire was not a philosophical idea like the reason of Kant's *Critique*, but a complex of sentiments and knowledge collected from widely different sources. We can understand it only by surveying the constituent factors. One of the most important factors for our purposes is the identification of a rational view of the world with the philosophy of Newton. During his residence in England, Voltaire was profoundly impressed by the philosophy of Locke and the physics of Newton; he studied the Leibniz-Clarke controversy with great care, and he later wrote, after his return to France, a presentation of the Newtonian system for the general reader.[20] The *Éléments de la philosophie de Newton* was not as detailed in the attack as the articles of the *Dictionnaire philosophique* and of the *Questions sur l'encyclopédie*, but it made the foundation of the attack more clearly visible than the later works. Hence an analysis of the *Éléments* is the best introduction to Voltaire's position.

The problem raised by the *Éléments* can be systematically formulated as follows: The Christian doctrinal symbols concerning the human soul, transcendental reality, and the relations between

---

20. Voltaire, *Éléments de philosophie de Newton* (1738), in *Oeuvres*, vols. 38 and 39. The edition used here is the critical edition, *The Complete Works of Voltaire*, vol. 15, *Éléments de la philosophie de Newton*, ed. Robert L. Walters and W. H. Barker (Oxford: Voltaire Foundation, 1992).

them are not a body of empirically verifiable propositions to be accepted as true after due examination. They receive their meaning as expressions of the spiritual process in which the soul responds with *caritas* to the supernatural aid of *gratia*. The *fides caritate formata* is constituted in this response, which opens the possibilities of reaching out understandingly into the supernatural. The soul develops the faculties of the *cognitio fidei*, the cognition by faith, concerning matters that are not accessible to natural reason.[21] Without the actuality of this spiritual process the theologoumena and the anthropology become empty shells. If the substance is lost, the professional theological preoccupation with them will tend to degenerate into the dubious controversies, both Catholic and Protestant, of the seventeenth century that have made scholasticism a byword for futility to the vast majority of Western mankind. When not only the substance is lost, but when also the active center of intellectual life has shifted to the plane of our knowledge of the external world, then the symbols expressive of Christian spiritual life acquire the opaqueness we discussed above. The symbols will either be abandoned entirely because they have become irrelevant or, when the sentiments of tradition are still strong, they will be submitted to rational simplification, psychological interpretation, and utilitarian justification. That last position—the combination of opaqueness of the symbols with traditional reverence for them—is the position of Newton and Voltaire.

When we now turn to the *Éléments* itself, we have to observe that the spiritual life of the soul in the Christian sense has disappeared, and with it the *cognitio fidei*. Knowledge of the external world, particularly in astronomy and physics, set the standard for what can be considered knowledge. Hence the discussion concerning Christian symbols cannot open with the analysis of a spiritual process. It has to open with a formula indicating the acceptance of God as a biographical fact in the life of Newton: "Newton was intimately persuaded of the existence of a God." The source of the persuasion remained for the moment obscure, and the next step was to offer a definition: "He understood by this word not only an infinite, omnipotent being, eternal and creator, but a master who has established a relation between himself and his creatures." The

---

21. See Saint Thomas Aquinas, *Summa contra gentiles* III, chaps. 151–52.

definition then was followed by the "reason" for the assumption that a personal relation existed between God and his creature: "Without that relation the knowledge of a God is but a sterile idea inviting to crime by the hope of impunity, for every *raisonneur* is born perverse."[22] These opening sentences of the *Éléments* set the style for the new attitude toward Christian symbols. The existence of God had become a human persuasion that has to be filled with a certain content in order to make it useful. The personal relationship between God and his creature had to be postulated because otherwise the trespasser would not be deterred by fear of punishment. Voltaire has indicated the line leading from fire-and-brimstone Christianity to the utilitarian pleasure-pain calculus. And the concluding remark offered one of the occasional profundities of Voltaire: that the man who reasons (the *raisonneur*) is perverse and needs the fear of punishment because his life is no longer transcendentally oriented by grace and love.

b. God and the Soul

Once these principles are established, the treatment of the sub-problem is logically more or less compulsory. The "persuasion" of the existence of God is due to a reasoning that draws from the order of the universe, as revealed in physics, the conclusion that "reason" ought to be persuaded of the existence of an artificer who created it. The Christian *credo ut intelligam*, which presupposes the substance of faith, was reversed into an *intelligo ut credam*. The existence of God becomes the object of a hypothesis with a high degree of probability. Furthermore, the basis of Christian theology, the *analogia entis*, has disappeared, and with it the possibility of speculation on the attributes of God. "Philosophy can prove that there is a God; but it is incapable of teaching what he is, or what he does."[23] The article on "God" in the *Dictionnaire philosophique* supplements this position by pragmatic arguments concerning the uselessness of metaphysical speculation: If I know whether God is a Spirit "would I be more just? would I be a better husband, father, master, citizen?" "I do not want to be a philosopher, I want

---

22. *Éléments*, 195. Subsequent editions declared, "Knowledge of God is but a sterile idea that leaves men without morals or virtue."
23. Ibid., 197.

to be a man."[24] The soul has to share the fate of God. The spiritual process, that is, the experiential reality designated by the symbol "soul," has ceased to exist. For Voltaire, there exists no Augustinian *anima animi* from which man reaches out in the *intentio*, into transcendent reality. The human personality has lost the integrating spiritual center with its phenomena of love, faith, hope, contrition, penitence, renovation, and acquiescence. The only human faculty that is left is thought *(le penser)*. And why do we have to assume a soul in order to explain the function of thought? Would it not be possible that thought is a function of matter, like gravitation? "Can reason alone give you sufficient light to conclude, without supernatural aid, that you have a soul?"[25] We cannot experience a soul, and if we had one we could not penetrate to its essence, for "God has given you understanding in order that you can conduct yourself well, but not in order to penetrate the essence of the things that he has created."[26] The freedom of the soul is disposed of in the same manner. Whether the soul is free to will or not, we do not know and it does not matter. In practice we act *as if* we were free.[27] Beyond that point speculation is senseless because, whatever we think, "the wheels that move the machine of the universe are always the same."[28]

c. The Foundation of Ethics

The spiritual obscurantism of Voltaire made it impossible for him to center a philosophy of morals in the idea of the spiritually integrated personality. The problems of ethics were dealt with under

24. Article *Dieu* in *Dictionnaire philosophique*. The edition used by Voegelin was the Flammarion reprint of the first edition of 1764. The volumes bearing the title *Dictionnaire philosophique* in the *Oeuvres* of 1785 contain the original *Dictionnaire* edited and fused with the articles of the *Encyclopédie*, the *Lettres philosophiques*, and other, minor pieces. The editors have mutilated the text frequently at their discretion. The edition consulted here is *The Complete Works of Voltaire*, vol. 36, *Dictionnaire philosophique*, vol. II, ed. Christiane Mervaud et al. (Oxford: Voltaire Foundation, 1994), 25–26. English edition: *Philosophical Dictionary*, trans. Peter Gay (New York: Basic Books, 1962), 1:239.

25. *The Complete Works of Voltaire*, vol. 35, *Dictionnaire philosophique*, vol. I, ed. Christiane Mervaud et al. (Oxford: Voltaire Foundation, 1994), 306; *Philosophical Dictionary*, 1:64.

26. *Dictionnaire philosophique*, 1:317; *Philosophical Dictionary*, 1:71. See also *Éléments*, pt. I, chap. 7, 233 ff., on Newton's ideas.

27. *Éléments*, 215–17.

28. Ibid., 218–20. See also "De la liberté," in *Dictionnaire philosophique*, 2:289–93; *Philosophical Dictionary*, 2:350–53.

the title of "natural religion": "I understand by natural religion the principles of morals that are common to the human species."[29] Such common rules are supposed to exist because they have their source in the biological structure of man and serve the purpose of making possible life in society. The fundamental rule is, therefore, a collectivized version of the Golden Rule: you should act toward others as you would wish them to act toward you. The rule has not been founded on the assumption of a spiritual person or of the recognition of the spiritual person in one's fellowman, but on the utility for society of conduct in accordance with the rule. "In every society one calls by the name of virtue that which is useful to society."[30] Voltaire denied expressly the legitimacy of a personalist ethics. "What does it mean to me that you are temperate? It is a rule of health that you observe; you will fare better with it and I wish you well. You have faith and hope and I wish you well still more: they will secure for you eternal life. Your theological virtues are gifts from Heaven; your cardinal virtues are excellent qualities that help you in your conduct; but they are not virtues with regard to your neighbors. The prudent will do good to himself, the virtuous to other men." The saint is neither good nor bad; he is nothing to us. "Virtue among men is a commerce of good deeds; who has no part in this commerce should not be counted."[31]

These passages grant perhaps the clearest insight into his inner-worldly religious sentiment as well as into the ideas of man and morality determined by it. The transcendental constitution of mankind through the pneuma of Christ has been replaced by faith in the inner-worldly constitution of mankind through "compassion." In this point Voltaire followed Newton closely. "Newton thought that the disposition that we have to live in society is the foundation of natural law." The disposition toward compassion in man is as general as his other instincts. "Newton has cultivated this sentiment of humanity, and he extended it even to the animals." "This compassion that he had for animals turned into true charity with regard to man. Indeed, without humanity, the virtue that comprises all virtues, a man hardly merits the name of philosopher."[32] Elements

29. *Éléments*, 219.
30. Ibid., 221.
31. *Dictionnaire philosophique*, 2:581–83; *Philosophical Dictionary*, 2:495–96.
32. *Éléments*, 222.

of Stoicism and Averroism obviously have entered into the belief in humanity as a rarefied biological instinct that serves the existence of the animal tribe.

The chattering discourse of Voltaire, furthermore, betrayed more openly than the more carefully considered formulations of later thinkers the relations between humanitarian tribalism and certain other phenomena. The attack on the saint as a prudent person who takes care of himself and forgets his neighbor is in principle indistinguishable from the Communist and National Socialist attack on the freedom and achievements of the spirit, as well as on the spiritual formation of personality, as socially useless, and perhaps even dangerous, private hobbies. The sphere of the socially valuable becomes restricted to the procurement of animal comforts and to scientific discoveries that may serve this purpose.[33] Behind the phrase that a man who is not socially useful in this restricted sense does not count looms the virtuous *terreur* of Robespierre and the massacres by the later humanitarians whose hearts are filled with compassion to such an extent that they are willing to slaughter one half of mankind in order to make the other half happy. The complacent assumption that charitable compassion is a general characteristic

33. See the praise of the Royal Society, founded in 1660, for its "useful and admirable inventions" in *Lettres philosophiques*, 1734, Lettre XXIV, "Sur les Académies." See particularly the following passage in this letter: "Je suis bien loin d'inférer de là qu'il faille s'en tenir seulement à une pratique aveugle; mais il serait heureux que les physiciens et les géomètres joignissent, autant qu'il est possible, la pratique à la spéculation. Faut-il que ce qui fait le plus d'honneur à l'esprit humain soit souvent ce qui est le moins utile? Un homme, avec les quatre règles d'arithmétique, et du bon sens, devient un grand négociant, un Jacques Coeur, un Delmet, un Bernard; tandis qu'un pauvre algébriste passe sa vie à chercher dans les nombres des rapports et des propriétés étonnantes, mais sans usage, et qui ne lui apprendront pas ce que c'est que le change. Tous les arts sont à peu près dans ce cas: il y a un point passé lequel les recherches ne sont plus que pour la curiosité. Ces vérités ingénieuses et inutiles ressemblent à des 'étoiles, qui, placées trop loin de nous, ne nous donnent, point de clarté" (I'm very far from concluding from these observations that it is necessary to be content with a blind practicality. But it would be a fine thing if the physicists and the geometers combined practicality and speculation as often as possible. Must one accord more honor to the human spirit in proportion to its lack of utility? A man possessing the four rules of arithmetic and common sense may become a prosperous merchant, a Jacques Coeur, a Delmet, a Bernard, whereas a poor algebraist may spend his life examining numbers for their astonishing but useless relations and properties and learn nothing in exchange for his efforts. Every art is a bit like this: there is a point beyond which research is undertaken only for curiosity. These ingenious and useless truths resemble the stars that, being positioned too far away from us, give us no light; *Oeuvres*, vol. 22, *Mélanges*, I, 186). Voegelin identified this text as part of the *Lettres Anglais*. Voltaire's *Lettres sur les Anglais* or *Lettres Anglais* is most often identified in the current discussion of Voltaire as the *Lettres philosophiques*.

of man abandons the healthy Christian cynicism that is aware of the precarious ascendancy of the spirit over the passions and takes precautions. The identification of the good with the socially useful foreshadows the compulsory goodness of the planner as well as the idea of revolutionary justice with its assumption that right is what serves the proletariat, the nation, the chosen race.

d. The Meaning of Reason

We must not fall into the mistake, however, of laying the evils of the future at the doorstep of Voltaire. Man can bend any religion to the purpose of war and persecution, a transcendental no less than an intramundane one, and Voltaire would have raised his voice against intramundane religious persecutions probably quite as vehemently as against the Christian ones of his age. Let us now return to the more immediate problems of Voltaire. Our analysis will have clarified somewhat the meaning of Reason. Reason is a symbol designating a complex of sentiments and ideas. The fundamental sentiment is the inner-worldly faith in a society that finds its coherence through compassion and humanity. Humanity is a general disposition in man, arising out of his biological structure. Negatively, the reasonable attitude is characterized by the absence of immediate spiritual experiences. As a consequence of this deficiency, the symbolic expression of spiritual experiences has become opaque and is misunderstood as depending for its validity on its resistance to rational critique. The monopoly of legitimate orientation in the world is arrogated, on principle, to the methods of natural science. The remnants of the Christian orientation toward the transcendent have to be justified, like the existence of God, in terms of a hypothesis based on the order of nature as revealed in physics, or, like the belief in supernatural punishment, on its pragmatic usefulness. The spiritual orientation and integration of personality is ignored as a problem, the principles of ethics are severed from their spiritual roots, and the rules of conduct are determined by the standard of social utility.

e. Philosophical Sectarianism

The implications of this complex designated by the name of Reason cannot be fully understood, however, unless one takes into account

Voltaire's opinion concerning its social function. In spite of the fact that Voltaire was a professional publicist, he seems to have been convinced that his ideas were relevant only to a comparatively small social circle and that they would not, and perhaps should not, penetrate into the consciousness of the masses. Voltaire's attitude bore some resemblance to that of Averroës and the Latin Averroists: the cultivation of Reason should be confined to a sect of intellectuals, whereas society at large, the people as well as the rulers, should remain in the orthodox faith.[34] In his conduct, however, he departed from the Averroist counsel of abstinence insofar as he intervened with intense aggressiveness in public affairs involving the orthodox faith. His intervention in persecution affairs gave to his work a public resonance that he disclaimed for it on principle. This peculiar suspense between an esoteric sentiment and aggressive intervention pervades the whole work of Voltaire and makes it frequently rather difficult to judge whether a particular declaration in favor of revealed religion is a political device to protect himself against unpleasant consequences or a sincere protestation of his respect for a religious sphere that he considers necessary for the orderly functioning of society. Public effectiveness on the European scale has become the predominant characteristic of Voltaire's work, but the undercurrent of esotericism, and perhaps the original sentiment of esotericism, must not be lost sight of. The problem deserves some attention, for in Voltaire's suspense we must recognize a late phase in the evolution of inner-worldly intellectualism of which an early phase is represented by the Averroist sectarianism of the thirteenth and fourteenth centuries. In the *Lettres philosophiques* of 1734, Voltaire still expressed the opinion that no philosophical sentiment would ever hurt the religion of a country. The objects of Reason and Faith are different, he said, and no Christian will cease to respect the mysteries of his religion because they are in conflict with reason. "The philosophers will never become a religious sect."[35] Why? Because they don't write for the people and because they have no

---

34. See particularly the revealing *Troisième entretien* of the *Catéchisme chinois* in the *Dictionnaire philosophique*, 1:449–59; *Philosophical Dictionary*, 1:132–37. See also the concluding passages on the article "Ame" in *Dictionnaire philosophique*, 1:317–19; *Philosophical Dictionary*, 1:71–73.

35. One should read this passage rather as "a successful religious sect." That Voltaire considered the philosophers, indeed, to be a sect will appear presently in the text.

enthusiasm. "The number of men who know the name of Locke is small; only very few of them read at all, and those who do read prefer novels to philosophical studies. The number of those who think is exclusively small, and they have no intention of bothering the world."[36] Nevertheless, he was clear about the sectarian character of the new philosophical movement. In the "Letter on Socianism" he wrote of the small English sect, consisting of a few clergymen and savants, who did not call themselves Arians or Socinians but who nevertheless did not at all agree with the Athanasian Creed and who placed the Father higher than the Son. Whatever one called these people, there was a distinct revival of Arianism in England, Holland, and Poland. Newton expressed himself favorably on it, "and the firmest advocate of Arian doctrine is the illustrious Clarke." The admiring characterization of Clarke seems to reflect Voltaire's own preferences: "This man is of a rigid virtue and a sweet character, more enamored with his beliefs than impassioned to make proselytes, exclusively occupied with calculations and demonstrations, blind and deaf for everything else, a veritable reasoning machine." The Arian revival, however, has chosen its time badly, for the age is preoccupied with sectarian disputes. The new sect is too small to obtain the freedom of public assembly, but it will obtain it if it ever becomes more numerous. Still, this is not the age "to succeed with a new or a revived religion." "It is not a nice state of things that Luther, Calvin, and Zwingli, all writers whom one cannot read, have founded sects that divide Europe among them, that the ignorant Muhammad has given a religion to Asia and Africa, and that Newton, Clarke, Locke, Leclerc, the greatest philosophers and best pens of their time, have hardly been able to collect a small troupe of followers."[37]

These passages illustrate the ambiguity of Voltaire's attitude. On the one hand, the philosophers were a small group and they did not want to bother the public. On the other hand, he hoped that they would have public meetings when their sect became more numerous. The comparison with the Reformers and Muhammad left hardly a doubt that he looked with some envy on the mass success of other religious movements. The remarks also betray

36. *Lettres philosophiques* XIII, "Sur Locke," in *Oeuvres*, vol. 22, *Mélanges* I, 124.
37. *Lettres philosophiques* VII, "Sur les sociniens, ou ariens, ou anti-trinitaires," in *Oeuvres*, vol. 22, *Mélanges* I, 100–102.

the sources of the ambiguity: Voltaire's understanding of his own position was limited. He saw in the philosophers' ideas a deviation from orthodox Christianity, and he classified it in dogmatic terms as a unitarian heresy, but he did not recognize the new inner-worldly religiousness as the force behind the innovation in dogma. He even denied the enthusiasm without which the movement would be inexplicable. The old faith was lost, and the new faith had not yet reached the level of a conscious, responsible will to order the world of man and society anew. We have observed earlier a haziness in Voltaire's reconstruction of the historical pattern: the *esprit humain* advanced somehow from medieval darkness to modern enlightenment, but the motive force of the advancement remained obscure. Voltaire did not see himself as the spiritual substance by means of which history advances. He was not a revolutionary spiritual founder, but remained in suspense before the revolution.

f. The Realm between the Spirits

Suspense before the revolution is perhaps the most intimate Voltairean sentiment. From this center we can gain an understanding of the connection between personality traits that otherwise would appear confusingly unrelated. We have to beware, in the case of Voltaire, of falling into the extremes of partisan judgment. Voltaire was neither neutral nor a great positive or negative force. One can, of course, make a long list of his more reprehensible qualities. He was deficient in spiritual substance and he was vulgarly irreverent. His surprising range of solid knowledge was coupled with an equally surprising ignorance concerning the more intricate questions of philosophy and religion. As a result his judgment was frequently superficial, though delivered with authority. He has set the style for brilliantly precise misinformation, as well as for the second-rater's smart detraction of the better man. He was ever ready to sacrifice intellectual solidity to a clever witticism. He has introduced to the European scene the unhappy persuasion that a good writer can talk about everything, that every unsound utterance has to be considered an authoritative opinion, and that irresponsibility of thought is synonymous with freedom of thought. In short: he has done more than anybody else to make the darkness of enlightened reason descend on the Western world. But all this does not add up to a demonic force for evil. If we subtract Voltaire's vitality, literary qualities, and intellectual temperament, there becomes visible in the distance the Homard of Flaubert's *Madame Bovary* or the exasperating Bouvard and Pecuchet who have to try their hands at everything. On the positive side we are in a similar difficulty. There we find the achievements of the poet, the master of elegant prose, the historian, the essayist, the correspondent, the reporter on England, the excellent popularizer of Newtonian physics, and the effective publicist. They certainly make Voltaire one of the greatest men of letters, but the range and quality of the performance can never quite anaesthetize our awareness of the ultimate defect of substance.

Still, Voltaire is not boring. There is in him a quality that is praised in such terms as his spirit of tolerance, his common sense, his indignation at scholastic obscurantism and at bigotry, his hatred of oppression and persecution, his advocacy of freedom of speech and thought. The praise is merited, indeed. Voltaire's strength lies in the twilight zone of procedural virtues that are peculiar to a man who has lost the old faith sufficiently to see its shortcomings as an outsider and to attack them without compunction. He did not have enough substance of the new faith to create the new law as its master, but he did have enough to fight with skill and courage for its establishment. This intermediate position is the soil for the style of critique and attack, of proselytizing and defense, sarcasm and satire, that Voltaire developed to perfection. It is a realm not of the spirit but between the spirits, where a man can live for a moment in the illusion that by discarding the old spirit he can free himself from the evil that inevitably arises from the life of the spirit in the world, and that the new one will create a world without evil. The protest against the world and the cry for light are futile if we expect to find the light in the world, but even this futility and illusion are still ennobled by the *contemptus mundi,* by a glimpse of the light and a sincere desire for deliverance from evil. The child-of-the-world's dream of a terrestrial paradise of compassion and humanity is only a shadow of the heavenly city, but still it is a shadow cast by the eternal light.

g. Compassion

And, finally, we must consider that Voltaire could dream of a paradise of compassion and humanity because he experienced these qualities actively in his person. However dubious his anthropology may appear as a systematic achievement, there can be no doubt that his compassion with the suffering creature was sincere. The religious wars of the sixteenth and seventeenth centuries, and the innumerable individual persecutions, perpetuated by the Catholic as well as the Protestant churches of all persuasions, were a stark reality. "Only the ignorant will scoff at the sacred and pious ring that the words Natural Religion, Enlightenment, Tolerance, and Humanity had for the men of those days. Then express a sigh of relief in a world that was on the point of succumbing to the oppression of the confessions."[38] The human situation will appear perhaps more clearly if we relate a simple case. In 1596, a poor artisan was tried in Amsterdam because his struggle with the Bible, in the two original languages, had led him to the belief that Jesus was only a man. Peter van Hooft, the mayor of Amsterdam, said in his defense speech: "I hear that he has been excommunicated because of his opinions. The church should content itself with the excommunication and proceed not further against the poor man. It is certain that a man who frequently visited his house saw his wife and his children on their knees in prayer before the meals. And that proves that he has brought them up in the fear of the Lord according to his lights. I believe that the life of a man should not depend on the subtleties of scholars."[39] The elements of the situation had not changed by the time of Voltaire; as far as the question of dogma is concerned, a Newton or Clarke might stand in the place of the artisan. There we see on the one side a poor fellow in his spiritual troubles, exerting himself to the extent of studying Greek and

38. Wilhelm Dilthey, "Das natürliche System der Geisteswissenschaften im 17. Jahrhundert," in *Gesammelte Schriften* (Stuttgart: Teubner, 1914), 2:95. On the problem and the history of persecutions see W. F. H. Lecky, *History of the Rise and Influence of the Spirit of Rationalism in Europe*, rev. ed., 2 vols. (New York: Appleton, 1914), chap. 4, pt. 1, "The Antecedents of Persecution," pt. 2, "The History of Persecution." As Lecky observed: "Indeed, even at the close of the seventeenth century, Bossuet was able to maintain that the right of the civil magistrate to punish religious error was one of the points on which both churches agreed; and he added that he knew only two bodies of Christians who denied it. They were the Socinians and the Anabaptists" (2:60).

39. Dilthey, "Das natürliche System," 101; the original source is Geeraret Brandt, *Histoire abrégée de réformation des pay-bas*, 3 vols., trans. from the Dutch (The Hague: Gosse, 1726), 1:331 ff. There is also a two-volume English translation and edition of the original four-volume Dutch work: *The History of the Reformation and other ecclesiastical transactions in and about the Low-countries* (London: Wood, 1720–1721).

Hebrew, and finally arriving at a heretical christological view. On the other side: the institutional machinery of church and state with its threats of excommunication and the death penalty. And then the reaction of compassion: it cannot be the purpose of Christianity to persecute such a man, to kill him, and to inflict infinite misery on his wife and children. The ecclesiastics who are responsible for the persecution appear no longer as defenders of the spirit but as intellectuals who bring human sacrifices to dogmatic subtleties that should be of secondary importance as compared to the substance of the faith. The earlier discussed inability of the churches to cope with the problems of postmedieval history reaches the breaking point where compassion turns against them and threatens to throw the spirit overboard together with the degenerative excrescences. Compassion for the suffering creature who is trampled underfoot by historical forces beyond his understanding and control is the great positive quality in Voltaire. And if his compassion had been less passionate and more spiritual, one might almost recognize a Franciscan touch in him: in the thirteenth century the mute creation had to be discovered and to be drawn into the orbit of spiritual sympathy. In the eighteenth century man in society and history had to be recognized as part of the God-willed creation and to be accepted in compassion. It may be considered unfortunate that the institutions of the spirit had sunk so low at the time that Voltaire had to devote himself to the task and to act with authority as the defender of man in historical society, but one cannot deny that he acted with grandeur the role of a *defensor humanitatis* against the professionals of the faith.

2

-ᴧᴛ ᴥᴦ-

The Schismatic Nations

§1. The Vacuum of Reason

The revolutionary movement of the eighteenth century broke with the idea of the unity of mankind in the spirit of Christ. In the previous chapter on apostasy we traced the transition from the Christian transcendental universalism of spirit to the intramundane universalism of reason, on the occasion of the great dialogue on universal history between Bossuet and Voltaire. In the work of Voltaire, the intramundane sentiment found its expression in two principal assumptions: first, in the assumption of a commonsense morality, motivated by the sentiments of humanity and compassion and guided by social usefulness as the criterion of right conduct; and second, in the assumption that the methods of science, which had proved their value in the creation of Newtonian physics, were the only methods leading to valid knowledge. The establishment of morality and knowledge on the new level was accompanied by the atrophy of Christian transcendental experiences. We considered as well Voltaire's spiritual obscurantism, which expressed itself negatively in the loss of cognition by faith and positively in attack on the symbols of faith that had become opaque as a consequence of the loss of the *cognitio fidei.*

As far as the evocation of reason on the general level of principles is concerned, the expression given to the intramundane sentiments by Voltaire is exhaustive. To be sure, consequences had to be drawn, corollaries had to be added, and special problems had to be elaborated. The nominal acceptance of opaque religious symbols could not last, and the evolution toward dogmatic atheism in the generation of Holbach and Helvétius was inevitable. The denial of cognitive value to spiritual experiences could issue only in the denial of the experiences themselves and in the development of a materialistic position. The ascription of a monopoly to the Newtonian method of science led, in the analysis of the mind, to the idea of association as the principle governing occurrences in the soul, in analogy to the principle of gravitation. The Newtonian humanity and compassion were to unfold in the theory of moral sentiments and in the ethics of sympathy. And social usefulness as the rule of right conduct was developed systematically in the calculus of pleasure and pain, in Bentham's "moral arithmetic," and in the philosophy of utilitarian radicalism. This universe of elaboration, however, does no more than embody the attitude that was fixed in its outlines by Voltaire. It brings immense consequences with it because it carries the attitude of enlightenment and reason into the details of a philosophical anthropology and into the critique of institutions. But it adds little or nothing to the penetration of problems on the general level of ideas.

While the theoretical elaboration of Voltaire's position is thus of minor interest, the apostatic revolt as such is significant because it released a movement of ideas that decisively shaped the political structure of the West. With the formal abolition of Christianity as the authoritatively unifying spiritual substance of mankind, the particular community substances could move into the vacuum. The mystical bodies of the nations, which had been growing ever since the high Middle Ages, had achieved by the eighteenth century a considerable coherence and articulation; and now with increasing effectiveness they began to substitute themselves for the mystical body of Christ. Nationalism had been a force in Western history for centuries, straining against the weakening bonds of church and empire, but only now could it unfold as a spiritual force, arrogating to itself the claims of absoluteness that formerly were the prerogatives of imperial Christianity. The separatist movement, which found its first expression in the formula of the *imperator in regno suo*, is now consummated by the evocation of the *imperium et ecclesia in natione*.

§2. The Irritation of Parochialism

The superficial but momentous symptom of the disruption of the West into schismatic politico-religious bodies is found in the development of the standard amenities by which members of the principal European nations express their disgust for each other's national peculiarities. Beginning in the eighteenth century, the national styles of intellectual expression become sufficiently differentiated to attract mutually unfavorable attention. In English-German relations, we find Scotch philosophers quipping about German "metaphysical madness," and we can observe the growth of an image of "obscurity," "mysteriousness," and "darkness" in German thought. In the nineteenth century the complaints begin to grow about Hegel's *Philosophy of Right,* which for its proper understanding would require "immersion" in Hegel's metaphysics—an obviously indecent demand. In the opposite direction, the Germans begin to develop the image of English "flatness" and we meet with such quips as Nietzsche's "John Stuart Mill; or the insulting clearness." In English-French relations complaints develop on the English side about French intellectual radicalism, about the inclination to follow a political idea to its logical consequences without regard to traditions and common sense, and such summary quips as Disraeli's "the rights of Englishmen are five hundred years older than the rights of man." On the French side, the stereotype is formed from English rambling, from the inability of the English to grasp principles and to follow through their implications, from their opportunism and their habits of improvisation. In German-French relations there appears on the German side the idea of French superficiality, of an accomplishment of form to which there does not correspond a weight of substance, of a rationalism and skepticism that does not penetrate to the concreteness of the spirit, of a certain levity and—an untranslatable gem—of *seelische Verschlampung* [spiritual slatternliness]. On the French side appear the German *fougue* [impetuosity], the *brumes du Nord* [Nordic obscurity], the complaints about idiosyncratic and whimsical vagaries, about a thickness of thought that never can elevate itself to the *clarté* of exposition.

§3. The Schismatic Cosmion

a. The Spiritual Closure of the National Cosmion

Such pleasantries are as partially right and as totally wrong as accusations of this kind always are. Nevertheless, while they are useless as a description of national characteristics, they are of value as symptoms of the irritation caused by the breakdown of the Western *koine.* They are the intellectual expression of the rise of parochial styles of thought that become increasingly unintelligible to each other. These parochial styles have little or nothing to do with the "national characters" that frequently are assumed to be ultimate and determining constants. They are the results of centuries of spiritual and intellectual differentiation in the various regions, and they represent aggregates of sentiments and ideas that have been laid down during the course of a long history. In the eighteenth century the process reaches a critical phase because then the national communities and their evocative ideas become active substitutions for the disintegrating imperial Christian evocation. Up to this point, the veil of the universal evocation had hidden the growth of the nations sufficiently to preserve the appearance of a general Western process unfolding through the medium of national variations. With the apostatic revolution this structure of the process changes fundamentally. Henceforth the evocation of the national cosmion enters into open conflict with the weakening evocation of a Western Christian mankind. The national communities are now able to close their particular evocations against each other; and the emerging, so-called national characteristics are the result of a closure that takes the constellation of sentiments and ideas at the critical time, which varies from nation to nation, as the fixed basis for a new evocative development. The nationally differing crosscuts at the time of the revolution dominate the further evolution of ideas, and the closed national units are driven farther and farther apart as a consequence until the tensions culminate in the catastrophe of the General Wars.

b. The French Case

We are still too close to the age of the Western national schism—indeed we are still involved in its liquidation—to have gained the proper perspective. We do not have sufficient knowledge to view it adequately either in its full course or in its details. Nevertheless, the dominant problems have become more clearly discernible in the light of twentieth-century events. The factor that differentiates decisively the several revolutionary evocations is the state and condition of Christianity in the various nations at the time of the schism. In the opposition between Bossuet and Voltaire, the apostatic break took the form of a transition from Catholicism to the

74

universalism of Reason. This type of transition is peculiar to France; it is not duplicated in England or Germany. And the character of an intellectual movement against Catholicism remains the signature of the French evocation of Reason throughout its history. Only in France do we find the attempt, during the Revolution, to elevate the cult of Reason into a universal religion in explicit opposition to Christianity. As late as the mid-nineteenth century, the anti-Catholic universalism of Reason, as embodied in the Revolution, inspired the hagiographic account of the Revolution by Michelet: "The Revolution adopted no Church. Why? Because it was itself a Church." This tinge of the reaction against Catholicism is again recognizable in Saint-Simon and in Comte, in their awareness of the necessity for a new *pouvoir spirituel* after the expiration of the Christian. France has become the classic country of the intellectual counterchurches: of Voltaireanism and Positivism, of romantic humanitarianism, and of the religion of solidarity under the Third Republic.

c. The English Case

The English spiritual and intellectual situation is entirely different. The brunt of anti-Catholicism was borne by the Anglican schism and the Puritan revolution. By the time of the apostatic revolution, "no-Popery" was a settled political issue. Anti-Catholicism was a datum in the situation from which the countermovement started. Hence the English transition does not move on the line from Catholicism to Reason. The tension plays rather between the poles of Puritan Independency and secularized individualism. England had no guardian of the old spiritual tradition, nor any intellectual expression such as that of Bossuet. Indeed, the established church had ceased to count as a spiritual force by the eighteenth century. In the Protestant climate of personal, idiosyncratic interpretation, the transition from Christianity to the intramundane faith took place gradually and by almost imperceptible steps. The lines become blurred between the defense of Christianity on the part of a liberal, deistic bishop and the incidental respect paid to the existence of God by a religiously indifferent layman. The atmosphere is favorable neither to a passionate materialism nor to a mystical enhancement of reason. A dogmatic atheism can hardly develop to a relevant degree if, on the one hand, its utterance is socially repressed because it would violate public decencies, and if, on the other hand, the urge for its expression is mild because dogmatic theism is little more than a matter of social respectability. In the face of such soothing efforts as Locke's *Reasonableness of Christianity*, or Toland's *Christianity Not Mysterious*, we cannot expect the spiritual zest that would produce a counterreligion of reason or unreason. Between the strength of English social forms and the self-reliant freedom of the individual within these forms, the life of the spirit moves in an even twilight of preservation and euthanasia.

d. The German Case

The German situation is complicated by the presence of three long-standing and interrelated tensions that enter into the history of the critical period as determining factors. The first is the tension between Catholicism and Protestantism, both entrenched regionally in the leading principalities in such strength that neither can form the nation to the exclusion of the other. The second is the tension between the imperial tradition and the plurality of territorial states, on the one hand, and the trend toward national unification and closure, in analogy to the schismatic nations of the West, on the other. The third is the tension between the colonial East and the old civilization of the South and West, which is precariously solved in the critical period by national unification under the leadership of Prussia.

From this initial situation a development is to be expected that will differ widely from the French and English. The absence of national political institutions and the regional division of religions made impossible a national revolution of reason as the French. The complex of reason-atheism-materialism-utilitarianism remained secondary in Germany until the 1830s. Only after the death of Hegel does materialism become of appreciable relevance, and only after the middle of the nineteenth century do the dogmatic antireligious sentiments become a component of increasing influence in political mass movements. Again, since Independency of the English type is absent from German Protestantism, the corresponding secular forms of individualism could not become a force in shaping institutions. The parliamentary political form, which in England is a creed sanctioned by the revolution of the seventeenth century, could become only a political technique in Germany, necessarily to be used in the age of democracy and national unification, but without roots deep in historically sedimented sentiments as in England. The main line of the German revolution, which parallels the French Revolution and the rise of English utilitarianism, is the great metaphysical outburst from Kant and Herder to Hegel and Schelling. The movement has its roots in Lutheranism and in the German mystical tradition. It acquires the characteristics of a revolutionary countermovement through its development of the Christian Logos-idea beyond orthodoxy in the direction of a new apocalypse. In Hegel we find the mystical speculation of Jacob Boehme translated into the dialectical movement of the Idea that reaches its self-conscious realization in the political forms of the present; Hegel's Reason is the speculatively purified Logos. With Fichte and Schelling we have to observe the explicit attempt at establishing a Christianity of the Johannine Logos as the Third Christianity after Catholicism and Protestantism. The adogmatic character of mystical speculation makes it possible for German thinkers to transcend the dogmatism of the churches critically and at the same time to recognize the relative historical validity of the church as a transitional phase in the evolution of the spirit. In this peculiarity of mystical speculation originate the characteristic traits of German intellectual history in the nineteenth century: the double aspect of historicism as a conservative and as a disintegrating, relativizing force, and the consciousness, particularly strong in Dilthey, that the *Geisteswissenschaften* are a final form of enlightened, critical Protestantism.

Furthermore, the mystical character of the metaphysical outburst determines the specifically German relation between the general level of political philosophy and the development of institutions. There is no parallel in Germany to the French relationship between reason and revolution, or to the English relationship between secular individualism and representative government. The mystical speculation on the spiritual substance of society cannot penetrate the institutions of a national polity because no such polity exists. We find instead an approach to the existing plurality of political institutions that moves between the poles of acceptance and rejection, typically represented by the extremes of Hegel and Marx. At the one extreme in Hegel, we have to observe the willingness to accept the territorial, constitutional state (which by no means is a national polity) as the objective manifestation of the

Idea; and at the other extreme, in Marx, we have to observe the revolutionary will to reject the existing society completely and to create a new, international community out of the mystically pure man, the proletarian. Between the acceptance of a subnational society within the territorial state and the supranational rejection of the historical structure of state and society that would have to enter a national polity there opens the chasm that was filled temporarily by the realpolitik of national unification. The unification, however, could not produce by itself a politically articulated nation. Instead, a political event of revolutionary proportions, comparable to the English Revolution of the seventeenth or the French of the eighteenth century, was required to solidify and articulate the national substance. The occasion offered itself in 1918, but as events have shown, the opportunity was missed. The workers' parties, which would have had to supply the strength of the revolution, were paralyzed by the anti-national, apolitical heritage of Marxism to a degree that incapacitated them as the bearers of a national revolution. The overdue revolution was finally realized, in 1933, borne by the middle class of an industrialized society and resulting in a national as well as an international catastrophe. The fact that the revolution of 1933 resulted in a catastrophe, for reasons that we analyze in a later context, must not obscure the insight, however, that in the immanent logic of the Western schism into national states a German revolution was due, and that the revolutionary ripeness of the situation was the overall factor that determined its initial success.

§4. The Time Structure of the Closing Process

a. The Problem of Closure

The survey of the three cases makes visible the common problem as well as the individual differences. To the common problem we gave the name "closure," and more specifically we have to speak of spiritual closure in order to distinguish this phase of the closing process from the legal and institutional closure that results in the form of the sovereign state, independent of the empire. The meaning of spiritual closure we have defined as the evocation of a schismatic cosmion that arrogates to itself the functions and claims of medieval, imperial Christianity. The problems arising from closure will come, therefore, under two general heads: the first complex of problems contains the relation of the new cosmion to its own, preschismatic past. The second complex of problems concerns relations among the plurality of the new evocations. The second complex is that of the disintegration of Western society and its destruction in the General Wars. We shall have to deal with it in detail in the last part of this study, entitled "The Crisis." The first complex is clarified in part by the foregoing analysis of the religious starting points, which determine the styles of the several national closing processes. Another aspect of the first complex, however, the time structure of the closing process, can be made visible only by a comparison of the differences in the several natural processes, and we must add, therefore, a few remarks concerning the time relations among the elements of the closed cosmion.

b. The English-French Time Structure

The first, and most obvious, line of differentiation has to be drawn between the English and French cases, on the one side, and the German, on the other. In the English and French cases, the growth of the unified national state precedes by centuries the spiritual closure. In the German case the time relation between the two phases is reversed. As a consequence, the institution of the national state is a datum in England and France at the opening of the critical period, and the spiritual closure is no more than a supervening event. The politically articulated nation can be taken for granted. In Germany, on the other hand, the spiritual closure partly precedes and partly runs parallel with national unification, and the two phases exert disturbing influences on each other. In spite of the actual unification, the imperial-federal construction of the central European area remained a live issue into the twentieth century, and the historical judgment on Bismarck's wisdom in forcing the issue in the direction of the national state, in imitation of the schismatic English and French developments, is still in suspense. By 1870 the value of the national state as the stable Western political form had already become dubious: Bismarck's addition of the German national state to the series of European Great Powers was accompanied by Nietzsche's dictum, "One stupidity more!"

c. The French-German Time Structure

A further differentiating line has to be drawn between England on the one side, and France and Germany on the other. Because of the peculiar English amalgamation of aristocracy and bourgeoisie, the revolution of the seventeenth century could lay the foundations for the parliamentary power of the bourgeoisie without abolishing the aristocratic structure of English society, or even a ceremonial monarchy. The transition from the aristocratic to the bourgeois republic has, therefore, in England the character of a gradual evolution, and the political form, established by the eighteenth century, has to date proved elastic enough to mold the political articulation of the lower middle class and the workers into its pattern. The style of the aristocratic ancien régime has remained the determinant of political form. The Revolution of 1789, on the other hand, broke the aristocratic structure of French society. The new form of the bourgeois republic, issuing from the revolutionary period, did not have the historical momentum of the English form, and after 1848 the process of attrition began, during the course of which the bourgeois republic was ground to pieces between the conquered, but not exterminated, prerevolutionary French tradition and the new forces of plebiscitarian democracy. In Germany we find no old national political form with historical prestige at all that would have been able to absorb the shock of mass democracy. Neither the survivals of the ancien régime in the territorial states nor the regional bourgeois republican forces proved strong enough to form institutions on a national scale, and the task of creating a political form devolved on the masses and their leadership, with the aforementioned catastrophic results. Accordingly, we have to distinguish between polities whose institutions develop in continuity with the ancien régime and those that have formed their institutions either by a revolutionary break with the aristocratic structure of society or by moving entirely beyond the aristocratic range. England, France, and Germany form a series of decreasing stability of political institutions in accordance with their distance from the aristocratic structure of Western society.

d. The Results

And, finally, we have to consider that the differences in the time position of the closing process entail differences of intellectual outlook that make themselves felt as determinants in the process. The oldest closure, the English, has most pertinaciously preserved the idea of the integral human personality, drawing its strength from such variegated sources as the aristocratic-feudal conception of the free man, the Renaissance conception of the autonomous individual, and the Protestant conception of the spiritually independent soul. The French closure, next in time, has preserved the idea of the integral personality with such strength that the conventional classification of France with England as the countries of "Western political humanism" is justified. Nevertheless, in French intellectual history the inclination is noticeable, more strongly than in England, to experience the idea of Reason as the legitimatizing source for imposing what is reasonable on other men, whether they are convinced that it is reasonable or not. And in the latest closure, the German, the economic and biological interpretations of man in society have determined a collectivist sentiment of such strength that the value of the integral personality is to a considerable extent destroyed.

3

Giambattista Vico—*La scienza nuova*

§1. Italian Politics

In the preceding chapter, on the schismatic nations, we have dealt with the reactions of several national societies to the problem of disintegrating Christianity, as well as with the marked differentiation of national "characters" in the age of Revolution and Crisis. The analysis extended, however, only to the English, French, and German instances; it did not include the Italian case. This is because the Italian history of political ideas differs so widely from the transalpine development that it cannot be presented as a variant solution to the same fundamental problem. On several earlier occasions we had to touch on the difference between the Italian and the northern historical structures. The political culture of the city-state, which in the north was superseded by the territorial state, remained the Italian political form and resisted integration into the national state until the latter part of the nineteenth century. In some respects this development is similar to the German, particularly with regard to the lateness of integration into the form of the national state. From this similarity stem the German and Italian parallels in the rhythm of the modern revolutions. There remains, however, the decisive difference that the German culture of the city-states had in principle been broken in the late Middle Ages so that the German plurality of states, preceding the national unification of the late nineteenth century, consisted of territorial states.

a. City-State and National State

This difference in political culture has caused serious tensions between Italy and the north, culminating in the foreign invasion of the late fifteenth century, and it has determined the intricate time lags and relations between Italian and northern political ideas. The hothouse atmosphere of the Italian city-states, with their political and economic revolutions, anticipated by centuries the corresponding development on the transalpine scale of the national state. The rationalism of the financial and bureaucratic organization of the Curia became the incentive for the rationalization of Western national states, and the plurality of city-states developed the principle of the balance of power in the cosmos of the peninsula before it was transferred to the relations between the northern territorial states. By the end of the fifteenth century relations between Italy and the north entered on the critical phase that we see reflected in the work of Machiavelli. The internal organization of the French and Spanish national states was sufficiently completed to become effective on the international scene. The superior military power of the large territorial states spelled the end of the Italian independent development. With the Milanese appeal to Charles VII, in 1494, the period of foreign invasions and occupations of Italy began.

b. Italian "Decadence"

The period from the French invasion to the Risorgimento is usually labeled as "decadent." While the term has its justification in view of the eclipse of Italy as a political power, it is entirely inadequate as a summary description of the highly complicated consequences of the disaster. Without qualifications, one can hardly call decadent the period of Machiavelli, Guicciardini, Bruno, Campanella, Galileo, Vico, and of a host of minor political thinkers and historians such as Boccalini, Paruta, Davila, Contarini, Sarpi, Pallavicino, and Giannone. Above all, the Italian breakdown has to be understood not as a purely internal phenomenon but as a state of disintegration and weakness that may be compared and related to the other European nations. Even the most intimate Italian aspect of the protracted weakness, the tension between the political culture of the city-state and the tendency toward national unification, is not a purely autochthonous problem, but it is caused by the northern development of the national state as the power unit of superior competitive value in international politics. Only if we make the quite unwarranted assumption that the national state is a model organization to which every people has to aspire can the

Italian failure to achieve this form in the critical age be considered a particular weakness.

A clash between two political cultures is a serious event. Institutions that have grown over centuries cannot be adapted to new demands overnight by the energy of solitary, intelligent individuals, so that when Machiavelli evoked the Prince as the savior who would transform Italy into another France, he overrated the possibilities of isolated intelligence and skill. The Japanese miracle of at least a temporary solution of an even graver historical problem is a rare occurrence in history. None of the Western nations has as yet shown a similar grasp of its political destiny in the face of imminent extinction. The clash between political cultures, moreover, was aggravated by the struggle between the Counter-Reformation on the one hand and the Reformation and secular science on the other. This problem cost France eight civil wars during the sixteenth century, participation in the Thirty Years War, internal repression of the Protestants under Louis XIV, and, finally, the Revolution with its aftermath of the intermittent civil war between the Left and the Right. In Italy, the imposition of this second problem on the first is sufficient to explain the difficulties of the period without recourse to the category of decadence.

c. Municipalization and Emigration

The net result of these tensions with regard to the problems that are our more immediate concern may be characterized as the cessation of intellectual life as the expression of a national Italian society. The trend of the Quattrocento toward a national intellectual life that in spite of the political competition between the city-states had its social basis in the interrelations of the Italian aristocracy was reversed. During this critical period, the intellectual life of the nation showed a distinct trend toward what has been called municipalization. Certainly, regional differences of Italian culture corresponding to the spheres of influence of the city-states had been strongly developed earlier, but during the fifteenth century they became marked and emphasized, indicating a curious regional withdrawal from national life. This is the period of the deeper differentiation between Venetian, Milanese, Romagnole, Tuscan, Roman, and Neapolitan cultural peculiarities. It is the period of Florentine insistence on the Tuscan variant as the model Italian language, of the counterdevelopment of a Venetian literary language in comedy, and of the new upsurge of Neapolitan patois poetry. To this process of municipal contraction corresponds a countermovement of Italian emigration, both compulsory and voluntary. The political contraction, as well as the pressure of the Counter-Reformation, drove energetic individuals out of the country. Men like the Socinis, who might have become the Italian reformers, had to emigrate. It is the time of the Medici influence in France, the time when, for a while, France was ruled by an Italian cardinal, and when the armies of the empire were commanded by dozens of Italian *capitani*. In the time of Vico, his younger contemporary Pietro Giannone had to leave Naples because he wrote and published his *Istoria civile del regno di Napoli* (1723), the first modern history of political institutions.

§2. The Work of Vico

The peculiar structure of the Italian intellectual situation has to be taken into account when we approach the work of Giambattista Vico (1668–1744). The new foundation of a science of politics and ideas by the Neapolitan thinker remained almost unknown in its own time and exerted little immediate influence. From the later eighteenth century, and throughout the nineteenth, traces of Vichian influence can be found more frequently, but they merge with the independent development of ideas in the north, which by that time followed lines similar to Vico's. While a more careful exploration of these influences may still render surprising results regarding certain details, it seems doubtful that the historical stature of Vico will ever be determined appreciably by the *influence* that he has exerted on the Western history of political ideas. There is no justification for the accusations that are sometimes leveled against men such as Spengler or Toynbee because they have not sufficiently recognized the extent to which their ideas stem from Vico's philosophy of history. Even if Spengler and Toynbee should have read Vico, it was not necessary for them to derive the idea of growth and decay of civilizations from the *Scienza nuova* because for the last two hundred years there runs a broad and increasingly loud debate over this question, beginning with the eighteenth-century controversy over the fall of the Roman empire. One, therefore, encounters the following problems: Wherein does the greatness of Vico lie? What prevented the effectiveness of his work in his own time? And what were the obstacles to his later recognition, obstacles that only in our time are being removed by an increasing body of monographic studies?[1]

a. Style and Mode of Expression

Beginning from the peripheral obstacles, we have to say that the *Scienza nuova* is not easy reading; the treatise is written in a terse, epigrammatic, rigidly constructed language that presents difficulties even to Italians. This idiosyncratic, nondiscursive style is certainly in part a result of the previously discussed municipalization of Italian letters; it is hardly conceivable that a French or English thinker of quality during this period would have expressed himself in a language that so strongly deviated from a national standard of intellectual discourse. The difficulties of the style, however, are interwoven inseparably with the mode that Vico chose for the expression of his ideas. His work is in substance a philosophy of history, but this substance is deeply embedded in a matrix of philological investigations, studies on Homer, a theory of language, a theory of aesthetics, and studies on Roman law and institutions. The access to the ideas proper is, furthermore, made difficult by a formidable apparatus of spurious authorities to whom Vico refers in order to legitimatize his ideas and by a signal absence of references to the true sources, references that would permit the reader to place Vico's ideas in a known universe of discourse and to distinguish between the tradition and his original thought. The reader who expects to find in Vico's work a straightforward, reasoned exposition of the author's ideas will be disappointed. To disengage Vico's ideas from the philological and juridical apparatus, and to place them correctly in the development of Western political ideas, requires considerable critical work and elaborate collateral studies. This mode of expression is in large part a consequence of the structure of the Italian environment and the place Vico holds in it. The philological and historical apparatus belongs to the style of Italian *erudizione*,

---

1. In the fifty years since Voegelin wrote this chapter, "Vico studies" have increased enormously. An annual journal, *New Vico Studies*, provides a regularly updated bibliography. See also Molly Black Verene, *Vico: A Bibliography of Works in English from 1884 to 1994* (Bowling Green: Philosophy Documentation Center, 1994).

accentuated in Vico because of his position as a professor of rhetoric who tries not to overstep the limits of his "department." In addition, however, the formidable scholarly apparatus, and particularly the misleading references to authorities, will have to be explained as precautions against the dangerous attentions of the Inquisition. And, finally, we must not neglect the problem presented by the subject matter itself. The prevalent style of an incipient critical historiography was still to collect materials; it was, therefore, a novel enterprise to develop a method of philosophical interpretation. To disengage the principles of the new method completely from the materials that were their first field of application was a task for future generations. We can hardly blame the genius who conceived the idea of the new science for not having given to it a definite, systematic form, which it has not gained even today, two centuries after its conception.

b. The Secularist Interpretation

The task of disengaging the principles of Vico's method from the materials to which it is applied creates a new problem that is apt to baffle the historian. In disengaging Vico's principles from the materials, one can go too far and discard as irrelevant problems that belong to the Vichian theory proper. This is a danger that has not always been avoided in the interpretations of Vico by his distinguished Neapolitan compatriots Benedetto Croce and Giovanni Gentile. Like every well-constructed theory of politics and history, the Vichian has for its center a philosophical anthropology. Having established this central theory, Vico interprets the course of history as an unfolding in time of the potentiality of the human mind. The various actualizations of the mind in society receive their meaning in history as the intelligible phases in the unfolding of a potentiality. The philosophical anthropology and the unfolding of the mind in a temporal process of the community are the inseparable parts of Vico's theory. However much of the philological apparatus we may reject as obsolete and irrelevant, and however freely we may recognize that the concrete historical construction is superseded by the advancement of historical science, the ideas of the anthropology and of the intelligible unfolding of the mind in history are the irreducible core of the theory. Nevertheless, both Croce and Gentile are inclined to discard the philosophy of history as of dubious value and to reduce the achievement of Vico to his philosophical anthropology. The sentiments that inspire this restrictive interpretation are worth some attention because Croce's monograph on Vico has become the starting point for the renewed interest in the Italian thinker and has exerted considerable influence through its English translation, and because, furthermore, these sentiments of Croce and Gentile are the same as those that prevented the influence of Vico even in the eighteenth century.

Croce and Gentile have misgivings about Vico's historical constructions because they are secularist progressives. They neither like the idea of a *corso* of history that ends in a barbarism of reflection worse than the initial primitive barbarism, nor are they willing to accept Vico's concern to keep his construction of profane history within the limits of Christianity or to recognize the problem of sacred history. The result of these sentiments is a curious evaluation of Vico's work. The philosophy of history, which does not please progressives, is pushed into the background, and the New Science becomes a "Nuova filosofia dello spirito e iniziale metafisica della mente" (new philosophy of the spirit and beginning philosophy of the mind).[2] This view in itself would not be more than a misjudgment concerning the relative importance of the parts of Vico's theory. But his progressive critics go further and berate precisely those aspects of the theory where Vico's instinctive genius shows itself most splendidly. They criticize him for not having explicitly drawn the conclusions from his conception of history with regard to the eternal recurrence of the *corsi*—whereas Vico's merit lies precisely in the good sense with which he avoids the trap of eternal recurrence, confines himself to the empirically observable *corsi*, and leaves the question of future *corsi* open. They criticize him because, in his analysis of the *ricorsi*, he indicates that our civilization has passed its *akme* and is approaching the phase of barbarism, and yet Vico does not express himself with what his critics think is appropriate pessimism concerning the future of Western civilization—whereas Vico's merit lies in his having the good sense to recognize that the *corsi* are not everything in history, that Christianity is a new factor that may influence the *corso* of

2. Benedetto Croce, *La filosofia di Giambattista Vico*, 2d ed. (Bari: Laterza, 1922), 150. English edition: *The Philosophy of Giambattista Vico*, trans. R. G. Collingwood (New York: Russell and Russell, 1964), 135.

our civilization, and that, because of the introduction of this new factor, the pattern of the Roman *corso* cannot be used as a basis for predictions concerning our own *corso* (Spengler's mistake). They criticize him because he did not push the metaphysics of the spirit in history into its pantheistic consequences—whereas it is Vico's merit to have avoided the impasses of gnosis and of a romantic philosophy of tragic existence that mar the achievement of Schelling. They criticize his having exempted the history of the Hebrews from the law of the *corsi*—whereas it can hardly be called a major achievement of Vico to have recognized what even the more obtuse have found out: that the history of the Hebrews presents a problem without parallel. And they criticize him, finally, because he has exempted Christianity and confined the *corsi* to the interpretation of profane history—whereas it is to Vico's credit that he has seen that the great irruptions of transcendental reality do not fall into patterns that can be constructed regarding the historical courses of human civilizations.

For this adverse criticism, the progressivists compensate by emphasizing the qualities of the *filosofia dello spirito*. We certainly have no objections to the praises bestowed on this part of Vico's theory, but the comparisons with other philosophers, incidental to the evaluation, distort the peculiar qualities of the Italian thinker quite as much as the criticisms. Both Croce and Gentile are obsessed with the desire to erect Vico into the Italian philosopher who compares in rank with Kant and Hegel. In fact, it had been observed already by Jacobi that Vico has found solutions for certain epistemological problems that even in their formulation "anticipate" Kant. Certainly, there is an appreciable core of truth in the exaggerated formula that with the Italian Hegelianism of Croce and Gentile Vico, has returned to Italy. Nevertheless, such comparisons can be overdone, and it is painful to see the idea of the *corsi* debased to a literary device when Croce presents the latter's history of ideas as *un ricorso delle idee di Vico*, beginning with the speculative movement from Kant to Hegel[3]—not so much because the comparison distorts the historical position of Kant and Hegel, but because the misuse of the idea of the *corsi* reveals a regrettable superficiality in the approach to Vico.

3. Croce, *Philosophy of Giambattista Vico*, chap. 20.

Mishaps of this kind are caused in part by nationalist rivalry. Vico, the Italian, has to be the equal to the German philosophers whom Croce and Gentile hold in highest esteem. But in their zeal to exalt an Italian who, through his philosophy of the spirit, is a rival for Kant and Hegel, the advocates of their national glory seem to have overlooked the possibility that Vico has a greatness of his own where the German philosophers cannot rival him—and this greatness lies in the very philosophy of history that his compatriots disparage. Vico can hardly be considered the equal of Kant as an epistemologist, or the equal of Hegel as a logician of the spirit, but as a philosopher of history he surpasses them both because his Christian awareness of the problems of the spirit guarded him against the Gnostic derailment of finding the meaning of history exhausted by the humanly intelligible structure of profane history. And in this respect, as we have said, he surpassed even Schelling, with whom as a philosopher of the myth in history Vico has much closer relations than with either Kant or Hegel. However, the affinity between Schelling and Vico is not stressed in the studies of Croce and Gentile because the work of Schelling is less well known to progressivist thinkers.

c. The Meditative Character of the Work

Difficulties for the interpretation arise lastly from the intimate, meditative character of Vico's work. The *Scienza nuova* is not a single, systematic treatise that may stand by itself; it is a process of thought that began about 1708, at a time when Vico had reached the age of forty. Its completion filled the remaining years of his life until his death in 1744, the year in which the work was published in its last form, the so-called "Third" *Scienza nuova*. In this period of thirty-six years he developed his ideas concerning a philosophy of the spirit in history by means of a process of meditation for which the various published works are the precipitations. The same general complex of problems is reworked with increasing clarity regarding the principal idea, but the later precipitations do not invalidate the earlier ones. Precisely because the later formulations reflect the stage that the process has reached at that moment, to be fully understood they presuppose the earlier ones as steps that have led up to the final form. For technical reasons of literary presentation it is helpful, as the historians of Vico have done, to distinguish between the first, second, and third phases of his thought, but the meaning of these phases is not exhausted by their character as successive steps in the clarification of an idea. They also contain elements that have to be considered as simultaneous parts of a system. The interpenetration of systematic simultaneity with successive clarification in this long-drawn-out process is perhaps the most serious obstacle to an adequate analysis of Vico's thought. It has not yet been mastered in a completely satisfactory manner by any presentation.

d. The Phases of the Meditation

The phases of this process are marked by the major works of Vico. The first is the *De antiquissima Italorum sapientia* of 1710. The work was planned in three books: on metaphysics, physics, and morals. Only the first of these books was published. The more adequate description of this work is given by its subtitle, *Liber Metaphysicus*, and we shall refer to it by this briefer title. In the form of an exploration of the meaning of certain early Latin terms, the book is a polemic against Descartes and established the principles of a new philosophy of mind in opposition to Cartesian scientism. The second phase is marked by two books, *De universi juris uno principio et fine uno*, of 1720, and *De Constantia Jurisprudentis*, of 1721. They are to be considered parts of one work to which Vico refers as the treatise *Diritto universale*. In the earlier work the polemic was directed against Descartes; now it is directed against the theories of natural law of Grotius, Selden, and Pufendorf. From the newly gained metaphysical position, Vico explores the institutions of Roman law. He shows with an immense philological apparatus that in the example of the Romans the origins of political institutions differ considerably from those imagined by the theorists of natural law, and he develops the course of Roman institutions as one that necessarily follows from the structure of the mind. This new jurisprudence assumes the character of a *universal* science insofar as it is the systematic science of things divine and human; that is, insofar as it shows divine wisdom, operating through the mind of fallen man, guiding the historical course of a people. The second of the works, the *De Constantia Jurisprudentis*, is subdivided into two parts, the *De Constantia Philosophiae* and the *De Constantia Philologiae*. This latter part contains for the first time the name "New Science."

Its opening chapter is entitled *Nova scientia tentatur*, and it defines the new science as a philology that explores the origins of things in exploring the origins of their names, for the names are created to signify things, and the things of society, the religious and legal institutions, signified by the names, flow forth from the mind of man. Philology is the instrument for understanding the origins and meaning of institutions: "hence the republic will derive great profit from the interpretation of the ancient language of religion and the laws." The third phase is marked by the "First" *Scienza nuova*, of 1725, entitled *Principi di una scienza nuova intorno alla natura delle nazioni*. The Roman course of history, which was explored empirically in the preceding work, is now erected into a typical course of the history of a people, it becomes a *storia eterna ideale* to which the histories of all nations conform. The further history of the work consists of emendations and enlargements, of which the edition of 1730 is counted as the "Second," and the final, most elaborate form of 1744 as the "Third" *Scienza nuova*.[4]

---

4. All references to the works of Vico in this chapter, unless noted otherwise, are to the edition of the *Opere* by Fausto Niolini, Benedetto Croce, and Giovanni Gentile, 8 vols. (Bari: Laterza, 1911–1941). Of the older literature, see Giuseppe Ferrari's *La mente di Giambattista Vico* (Milan: Società tipog. de' classici italiani, 1837). As far as the interpretation of Vico is concerned it has been superseded by later, more critical works, but it is still worth reading as a product of the Risorgimento, and it gives a good impression of Vico's place as a treasure in the national shrine of Italian spiritual glory. The French edition of 1839, the title of which Ferrari changed into the war cry *Vico et l'Italie* (Paris: Éveilard, 1839), conveys this impression even more strongly. Of the modern literature the authoritative guide to understanding Vico is still Benedetto Croce's *Philosophy of Giambattista Vico*. The reader should beware, however, of the secularist and progressivist bias discussed in the text. For a more thorough exploration of special problems, Giovanni Gentile's *Studi Vichiani*, 2d ed. (Florence: Monnier 1927), is invaluable. His *The History of Political Philosophy* (Manchester: Manchester University Press, 1925) should also be mentioned, and the fine study by H. P. Adams, *The Life and Writings of Giambattista Vico* (London: Allen and Unwin, 1935). By no means should one neglect the literature on Vico that has sprung up during the Fascist period. Walter Witzenmann's *Politischer Aktivismus und sozialer Mythos, Giambattista Vico und die Lehre des Faschismus* (Berlin: Junker und Dünnhaupt, 1935) certainly distorts the figure of Vico by accentuating the elements of his thought that could be developed into a philosophy of activist existence; but, incidental to the distortion, aspects of Vico's work are explored that have not received the same attention by idealists and progressivists. Finally we should mention the English translation of *The Autobiography of Giambattista Vico*, by M. H. Fisch and T. G. Bergin (Ithaca: Cornell University Press, 1944). This book contains a valuable introduction, and the sections on Vico's influence in England and the United States and on the Marxist tradition are particularly useful since they contain materials that cannot be found elsewhere. [A revised version was published in 1963. When available, translations of Vico are also cited. For the *Scienza nuova* it is necessary only to cite

§3. The Idea of a New Science

We have surveyed, first, the Italian political situation in the time of Vico, and then the peculiar structure of his work and some of the difficulties it offers to the interpreter. When we now proceed to the analysis of Vico's theory itself, the reader should be aware that it is not our task to present the vast cosmos of Vico's thought in its full expanse, including the theories of language, of aesthetics, of the myth, and so forth. We shall discuss only those aspects of the work that will permit us to clarify Vico's position in a general history of political ideas. This analysis of specific doctrines, however, has to be preceded by a few remarks on the idea of a New Science in general.

a. Ambivalence and Pathos

The title of *Scienza nuova*, which Vico gave to the final form of his work, was influenced by Bacon's *Novum Organum* as well as by Galileo's *Dialoghi delle scienze nuove*. The filiation of the name indicates a certain ambivalence in Vico's idea. The *Scienza nuova* is a true science of substance in opposition to a science of physical phenomena, while, at the same time, it is a science of politics in emulation of the imposing new science of nature. This ambivalence is also a factor in Vico's relation to Descartes. In his *Autobiography*, Vico dramatizes his intellectual life by the contrast between the nine years of seclusion at Vatolla (as tutor with the Rocca family) and his return to Naples in 1695 into an environment dominated intellectually by the philosophy of Descartes. Vico's biographers have suggested correctly that the seclusion at Vatolla was not un-broken, that several sojourns at Naples must have acquainted Vico quite well with Cartesianism before his permanent return to the city, and that the year of his return does not mark an epoch in the sense that a mind that had grown to its full stature in solitude now emerged as the protagonist in a struggle against Cartesianism. The anti-Cartesian attitude became articulate more than a decade after

---

the marginal paragraph numbers, which are identical in the translation, *The New Science of Giambattista Vico,* unabridged translation of the Third Edition (1744) with the addition of the "Practice of the New Science," trans. Thomas Goddard Bergin and Max Harold Fisch (Ithaca: Cornell University Press, 1968). As indicated in the Editor's Introduction, Voegelin's translations are retained.]

the return, while the stress on the nine years at Vatolla is a bit too reminiscent of the nine years Descartes spent in the solitude of Holland at the end of which time he emerged with his *Discours de la méthode*. This ambivalence can be felt in the depreciation of the truth of physics, on the one hand, and the arrogation of the true *certezza* for the New Science, on the other. Furthermore, it is pervasive in the attack on the Cartesian meditation, with its point of certainty in the *res cogitans,* and in the philological countermeditation with its *constantia in Deo.* In spite of the element of triviality that seems to enter the tension, it must not be taken lightly nor be considered as merely a personal rivalry.

The projection of the tension into the past occurs at a time when Vico had completed the "First" *Scienza nuova,* and it reflects the pathos of his achievement. At this time, the real achievement had placed Vico beyond a mere rivalry with Descartes and beyond a mere competitive attempt to create a science of politics in emulation of physics. Vico had become aware of the weight of his achievement on the European scene, and the opposition to Descartes had become a minor factor in his conscious and proud counterposition to the transalpine intellectual development as a whole, that is, to the scientism of the Cartesians as well as to the Protestant speculation on natural law, represented by Grotius, Selden, and Pufendorf. Of the *Scienza nuova,* Vico says at the same time in his *Autobiography* that "by this work, to the glory of the Catholic religion, Vico has procured for our Italy the advantage that no longer does she have to envy Protestant Holland, England, and Germany their three princes of this science, and that in this our age, in the bosom of the true Church, have been discovered the principles of the gentile wisdom of things human and divine."[5]

b. Reversal of the Apostatic Movement

The Italian and Catholic elements in the pathos of Vico are inseparable. Something has happened in Italy that outweighs the transalpine achievements in science, and this something is animated by the Catholic spirit of Vico. What is this something? We can express it briefly as the insight into, and the reversal of, the Western apostatic movement. Unfolding the implications of this brief formula, we

5. *Autobiografia,* in *Opere,* V:53; *Autobiography,* 173.

94

would have to say that Vico had perfect insight into the hubris of disoriented man who is obsessed by his *amor sui*. He had this insight in the same manner as Hobbes and Pascal (whose *Pensées* he mentions occasionally as *lumi sparsi* of a Christian protest),[6] but by his time the hubris had gained a social and literary body that made it possible for a disciplined intellect to discern the disaster. Vico was able to sense the consequences of the scientism of the Cartesian movement and of Protestant political speculation that became fully visible only in his own lifetime and in the following century, namely the sensualist psychology that arose in the wake of Locke, in the spiritual obscurantism of Voltaire, in utilitarian ethics, in the progressive philosophy of history, and in the break-down of reason followed by romanticism, by the new gnosis, by the philosophy of tragic existence, and by economic materialism. His genius did not have to wait for the course of enlightenment and revolution to see the aftermath of the crisis, and his unbroken Catholicism, combined with the Italian sentiment of resistance against the transalpine success story, gave him strength to under-take the persistent elaboration of his vision.[7]

These last remarks ought to clarify the question of the so-called anachronism of Vico's thought. It is quite true that the *Scienza nuova* is an attempt to restore the order of the spirit that, on the same level of insight and metaphysical strength, we do not find in the North before Schelling's *Weltalter* of 1812. This time

---

6. *Autobiografia*, in *Opere*, V:19; *Autobiography*, 130.

7. The awareness of the religious crisis and its consequences for a social crisis finds expression in numerous passages in the work of Vico. A concise statement of his view is contained in a letter of November 8, 1724, to Monsignor Filippo Maria Monti. In discussing the principles of public law, Vico says: "Quindi i princípi di tal dritto si vanno a ritrovare dentro quelli della sacra storia, che anche per umana credenza è la più antica di tutte che a noi son giunte, anche la favolosa dei greci; e quivi umanamente si stabiliscono con la dottrina platonica che serve alla Provvidenza, e si difendono contro il fato degli stoici, il caso degli ipicurei, e si confermano contro Obbes, Spinoza, Bayle et ultimamente Lock, i quali tutti, conquelle stesse loro dottrine con le quali oppugnano le massimi civili cattoliche, se dimostrano andar essi a distruggere, quanto è per loro, tutta l'umana società" ("So the principles of such [public] law are to be found in [the principles'] sacred history, which according to human belief is the most ancient of all those that have come down to us, including the fabulous history of the Greeks, and [here] they are in harmony with Plato's doctrine, which supports the idea of providence; and they defend themselves against the doctrine of fate of the Stoics, and the doctrine of chance of the Epicureans; and they provide sanction against Hobbes, Spinoza, Bayle and finally Locke, all of whom, with their similar doctrines, oppose Catholic civil principles, and, so far as it is in them to do so, show themselves capable of destroying the whole of human society; "*Carteggio*, XXVI," in *Opere*, V:168).

difference of approximately a century, however, does no more justify the use of the term *anachronism* than the peculiar Italian
political development justifies the use of the term *decadence*. Just
as an Italian political decadence can be construed only under the
assumption that a people are obliged to develop a national state
at the proper time, the appearance of Vico can be construed as an
anachronism only if we assume that a people and its thinkers are
obliged to run the course of enlightenment and revolution before
they are permitted to find out that something is wrong. The time
difference between the appearance of Vico and the general European
movement for spiritual restoration is of the same type as the time
differences in the formation of the schismatic nations and in their
revolutions. It is merely a symptom of the degree to which the
unity of Western civilization had already been destroyed at the
beginning of the eighteenth century. The cleavage is so deep that
the intellectual development in the various schismatic bodies can
show time differences of a century.

§4. The Steps of the Meditation

The discussion of Vico's theory has to begin with the famous
formula *verum esse ipsum factum*. Chronologically, the formula
marks the beginning of the long meditation inasmuch as it occurs
in *Liber metaphysicus* I.1.[8] Moreover, it is embedded in an argument that shows in a perfect manner the typical steps of Vico's
meditative procedure. Hence we shall first present the argument
itself, following the text closely, and then we shall proceed to the
interpretation of the successive meditative steps.

a. Verum Est Factum

The argument of *Liber metaphysicus* I.1 is as follows: For the
"Latini," the terms *verum* and *factum* seem to have been inter-
changeable. This appears from their synonymous use of the terms
"understanding" *(intelligere)*, "to read perfectly" *(perfecte legere)*,
and "to know plainly" *(aperte cognoscere)*. The term *cogitare*, on
the other hand, was of lesser dignity, meaning no more than simply

---

8. *Liber metaphysicus*, chap. I.1, in *Opere*, I; translated by Leon Pompa in *Vico:
Selected Writings* (Cambridge: Cambridge University Press, 1982), 50–52.

"thinking" or "believing." Since words are symbols of ideas, and ideas symbols of things, it follows that reading means to collect the elements of script in order to compose words, and understanding means to collect the elements of things in order to compose a perfect idea. To be in the perfect and understanding possession of an idea means to be in the perfect possession of the thing itself. Perfect understanding can be achieved only through the identity of fact and idea.

From this insight follow the distinctions of divine and human knowledge. God is the *primum verum* because he is the *primus Factor*. Since knowledge *(scire)* consists in the composition of things, the mind of man is capable only of thinking *(cogitare)*, while true understanding *(intelligentia)* is reserved for God. God reads the things perfectly because he contains and orders them. Man, with his finite mind, can only think about them because man merely participates in reason, but does not possess it.

This doctrine of the "Latini," however, requires a qualification in order to be acceptable to the Christian thinker. The ancient philosophers of Italy could identify *verum* and *factum* because they assumed the world to exist uncreated from eternity, and because, consequently, their God operated always *ad extra* in an existing world. This is unacceptable in Christian theology because the world is created ex nihilo. Hence the Christian has to distinguish between the *verum creatum* and the *verum increatum;* only the *verum creatum* is identical with the *factum*. The *verum increatum* is not *factum* but *genitum*. The Holy Scripture, therefore, calls the Wisdom of God the *Verbum*. In the Word the truth and the comprehension of the elements of all possible worlds are identical, and of this cognition in the divine omnipotence consists this most exact and real word, which "as it is known from eternity by the Father, is from eternity born from him."

b. The Philological Origin

I have rendered this fundamental argument of Vico in its full extent because it reveals the constant style of Vico's speculation as well as the ideas that dominate it throughout its course. The speculation begins with a reference to the synonymous use of certain terms by the Latins. This opening implies the first principle of Vico's speculation. Man is not an isolated individual who can attain truth through the analysis of his mind in the manner of the Cartesian meditation (as Vico understood it). Man exists in history. The language of the myth, or poetry, and of civil institutions, as it is thrown up by man in unreflected creation in the course of historical existence in community, is the authoritative source for the understanding of the mind of man and its place in the cosmos. The reflective, Cartesian approach leads to the false picture of man as a rational being who enters into society by means of a contract. We cannot construe history by projecting into the past the reflective symbolizations of our own time. On the contrary, we have to correct our false picture of rational man by having recourse to history as the field of symbolic expressions in which the unreflected nature of the human mind is accessible to us in its immediacy. The speculation of the philosopher must not use the instrument of reflective meditation, but must start from the unreflected symbols given in history and rise to the speculative penetration of their meaning.

c. The Conjecture on the Pagan Level

The second step in the argument is the speculative penetration of the symbols of language. The identity of meaning in the terms *intelligere, perfecte legere,* and *aperte cognoscere* becomes the basis for a conjecture *(hinc coniicere datur)* that *verum* and *factum* must be "convertible" terms for the Latins. From this conjecture Vico derives the epistemological principle that remains constant throughout his work, though the later treatises elaborate it beyond the form it received in the *Liber metaphysicus.* True understanding is possible only if the knower of the object is identical with its maker. This is possible only for God. Man can touch the creation only from the outside through his *cogitationes.* Nevertheless, there are differences of certainty between the various human sciences. Most certain are the sciences that proceed analogically to divine creation by producing their object while understanding it. These are the mathematical sciences that proceed from definitions made by the mathematician himself to the theorems derived from them. Certainty decreases with the extent to which the sciences leave this level of abstraction and immerse themselves in matter. The sciences can, therefore, be arranged in an order of certainty from mathematics, through mechanics and physics, to morals. The moral sciences are the least certain because the movements of the soul are most deeply buried in matter. This is the epistemology of the *Liber metaphysicus;* it is directed against the physicists' claim of certainty for the results of their science, and particularly against the Cartesian *cogito* as the point of certainty in meditation. The later work of Vico retains the order of the sciences of the external world, but it changes it fundamentally with regard to the moral sciences. In the later phases of the *New Science* the realm of the mind in history becomes the field of true *certezza* in science because in history man is the maker as well as the scientist. In historical science man understands the product of his making.

d. The Christian Level

The third step goes beyond speculation on the basis of the Latin materials and carries the argument into the context of Christian metaphysics. This third step again is a constant element in Vico's meditation, and the principles developed on this occasion belong to the permanent, dominating ideas in his philosophy of history. Regrettably, it is frequently overlooked by the secularist interpreters; or, if it is not overlooked, it is dismissed as an irrelevancy, or as a deviation from the main direction of his thought. This attitude, which is inadmissible in science, has become the principal source of misunderstandings concerning Vico's theory. Hence we shall have to stress with particular care the importance of this third step. The formula *verum esse ipsum factum,* which results from the speculation on the philological materials, is usually quoted as Vico's formula, without further qualification. As a matter of fact, we have already seen that Vico does not himself accept the unqualified formula. On the contrary, he characterizes it as a result, on the level of the *ethnici philosophi* of the pagan philosophers. The Christian thinker has to restrict the identification of *factum* with *verum* to the *verum creatum;* the *verum increatum* is not *factum* at all, it is *genitum.*

The distinction has several important consequences for a philosophy of history. First of all, it draws a clear line between a Christian philosophy of history and a pantheistic or Gnostic one. The distinction of the *verum creatum* and *increatum* preserves the Christian tension between the transcendental existence of God and the created world. God has created the world out of his Wisdom, God has revealed himself to the world through the Logos, God guides the world through Grace and Providence—but God is not the *anima mundi,* his existence is not absorbed in the world. God is not absorbed in the world as a whole, and still less so in any part of it, and particularly not in history. Reason in man bears the imprint of the *ratio aeterna* (to use the term of Saint Thomas), but it is not the *ratio aeterna* itself. The preservation of the tension makes ontologically impossible a construction of history as a process in which the divine Logos comes to its self-reflective fulfillment; and it makes epistemologically impossible a Gnostic philosophy of history according to which the meaning of history can be penetrated fully by the mind of man because in the reflective, spiritual consciousness of the thinker the identity of the human mind with the historical Logos is achieved. This is the decisive point of difference between Vico and Hegel.

Of Hegel's philosophy of history, it could be said with much more justification than of Vico's that it is based on the principle *verum esse ipsum factum.* For Hegel expressed in two famous propositions a principle that abolishes the tension between God and the world. He indeed proposed ontologically that the Logos has become reality *(Was vernünftig ist, das ist wirklich);* and epistemologically he said that reality contains the Logos and hence is intelligible *(und was wirklich ist, das ist vernünftig).* Vico would not agree with these propositions. For him the Logos is not absorbed in the *factum* of creation; it was born from eternity and can be revealed to creation.[9] The distinction of *genitum* and *factum* enables him, as far as the philosophy of history is concerned, to distinguish between profane history (or gentilician history), which is a science of the *verum creatum,* and sacred history, which rests on the authority of the revealed Logos. Only the history that runs its course in the *factum* of creation can be the object of the New Science. Sacred history, in which the Logos is revealed beyond the *factum creatum,* cannot be penetrated by the powers of the human mind. From Vico's position, all philosophies of history that merge sacred and profane history into one intramundane line of historical meaning would be equally reprehensible, whether it be a progressivist philosophy that exhausts the meaning of history by the progress of reason, a Protestant gnosis of Hegel's or Schelling's type, the late form of this gnosis in Dilthey, or a dialectical materialism of the Marxian type.

9. *Liber metaphysicus* I.2.133; *Vico: Selected Writings,* 52–53.

Moreover, this stratum in the speculation of Vico makes sense-less all attempts to press him into the role of an authority for an activist philosophy of existence of the Fascist type—as has been done. The activist attempt to create a *verum* through the *factum* of political action cannot claim the authority of Vico even on the "pagan" level of the identification of *verum* and *factum* because the process of history is unreflective and beyond conscious planning. The political action of the activist certainly creates a historical *factum*, but the *verum* it contains is not the intention of the actor. It is a *verum* beyond his foresight, and it will quite possibly differ widely from his expectations. Reflective reason in action does not produce reason in history. On the contrary, according to Vico's observations it produces barbarism. Still less, of course, is the activist attitude compatible with the Christian qualifications of Vico: to have the *verbum genitum* of the leader revealed to creation and, at the same time, to have it imprinted as a *verum creatum* into the *factum* of history is a fascinating *imitatio Dei* as well as an intricate exercise in theology. But it certainly has nothing to do with Vico.

e. Neoplatonism

It will not have escaped the reader that the obscure point in this meditative course lies in the transition from the philological materials to the speculative conjecture. Certain questions impose themselves: Do, indeed, the materials lend themselves to the conjecture? And if so, are not perhaps other speculative interpretations equally possible? And are the materials the only determinants that lead to the speculative results? Where is the second premise that permits Vico to draw the conclusions from his materials that he actually draws? In brief: do we not have to search for a source of Vico's thought beyond the materials of philology and beyond Christian metaphysics?

Such questions are entirely justified. There is no doubt about Vico's obscurity, and we have to stress again that it is not peculiar to the argument under discussion. Rather, this obscurity is one of the constant problems in Vico's thought. Throughout his work, the results at which he arrives point to a motive of thought beyond philology and Christianity. And there is, of course, such a source: it is the speculative tradition in which the thinker moves. It remains obscure because Vico is reticent about it. We have mentioned before that he does not place his ideas in a universe of discourse and that, as a consequence, his ideas have the appearance of springing out of nowhere. The cause of this reticence is the nature of the speculative tradition Vico continued. We are referring to the tradition of the Italian Neoplatonists, and it would hardly have been prudent of him to stress this heretical ancestry. On this question, however, we are now sufficiently well informed by Croce in his *Le fonti della gnoseologia vichiana* and by Gentile in his *Studi Vichiani.* The Neoplatonic tradition has simply to be inserted as a further determinant into the speculative process. Only by means of contact with this tradition do the philological materials entail the result of the *New Science.* This tradition is the missing premise that always has to be presupposed in the argument leading to Vico's conclusions.

§5. The Continuum of Western Ideas

Beyond its systematic function in Vico's thought, this strand in the *Scienza nuova* is relevant for the purposes of this study in two respects. First, it permits us to place the thinker more clearly into the tradition of Marsilio Ficino, of Cardano and Giordano Bruno, as well as of the Spaniard Sánchez. As a consequence, the *New Science* loses much of the appearance that induces the view of Vico's work as an "anachronism." Without this background, seen only in the perspective of the future, Vico is the isolated figure, the solitary genius who anticipated by a century the revolt against enlightenment and reason. Placed into the Neoplatonic tradition, his work is more intimately linked to Italian intellectual history. It still has the character of a revolt, but the revolt has the momentum of a past; it reasserts an older position, preceding scientism and the Protestant speculation on natural law, and it represents the attempt to use intellectual instruments that had been developed before the irruption of Cartesianism to cope with the new problems.

Second, the connection with the Italian tradition is of importance because it casts new light on the general structure of the Western history of ideas. Generally speaking, we are still accustomed to understanding this structure according to categories developed in the seventeenth and eighteenth centuries. The age of Descartes and Newton appears as the great epoch: what lies before it is an intellectual prehistory, and what comes after is the truly modern age of mathematized science and critical method. If this pattern is accepted, the bearers of the great countermovement to Enlightenment must appear as thinkers who could not free themselves from the shackles of a past that had gone. They must appear as reactionaries, as pessimists, as men who struggled against the current of progress but who would be swept aside. If they are of sufficient stature, they will either be disregarded, as Schelling was, or wildly misunderstood, as Nietzsche. This construction is inadmissible in a critical history of ideas because it endows the epoch of mathematized science and reason with a specific authority and interprets other periods and movements by orienting them toward the authoritative period.

Widely different constructions will prove necessary if we pay proper attention to the continuum of ideas itself and do not accept the self-interpretation of a particular period as obligatory for the historian. Schelling, for instance, was of the opinion that the period from Descartes to Hegel was a huge aberration of the human mind and that only in his own time, after the aberration had run its course, was it possible to resume again consideration of the problems of the spirit at approximately the point where they had been left by Giordano Bruno. This construction of Schelling, while it is not the exhaustive answer to the problem presented by the classic age of modern philosophy, has at least the merit of pointing to a continuum of Western ideas that encompasses in its vaster range the age of physics and reason as an ephemeral irruption. In the present context we cannot go into the details of this question; for a full exposition of the problem the reader should refer to the earlier chapter on "Man in History and Nature" and to the subsequent "Part Eight: Last Orientation."[10] Nevertheless, we have to be clear in principle about this structural problem of Western history. In transalpine Europe we have to observe a continuity of ideas in which the intellectual situation of 1800 is linked, after an interruption of two centuries, with the situation of 1600. Schelling resumed Bruno's speculation on the substance of the universe across this vast gap and elaborated, on this restored basis, his philosophy of

---

10. See *The Collected Works of Eric Voegelin*, vol. 23, *History of Political Ideas*, vol. V, *Religion and the Rise of Modernity*, ed. James Wiser (Columbia: University of Missouri Press, 1998), chap. 5, and *The Collected Works of Eric Voegelin*, vol. 25, *History of Political Ideas*, vol. VII, *The New Order and Last Orientation*, ed. Jürgen Gebhardt and Thomas A. Hollweck (Columbia: University of Missouri Press, 1999).

history and politics. Under the peculiar Italian conditions, on the other hand, the gap is not quite so vast. Here, Neoplatonic philosophy was part of the national tradition, whereas Cartesianism and Protestant political speculation bore the stigma of "foreign" intellectual developments. Hence, on the European scene at large, the work of Vico could become the halfway mark on a line that connects Bruno and Schelling.

§6. The Model of Nature

The question of the Neoplatonic tradition becomes acute on the occasion of Vico's speculation on the substance of the *creatum*. His argument is directed against the claims of Cartesians concerning the value of the new science of physics as a new philosophy of nature. It is, in principle, the argument of Bruno against the science of "the accidences of the accidences," with its insistence on the necessity of a new philosophy of substance that has to replace the speculations of the alchemistic type. In the *Liber metaphysicus* this argument culminates in the theory of the metaphysical point and of the *conatus* as substantial origins of phenomenal extension and movement; in the later phases of Vico's work the position is extended to the philosophy of the mind in history.[11]

a. The Metaphysical Point and the Conatus

Again the argument begins with philological references to the identical meaning of the terms *essentia, vis,* and *potestas,* and again it proceeds to a conjecture: that the ancient philosophers of Italy considered the essences of all things to be eternal and infinite *virtutes.* Then the conjecture broadens out into corollaries. Because of the eternity and infinity of the *virtutes* the people called them "immortal Gods." The sages, however, attributed them to a highest divinity.[12] Having thus passed from the polytheistic to the metaphysical phase, Vico assumes that the ancient philosophers

---

11. *Liber metaphysicus* IV.152–59. For an extensive discussion of the problems of substance and phenomena in modern speculation see the chapter on "Phenomenalism" in vol. VII, *The New Order and Last Orientation,* Part Eight.

12. *Liber metaphysicus* IV.1. The reader will notice in this passage the implied theory of levels of consciousness that are distinguished by the degree of rationality. In the elaborated philosophy of history this theory assumes a form that in substance is the same as Turgot's and Comte's law of the three phases.

considered metaphysics the true science because it deals with the eternal *virtutes* of the phenomena. These *virtutes* are the *conatus*[13] as the *virtus* of motion, and the metaphysical point as the eternal *virtus* of extension. "As body and motion are the proper subjects of physics, thus *conatus* and *virtus extensionis* are the proper subject matter of metaphysics." Beyond phenomenal motion and extension lie their divine *virtutes*. But in God motion is not motion, and extension is not extension. The *virtus* of motion is quiet in God, the author of the *conatus*, and the metaphysical point, the *prima materia*, is the purest, but inextensive, mind, in God, the creator of matter.

The Neoplatonic character of this speculation is obvious. It becomes evident beyond doubt through a passage in the *Autobiography* where Vico sets in opposition to each other the Aristotelian and Platonic approaches to the problem. The speculation of Aristotle leads to a material principle from which the particular forms are drawn, and this "makes God a potter who works at things outside himself." The Platonic speculation leads to a metaphysical principle, to "the eternal idea that brings forth and creates matter itself, like a seminal spirit which itself forms the egg."[14] The so-called Platonic speculation is hardly Platonic. It is a mixture of Neoplatonic and Stoic elements, and it finds its ancestry in the Renaissance. We need not go into the details of the sources. The previously mentioned studies of Croce and Gentile bring ample references to Ficino's *Theologia platonica* and *In parmenidem*, to Cardano's *De acarnis aeternitatis*, to Sánchez's *Quod nihit acitur*, and to Bruno's *De la causa*. The important point is that the revolt against scientism begins with a renewal of the pre-Cartesian philosophy of nature. In breaking the phenomenal network of mathematized science, Vico re-creates the model of a substantive process. Behind the veil of phenomena lies the reality of nature, behind extension and movement lie the inextensive principle of extension and the unmoved principle of motion. These principles, the *virtutes*, are

---

13. *Conatus* literally means striving or endeavoring. It is used technically by Hobbes and Spinoza as well as by Vico. In Vico's usage, it symbolizes both the participation by humans in the divine order and the divine assistance needed by humans to rise from the status of *stulti*, fools, to *sapiens*. See the discussion in Gino Bedani, *Vico Revisited: Orthodoxy, Naturalism and Science in the "Scienza nuova"* (Oxford: Berg, 1989), 267–74. See also *Scienza nuova*, nos. 340, 504, 1098.

14. *Autobiografia*, in *Opere*, V:11 f.; *Autobiography*, 121.

in God, the *Factor* of nature, the eternal and infinite existence in whom knowledge and power of the creation are one. It is nature that serves as the model of the substantive process, which is not yet the human mind in history, but obviously the model can be transferred, and that is what Vico does in the later phases of his meditation.

b. The Systematic Function of the Model

With the transfer, however, the model of nature has not become irrelevant; one cannot concentrate an interpretation of Vico on the final form of the *Scienza nuova* and expect to understand the peculiar problem of the New Science while neglecting its origins. The balance of Vico's thought would be destroyed and the component elements would fall apart into conflicting doctrines. This is the previously discussed difficulty that arises from the systematic simultaneity of the successive phases. As a matter of fact, Vico's thought has fallen apart in the equally inadmissible interpretations of the *Scienza nuova* as a metaphysic of the spirit and as a cycle theory of history. Such erroneous interpretations are inevitable if the systematic function of the Neoplatonic model of nature does not receive proper attention. Taken in itself the Neoplatonism of the philosophy of nature is so closely related to Bruno's *anima mundi* that it becomes flatly incompatible with the orthodox Christianity of Vico's thought. And again, if we transfer the Neoplatonism directly to history, we arrive at an intramundane construction of history as a perpetual repetition of cycles. The orthodox Christian element, however, is nevertheless present, and from its presence it follows for a critical interpretation that the Neoplatonic element must not be fully pushed to its final consequences. This incompatibility of Neoplatonic and Christian elements (of which, as we have seen, Vico is quite aware) must be interpreted genetically in such a manner that the systematic intention emerges clearly beyond the conflicts that result from the genesis of the system. About this systematic intention there can be no doubt: a series of facts had entered the historical scene and precipitated a crisis in the sense that the traditional intellectual instruments had become inadequate for coping with the new situation. These new facts were: (1) the advancement of mathematized science; (2) the evocation of a new idea of man in the seventeenth century, particularly in Protestant political speculation; and (3) the enlargement of the historical horizon. The New Science is an analysis of the crisis as well as a systematic attempt at its solution. Vico's crisis is an early phase of the same crisis whose late phases we witness during our time, and Vico's attempt at a solution is of the most intense interest for us because it is an attempt in which we are still engaged today.

c. The Attack on Phenomenalism

If we interpret Vico's meditation as an attempt to cope with the crisis, the systematic function of the model of nature immediately becomes clear. In the science of politics the crisis had taken the form of a transfer of the ideal of mathematized science to the problems of man in society. A science of politics was impossible as long as a science of substance pursued the ideal of a science of phenomena. The establishment of a science of politics presupposed (and still presupposes) under these circumstances a critical attack on the ideal of a science of phenomena; only when the methodical ideal of physics is critically destroyed can a science of politics begin. This purpose Vico achieves through the creation of his Neoplatonic model of nature. That it became Neoplatonic is determined by Vico's historical position. Today we would use a different approach; but however we construct the model in speculation, the problem of a science of phenomena has to be disposed of before we can attack the problem of a science of politics. This systematic purpose in the solution of the crisis is, therefore, the point that has to be stressed, not the more or less accidental Neoplatonic form that the attempt has assumed in its execution.

d. The Attack on the Cogito

In the same manner, the closely related attack on the Cartesian *cogito ergo sum* has to be understood functionally. There is a bit more to Descartes's *Meditations* than would appear in Vico's critique; but again, what matters is the point of attack: that the *cogito* is not a point of certainty, in which the substance of man would be given in its immediacy, because the *cogito* belongs to the realm of phenomena. The *cogitare* is a reflective "thinking about." It is not an unreflective, creative evocation of symbols that express a deeper stratum of human substance. In the reflective meditation of Descartes, Vico sees a symptom of the "barbarism of reflection," which is the signature of the crisis. His search for a counterposition in the creative world of myth, poetry, and institutions is in substance the approach of Schelling to the problem, namely the search for a philosophy of the unconscious. In its execution, this systematic intention of Vico again shows certain imperfections that are a consequence of his historical position, but the intention itself is clear in the transfer of the model of nature to the mind in history. The process of the mind, just as the process of nature, has a depth-structure that reaches from the surface of the *creatum* into the depth of the *virtutes*. The transfer of the Neoplatonic model is Vico's remedy against the illegitimate transfer of the ideal of physics to the science of politics. The *virtutes* of nature become in this transfer the *aeterni veri semina* that operate *(conantur)* against the corruption of the *amor sui;* and because of their force *(vis)* they are called *virtus.*[15] Even in the terminology of *semina, conatus* and *virtus,* the model is followed in the description of that stratum in the human substance that gives direction to the course of the mind in history.

e. The Transfer of the Model to History

The third factor in precipitating the crisis is the enlargement of the historical horizon. We have discussed this problem extensively in the chapter on apostasy, and we have seen how Voltaire attempted to solve it through the evocation of secular history in which profane history is endowed with the meaning of sacred history. Secular history in this sense implies the merger of nature and grace in the idea of an intramundane history in which the rise and fall of empire is at the same time a process of salvation. Vico copes with this problem through the transfer of the model of nature to the process of history. The historical unit to which he transfers the model is not mankind at large; it is a "people." Every unit of this type runs its course in history in accordance with the "nature" of a human community. Such courses may run parallel, or they may follow each other in time. Through this transfer of the model to the finite community of a people, Vico solves the difficulty that causes the breakdown of the intramundane constructions, whether they be Voltairean, or Comtian, or Marxian. He is not compelled to find the

---

15. *De uno universi juris principio,* 34 and 36, in *Opere,* II-1:49–50.

meaning of history in the empirical rise and fall of nations, but he has nevertheless gained the instrument for interpreting a pluralistic field of historical phenomena. The ultimate meaning of human history remains sacred, but at the same time profane history ceases to be a dubious string of meaningless events. China and Russia can have their meaningful, intelligible courses of history, just as Rome or France, because the "nature" of the community has become the source of its meaning in history. Hence, the function of the transfer is the articulation of the enlarged field of history through the construction of finite lines of meaning, and it is in the light of this function that we have to interpret the Neoplatonic model of nature. It is definitely *not* the purpose of the model to replace the Christian sacred meaning by a new intramundane meaning of history. With a clear consciousness of his method Vico tries to establish a *storia ideale*, that is, a *typical* course of history that can be observed *empirically* as the course followed by nations in their history. Whether there is a universal meaning transcending the finite, simultaneous, and successive courses is a question beyond empirical science. As far as the Neoplatonic element would imply an intellectually penetrable logos in history, comparable to Hegel's *Vernunft*, it has again to be considered accidental, and it must not be construed as the systematic intention of Vico's philosophical position.

§7. The *Mondo Civile*

a. The Science of History

The Neoplatonism of the model of nature is in conflict with the Christian metaphysics of Vico. Hence the transfer of the model to the realm as history is not such a simple affair. History must not be understood as a process with a self-sufficient, immanent meaning. The *corsi* of the peoples take place in a created world, and these finite *corsi,* therefore, are related to the all-embracing *factum* of creation. Man in history is created, and he is created in the image of God. From this fundamental doctrine, two principles follow for a science of history. The first is the ontological principle: that the process of the human mind in history is part of the process of divine creation. The second is the epistemological principle: that the operation of the human mind in history can be understood as an analogue of the operation of God in his creation. A complete science of the historic process has to consist, therefore, of three parts: (1) a first part dealing with *Origins* (that all things proceed from God); (2) a second part dealing with the *Circle* (that all things return to God); (3) a last part dealing with *Constancy* (that all things rest in the truth of God). This analogue of creation is used, indeed, by Vico for the organization of subject matter in his *Diritto universale.* The plan, however, is obscured somewhat in the execution because the external structure of the work does not correspond exactly to the internal organization. Externally, the work is organized into the *De uno universi juris principio et fine uno,* and into two more slender studies, united in the *De Constantia Jurisprudentis.* Internally, the *Origins* fill the first two pages of the *De uno,* and the part on the *Circle* fills the rest of the book, beginning on the third page. The part on *Constancy,* finally, is contained in the *De Constantia.*[16]

In the *Proloquium* Vico narrates how the idea of the transfer occurred to him in reading a quotation from Varro in Saint Augustine's *Civitas Dei:* if he (Varro) had the power to give the Roman people a religion, he would choose a God according to the *formula naturae,* that is, an incorporeal, infinite God, not innumerable, finite idols. In reading this passage it came to Vico in a flash that the formula of nature is valid not only for theology but that legal institutions in history can be conceived as a *formula,* or *idea veri,* which is transparent for the truth of God *(quae verum nobis exhibit Deum).*[17] It is transparent for the truth of God in the double sense indicated previously: as a finite analogue to God in his creation, and as a part of this creation itself. From the first transparency follows the great principle of the *Scienza nuova:* "In the dense night of shadows, by which at first is hidden from our eyes the most remote antiquity, appears the eternal light, which never fails us, of this truth beyond doubt: that this world of history is most certainly made by man, and hence we can find, we must find, its principles in the modifications of our own human mind."[18] Man is the creator of the *mondo civile* as God is the creator of the

---

16. The division of the science of history into the three parts is set forth in *De uno universi juris,* "De Opera Proloquium," sec. 28, *Opere,* II-1:34–35. All references to the *Diritto universale* are to this edition. The *De uno* forms vol. II-1 of this edition and the *De Constantia* forms vol. II-2.

17. "Proloquium," sec. 24, in *Opere,* II-1:33.

18. "Third" *Scienza nuova,* in *Opere,* IV:1, 117. Cited hereafter as *Scienza nuova* by paragraph number.

mondo naturale, but this human creation is known to us from the "inside," whereas nature can be known only by its phenomena. "We cannot wonder enough, therefore, that all the philosophers have endeavored seriously to pursue the science of this *mondo naturale,* of which God only, since he made it, has the science; and that they have neglected to meditate on this *mondo delle nazioni,* or *mondo civile,* of which men can pursue the science since they made it."[19]

b. Vico's Anthropology

The *mondo civile,* thus, is an intelligible creation, produced by man and accessible to science. This principle, however, must not be taken in isolation, as has been done so frequently by Vico's interpreters. The principle is of absorbing interest to Vico because the human analogue of divine creation is, at the same time, part of divine creation. That is, in the principles of human creation, the principles of divine creation themselves become visible. This ontic relation between the two creations is the subject of the *Diritto universale.* Vico opens the systematic discussion with the Augustinian characterization of God as the *Posse, Nosse, Velle infinitum* (§2). The source seems to be *Civitas Dei* XI.24–28. In particular, the wording of 26 suggests the Vichian formula; the formula itself, however, is not to be found in Augustine. The reader should compare the Augustinian text with the Vichian definition. The comparison is very illuminating as an indication of Vico's imaginative treatment of his sources. Man has the same characteristics, but he consists of mind and body. Since mind is spiritual and cannot be circumscribed by corporeal limits and since the body is a corporeal limitation, man is *nosse, velle, posse finitum quod tendit ad Infinitum* (§10). Infinite being, however, is God. Man, therefore, tends to return to God as he has proceeded from him (§11). This, however, is fully true only for the integral nature of man before the Fall. If man had remained in this prelapsarian state, human life would have consisted in the *humana beatitudo* (§20) of following, in *heroica sapientia* (§19), his tendency toward union with the eternal truth of God (§16). Human nature, however, has been corrupted by the Fall, with the consequence that the human *velle* is in opposition to the human *nosse* (§21); this will in revolt is called *cupidity* (§22), and

19. *Scienza nuova,* no. 331.

cupidity breeds the *amor sui* (§23). The satisfactions of cupidity lie in the field of the corporeally useful (§24). Hence man in the fallen state is dominated by utilitarian interests (§31).

If the anthropology of Vico were to stop at this point, we would have reached the problem of disoriented man as it presented itself to Pascal and Hobbes. Man dominated by his *amor sui* is the object of the new psychology of the seventeenth century, and on this model of disoriented man is built the political theory that lets the structure of society arise out of the utilitarian interests of the single individual. But Vico does not stop at the utilitarian level. He links the human process with the process of divine creation through the permanent presence in history of Providence (§§ 6 and 8). The "principle of all humanity" is that man can never lose sight of God completely. If the light of God is not reflected in the things that proceed from him, at least some refraction of its rays is still discernible. Even when man deceives himself, he still does so under some image of the truth (§33). The seeds of eternal truth are not quite dead in corrupt man, and by the Grace of God they can operate *(conantur)* against the corruption of nature (§34). Reason in man is this spark of truth (§35), and insofar as it is a force it is called virtue (§36). This force, the *vis veri*, or *ratio*, is called virtue when it struggles against cupidity in the individual soul. It is called justice when it directs and equalizes the utilitarian interests of a multitude of men. Justice in this sense is the *unum universi juris principium, unusque finis* (§43). This principle of an *aequum utile*, measured by a reason that participates in eternal truth (§44), can become the ordering principle among men because man is capable of communication. Man is by nature made to communicate with other men about his utilitarian interests (§45). These utilities of the body are in themselves neither good nor bad. Only their social inequality is dishonest *(turpis)*, whereas their equality constitutes *honestas.* This principle of equalizing honesty is eternal in its origin and cannot be derived from the fleeting utilities of the body. Hence, justice cannot be derived from, or caused by, interest. The utilitarian interest is the *occasion* of justice, not its *cause,* "a point that Grotius has not seen." Utility was never the principle of law or human society, nor was it necessity, or fear, or want, as believed Epicurus, Machiavelli, Hobbes, Spinoza, and Bayle. Utility was the occasion when men, who by their nature are social, were induced to actualize their social nature. *Usus* and *necessitas* were the occasions by which Divine Providence, by using the pressure of circumstance *(rebus ipsis dictantibus)*, brought corrupt man to the realization of justice and the cultivation of society (§46).

c. *The Autonomy of the Spirit*

We do not have to provide an elaborate commentary on this part of Vico's theory. The importance of the new position is obvious, if we list only the principal implications of these paragraphs. The psychology of disoriented man is rejected as a basis for political science: even if man is disoriented, and even if empirically we live in a state of society where the character traits of the *amor sui* are predominant, this is no reason to lose our heads and to adopt a new philosophical anthropology that erects a spiritual disease into a human norm. The spirit retains its autonomy in face of empirical defection, and it retains this autonomy because man, in the Vichian language of Revelation, is the image of God, however much he may be in revolt, or, in the language of metaphysics, because through his *ratio* man is linked with the infinite transcendental reality. In this position, Vico does not go very far beyond a Christian metaphysics of the Thomistic type. He develops, however, a corollary, which is of the utmost importance for the method of history, when he insists that man, even if he deceives himself, must do so under some image of truth. From this corollary, which is inspired by Saint Augustine, follows the principle of interpretation for the history of ideas: the structure of the spirit cannot be abolished through a revolt against the spirit. The revolt itself must assume the structure of the spirit. In the chapter on apostasy, for instance, we have seen that the spiritual obscurantism of Voltaire cannot produce a nonspiritual philosophy of history. When the problem of a sacred history is rejected in its Christian form the resulting alternative is not an empirical science of universal history but a new sacred history of the progressive type. The revolt cannot result in "enlightenment." It can result only in dilettantish metaphysics with the very same structural forms against which the revolt is directed. This principle of the identity of spiritual structure in all modifications of the spirit, right into the revolt against it, is the basis for a *history* of ideas, understood as an intelligible line of meaning in time. Without this principle, the various manifestations of the mind would be disconnected events in external time.

Vico, furthermore, copes successfully with the problems of the somatic basis of the spirit in history. The utilitarian interests, the necessities, are duly recognized as the motive power of history. But this motive power is not made the cause of the structure of history. The utilitarian calculus of pleasures and pains is rejected before it is even conceived by Helvétius and Bentham, and in the same manner the economic materialism of the future is disposed of through the distinction between *cause* and *occasio.* The necessities are not more than the occasions for the realization of spiritual order. They are not its determinants. The "superstructure" in the Marxian sense takes a course of its own, even if this course, in its realization, is occasioned by material interests. Whether we interpret this relation between spirit and material interests as the operation of Divine Providence, as Vico does, or use Hegel's formula of the *List der Vernunft* will depend on our general metaphysical position. However we interpret it, a recognizable order of the spirit, which inexplicably rises above the interplay of material occasions, is a stark fact of history. In short, Vico reestablished the principle of historical science long before its disestablishment by utilitarianism and economic materialism had even run its course.

d. The Recursus

On the basis of this anthropology, Vico develops in the *Diritto universale* the theory of the *recursus.* This *recursus* is not identical with the *ricorso* of the later *Scienza nuova.* The *recursus* is the course of history, moving in the Circle that proceeds from God and returns to God; the *ricorso* is the historical course of the nations after the migration that follows in time the course of the nations of antiquity. Although on the surface the two concepts have nothing to do with each other, there exists nevertheless a subtle relationship between them that we shall discuss presently.

The *recursus* of the *Diritto universale,* that is, the cyclical course of Roman history, shows in principle the sequence of phases that we find in the *Scienza nuova* erected into the *storia eterna ideale.* The course of history itself is preceded by the solitary existence of fallen man (§98), the *stato ferino* of the *Scienza nuova.* From this hypothetical, savage state emerge social nuclei, the *gentes,* through the aggregation of certain material and spiritual elements.

The material core is the family as a sexual and economic unit, consisting of the paterfamilias, his wife, and his children (§§100–103). These family centers grow further through the integration of a clientele into the unit, that is, persons who are not strong enough to hold an independent status but enjoy, in return for their services, the protection of the.*gens* (§104). Such nuclei presuppose for their existence a principle of order that fixes and sanctifies the social relations between husband and wife, father and children, the order of heredity, etc. This principle of order is furnished through the awakening of religious awe and the creation of the *falsi Dei* of the pagans, who are the symbols of the sanctity of social relations. Thus legal institutions are at the same time religious institutions. This is the material and spiritual origin of the primitive social unit, of the *gens* (§104). All subsequent history is the course of events that flows from the structure of the *gens*. For Vico, history therefore is the course of *gentilician* history.

The phases of political history proper begin with the formation of the gentilician republic by which the heads of the *gentes* meet the threat of a revolting clientele. The republic is organized as the *ordo* of the *gentes*, with a *rex* who is elected in recognition of his personal charisma. The nongentilician people are the *plebs*. In the struggle between patricians and plebeians (the *contese eroiche* of the *Scienza nuova*), the latter finally achieve legal and religious status and the aristocratic republic passes into the state of the democratic republic. With the growing inability of the plebeians to preserve the order of the republic, power passes to a single individual, the *princeps*, at first of a regal, later of a tyrannical, type. The cycle is complete from the *rex* of the patricians to the monarch of the period of social disintegration (§§104, 152, 153). Moreover, in the period of disintegration we witness the rise of Christianity. The gods of the *gentes* and the gods of the democratic republic give way to a monotheistic idea of God, and correspondingly to the idea of a republic of mankind, through the influences of Stoic wisdom, through the dispersion of the Jews and the propagation of their monotheism, and, finally, through the growth of Christianity itself and its adoption as the religion of the empire. Thus the divine circle closes with the political circle: gentilician history started with the spark of religious insight that created the gods of the *gentes*, and it ends with Christianity.

§8. *Recursus* and *Ricorso*

Obviously, this theory of the cycle is inconclusive as a philosophy of history. What happens after gentilician history has returned to God in Christianity? Will the same cycle be repeated with the new communities? Will a new religion, comparable in its function to Christianity, again bring a return to God? Will this sequence be repeated without end? This is the point where the theory of the *recursus* is linked with the theory of the *ricorso*. In order to understand this crucial point in Vico's philosophy of history let us go through the successive formulations that he has given to the problem.

a. The Problem in the Diritto universale

In the *Diritto universale* we find (§219) an interesting comparison of the course of mankind in history with the phases of human life. *Pueri* are dominated by their desire and act with violence; *adolescentes* abound in imagination; *viri* judge things with mature reason; *senes*, with firm wisdom. In the *genus humanum* we find a corresponding series of phases. Because of its original vice, the *genus* started from a weak and solitary state. In the beginning, it had to grow in an easy manner, by unbridled liberty. Then, through imagination, it had to find the necessary, useful, and pleasant things of life—"this was the Age of the Poets." And, finally, reason and wisdom had to be cultivated—"this is the age where the philosophers taught the duties of human life."

The passage is overloaded with meaning. In the first stratum of meaning we can discern the division of the *corso* into the Poetic and Human Ages, which is the final form of the theory in the *Scienza nuova*. In a second stratum we find that the characterization of the ages is linked to Vico's anthropology. The *velle, nosse, posse*, which characterizes the mind of man, is in history distended into an age of predominant *velle*, followed by an age of predominant *nosse*. And, finally, we are reminded of the Augustinian ages that extend from infancy to senescence.

The combination of these three meanings seems to be the key to the understanding of Vico's problem. The first and second strata of meaning connect the theory of the finite course of a people— from its mythical evocation to the disintegration of the myth—to a philosophical anthropology. The third, the Augustinian meaning, introduces as the subject of the course the *genus humanum*. If the theory of the *corso* were no more than the theory of the course of a people from evocation to disintegration, then such courses could follow each other in time without limitation of numbers. If the *corso*, however, has a universal meaning for the *genus humanum*, then the Augustinian problem of sacred history cannot be wholly dissociated from it. Let us now consider the later formulations in order to clarify this open question.

b. The Problem in the "First" Scienza nuova

In the "First" *Scienza nuova* the problem of the *corso* is bent in the direction of the finite course of a people. The course is now clearly understood as the movement from myth to reason. It begins with the *sapienza volgare*, which crystallizes in religious and legal institutions, and it moves toward the reflective penetration of this stock of wisdom in the sciences of divine and human things, that is, in metaphysics, mathematics, physics, and in the human sciences of morals, economics, and politics. When the reflective penetration is completed, the *akme* of the course is reached; the *akme* is the perfect state of the nation when the arts and sciences, which have their origin in religion and law, all serve religion and law. When the *akme* of this perfect balance between myth and reason has passed, reflection begins to turn against its origins—through deviation, as in the Stoics and Epicureans, through indifference, as in the skeptics, or through revolt, as in the atheists. This is the phase during which nations decay. They lose their religion and their law, and since they have lost their civilizational personality they become incapable of governing themselves. And thus, by the eternal law of Providence, which wants to preserve mankind, we return to the natural law of the heroic age because there can be no reasonable equality between the independent weak and strong.[20]

c. The Problem in the "Third" Scienza nuova

The account of the "First" *Scienza nuova* has the strong touch of a critique of the age. This is not only a description of the Roman decay

20. *La scienza nuova prima* II.68, in *Opere*, III:142.

but also a description of Vico's own age. The *corso*, thus, seems to repeat itself. We are surpassing the *akme*, and we are drifting toward the barbarism of reflection, which can be overcome only by a new barbarism of heroes. The second *corso* does not seem to be the last. Perhaps a third one will follow? The pendulum of Vico's thought has swung far toward the assumption of indefinitely repeated *corsi*. In the "Third" *Scienza nuova*, however, we find that the accents have shifted. To be sure, the parallel between the ancient and modern *corsi* is stressed even more strongly than in the earlier work, and a whole book (the fifth) is devoted to the elaboration of the parallel in detail. Nevertheless: "We show at the same time how the Almighty has made the counsels of his Providence serve the ineffable decree of his Grace." The "counsels of Providence," as we have seen, guide the gentilician history, while the decrees of Grace concern sacred history. How can the two orders be made to support each other? Vico's answer: "When God, by his supernatural ways, had clarified and established the truth of Christian religion (by the virtue of the martyrs against the Roman power, and by the doctrine of the Fathers and the miracles of the Saints against the wisdom of the Greeks), and when the armed nations arose from all sides to combat the true divinity of its Author, then God permitted a new human order to be born among the nations so that, according to the natural order of human affairs itself, this religion would be firmly established."[21]

d. Vico and Saint Augustine

According to this final formulation, the *ricorso* is not simply another *corso* to be followed by still others *in infinitum*. It is a second *corso*, and it has the definite function of securing the historical existence of Christianity. Gentilician and sacred meanings merge in this second *corso* insofar as revealed Christianity has become the myth of the *gentes* of the Middle Ages. The *ricorso* follows the same pattern of a *storia ideale* as the *corso*, but the pagan myth is supplanted by Christianity. While the second course follows the typical pattern, it is enacted on a higher level of spiritual consciousness.

We can see now in what manner the *recursus* of the *Diritto universale* is linked with the *ricorso* of the *Scienza nuova*. The parallel, in the earlier work, with Saint Augustine's periodization

21. *Scienza nuova*, book V, nos. 1046–47, 397.

of history proves to have been not accidental because Vico's divine cycle of ancient history ends with the senescence of mankind in the Roman empire. This Vichian age of senescence corresponds to the Augustinian *saeculum senescens*. The *recursus* of gentilician history, thus, issues forth in the last period of Augustinian history. By his theory of the *ricorso*, however, Vico does not abolish Saint Augustine's periodization, because the result of the *recursus*, that is, the return to God in Christianity, is preserved. The *ricorso* is unfolding on the new level gained by the *recursus*. It has precisely the function of serving as the natural, human substructure for the preservation of this level. Hence, seen in the perspective of the Augustinian philosophy of history, the *ricorso* is the natural structure of the *saeculum senescens*, whereas, seen in the perspective of Vico's philosophy of history, the *ricorso* is the instrument of Providence for the historical perpetuation of the *recursus*.

The theory of the *corsi*, thus, is more than an attempt to describe empirically the typical course of civilizations from evocation to dissolution. Rather it is an attempt to give a new solution to the problem of universal history in the Augustinian sense. By the eighteenth century, as we have seen, the Augustinian construction had become unsatisfactory in several respects. Inevitably, because of his position in time, Augustine could not give an interpretation of the course of Western civilization from the migration onward. Moreover, he had concentrated the meaning of history entirely within sacred history, and consequently had left the rise and fall of empire in profane history with little meaning beyond that of an object lesson for pride and humiliation. As a result of these two shortcomings, finally, the Christian era had to be understood as a time of waiting for the second coming of Christ, and thus as lacking a profane, civilizational meaning of its own.

The construction was experienced as unsatisfactory even in the high Middle Ages. The first attack on the problem was that of Joachim of Fiore, through the evocation of the Third Realm of the Spirit. With the prediction of a new Christ-like figure, the *dux*, who would inaugurate a further period of spiritual meaning, this attempt by Joachim was in substance a revision of sacred history. The attempt proved a failure in practice as well as in theory. It was a failure in practice because saviors do not appear at the bidding of speculative systems, and it was a failure in theory because it tried to solve the problem of profane meaning on the level of sacred meaning—which is the domain not of the philosopher but of God. Nevertheless, the problem of Vico is contained in the speculation of Joachim because the attempt to solve the problem of historical meaning through a reconstruction of sacred history implies the recognition that Christianity has become embedded in the structure of history and that a solution of the problem is impossible without considering this strand of meaning that has become a historical fact. This, however, is precisely the implication of Vico's theory of the *ricorso*. The hesitations of Vico, and his reticence with regard to the future course of Western history, are a result of the insight that the meaning of the second course goes beyond being a repetition of the first one and that, therefore, predictions concerning Western history cannot be based on our knowledge of the course of ancient history. The unfolding of the *ricorso* on the level gained by the *recursus* means that the structure of profane history has been affected by the historicity of Christianity.

While the Vichian problem is implied in the speculation of Joachim, it certainly is not solved by it. On the contrary, the transposition of the problem to the level of sacred history foreshadows the possibility of a solution on the level of profane history. Why should the problem of sacred history not be discarded altogether and the meaning of history be found in the intramundane rise and fall of nations or civilizations? This is the possibility that, after many tentative and partial constructions, has ultimately been realized in Spengler's philosophy of history. The realization of this possibility means the return to the pre-Christian, pagan interpretation of history. The value of Spengler's construction lies in its admirable, anti-Christian cleanliness: it mercilessly reveals what happens to us if the problem of sacred history is simply ignored. The abolition of mankind as the subject of history, and its replacement by the plurality of cultures, is of course unacceptable to the Christian. But it also must arouse, and has aroused, the particular wrath of anti-Christian intellectual movements that at the same time are ready to supply a new intramundane meaning to history—namely, the Progressives, the Communists, and the National Socialists. The bluff of anti-Christianity is called when the profane, antispiritual interpretation of history is applied relentlessly, not only to the Word that has become flesh but also to the flesh that wants to become a Word in rivalry with the *verbum genitum*.

The extreme positions of Joachim and Spengler bring into clearer focus the problem that the philosophers of the eighteenth century tried to solve. We can express it briefly as the search for a formula that would harmonize systematically the universalist meaning of Christian sacred history with the finite meaning of the profane rise and fall of civilizations. The constructions of the Voltairean and later Progressivist type solved the problem through the transfer of sacred meaning to the most recent phase of Western civilization. We discussed this secularist solution in the chapter on apostasy and shall discuss it at greater length in the chapter on Positivism.[22] Vico solves the problem through building the "gentilician" *ricorso* into the *saeculum senescens* of Augustinian sacred history. Obviously, the Vichian construction is superior as an empirical theory of history because it does not have to ignore, or deprive the great spiritual events of human history of, their unique character. Nevertheless, the secularist construction contains an important empirical element that is not emphasized sufficiently in Vico's solution, namely the insight that sacred history has, indeed, become *history* and is inseparably blended with the course of profane history in Western civilization. This element is not altogether missing in Vico, as we have seen, because the *ricorso* is distinguished from the *corso* owing to the fact that Christianity has become the "myth" of the *gentes*. Still, the repetitive character of the *ricorso* is so strongly stressed that the previously mentioned hesitations and reticences of Vico with regard to the future course of Western civilization must be considered a symptom of his embarrassment in face of the theoretical conflict between the profane cycle and the sacred straight line. The *ricorso* ought to have a *recursus*, and where would the *recursus* lead us if not to a new Christ?

This is the open problem in Vico's construction. It has remained an open problem to this day—even in Toynbee's *Study of History*—for the same reason that Vico had to leave it open. This reason is the temptation to generalize on the basis of too limited historical materials. Vico runs into his impasse because he construes his *storia ideale* on the basis of one single instance of a civilizational course, that is, the course of the Romans. And the model of

---

22. *The Collected Works of Eric Voegelin*, vol. 26, *History of Political Ideas*, vol. VIII, *Crisis and the Apocalypse of Man*, ed. David Walsh (Columbia: University of Missouri Press, 1999), chap. 2.

Greco-Roman history with its impressive course from the heroic kingship to the empire, and from the pagan pantheon to Christianity, still exerts its influence on historical construction, although our vastly enlarged knowledge has taught us that the problem of the *corsi* is not to be exhausted by the construction of a pattern that would fit all civilizations.

If we take into proper account the structure of Eastern history, the problem of the *corsi* presents itself in a somewhat different light. For only Western history shows the deep incision that clearly sets off the Greco-Roman civilization against the Western civilization on the new ethnical basis provided by the Great Migration. In Chinese history, for instance, the problem of the succession of *corsi* is so obscure that traditionally we speak of only one Chinese civilization, whereas in fact Toynbee could show that Chinese society has run the full courses of two civilizations, which he distinguishes as the Sinic and the Far Eastern. And the Chinese case is still comparatively clear because the incision between the two civilizations is well marked by the interregnum at the end of the Han empire and the refoundation of civilization by the barbarian invaders aided by Mahayana Buddhism. In the case of Babylonian history, for instance, the problem of the *corsi* is even more obscure. Again Toynbee thinks that he can distinguish two courses, which he calls the Sumeric and Babylonic civilizations, separated by the Kassite rule in Babylon. But while there is a well-marked interregnum, and while ethnically the neo-Babylonian empire is built on the amalgamation of the people of the city-states with the Chaldean nomad invaders, there is signally absent a new element of spiritual cohesion comparable to Mahayana Buddhism in the second Chinese civilization, or Catholicism in the medieval West. The Babylonic civilization is built on the same religious foundations as the preceding Sumeric.

The comparison with the structure of Eastern history shows that civilizational courses do not necessarily have the dramatic qualities of the Roman. In the Chinese case, we do not find the violent geographical dislocation that in an external, physical manner sets off Western from Greco-Roman civilization. Nor does Mahayana Buddhism dislodge the Confucian ethos of governmental organization in the same manner that Christianity superseded Roman Stoicism. The Sinification of the barbarians was sufficiently thorough to preserve a cultural continuity that is apt to obscure the fact that the interregnum after the Han empire was followed by a second political course that culminated in a new empire period in the time of the Mongol conquest. And in the Babylonian case we do not even find the higher religion that sets off clearly the second Western course against the first. In light of this comparison, the problem of the *corso* requires a redefinition. The regularity of the courses (which actually can be observed, though even Toynbee's study will require many corrections in detail) is confined to that stratum in history that, for lack of a better term, we may call the dynamics of pragmatic history. The repetitive regularity of the courses does not extend to the history of the myth that gives sacramental coherence to a civilizational society and its subdivisions, nor does it extend to the evolution of the spirit in the history of mankind.

Vico's concept of the gentilician *corso* is methodologically vitiated through the blending of the course of Roman pragmatic history with the segment of the spiritual evolution of mankind that fills the course of Greco-Roman civilization. To be sure, every civilization has its myth. Hence we may accept as substantially correct the insights of Vico's genius, that the *akme* of a civilization is reached when the myth is penetrated by rational speculation and that a civilization declines with the rational exhaustion and dissolution of its myth. But that a myth, and through it a civilizational community, is evoked at all, that it has a specific, spiritual content, and that through the simultaneous and successive growth and decay of civilizations mankind has a spiritual history—all these are problems that transcend the immanent regularities of a civilizational course. Indeed, these problems belong to a philosophy of the theogonic process. Hence in the search for historical regularities it is methodologically inadmissible to include the mythical structure of a specific civilization in the construction of a typical civilizational course.

Vico committed this methodological sin when he generalized the Roman *corso* into a *storia ideale,* and he aggravated the mistake as well as complicated it when he made the compromise with sacred history in the Augustinian sense. The sacred history of Saint Augustine is in itself a quite legitimate attempt to give systematic expression to a decisive phase in the spiritual history of mankind on the basis of the historical knowledge of his time. The history of Israel and Christianity is, indeed, such a well-circumscribed phase. There have been many a nomad people and many a temple-state in Asia Minor, but only in one instance has there been realized historically the spiritual evolution that was carried successively by Hebrew, Israelitic, and Jewish religiousness. And there has been more than one higher religion, but only in one instance has the representative suffering of the Logos for the guilt of man been realized historically. Even today, when the advancement of science allows us to place the history of Israel and Christianity in a larger context than the Augustinian, no critical objection can in principle be raised against the project of isolating theoretically this evolution of religious consciousness as the most important event in the spiritual history of mankind or of setting it off against the profane *corsi* of the civilizations. The difficulties of the Augustinian position, and consequently of Vico's, do not arise from the theoretical isolation of a spiritual history as distinguished from pragmatic history. Rather, they arise from the fact that the isolation has not been driven far enough. Just as in Vico's idea of gentilician history the problem of the typical pragmatic *corso* is obscured because it is insufficiently separated from the peculiar problems of the pagan myth, so in Saint Augustine's idea of sacred history the problems of the spirit are obscured because they are insufficiently separated from the pragmatic course of Hebrew and Roman history. The methodological crack in the Augustinian construction makes itself most painfully felt at the very point where Vico links the *recursus* with the *ricorso*, that is, in the idea of the *saeculum senescens*. In the idea of the *saeculum senescens* a phase of spiritual history has blended with the pragmatic substructure. Spiritually it is the age between the first and second comings of Christ; pragmatically it is the age of waiting for the end of human civilization without a meaning of its own. The age is senescent, not because there is anything senescent about the spirit, but because the course of Roman civilization draws visibly toward its close and because the attempt to make the people of the Roman empire the carrier of the spirit of Christ in history has failed. The Augustinian pessimism is justified insofar as it implies the insight that the spirit can exist historically only through embodiment in a community; it is unjustified insofar as it reflects the sentiment that the end of the historical world has come when a civilization has run its pragmatic course. The possibilities of social existence in history are not exhausted by the power organizations that succeed each other typically in a pragmatic *corso*. On the contrary, the spirit can form its own social bodies beyond the order of the *corsi,* and the church has, indeed, survived the political organizations of the Greco-Roman world and become the chrysalis (Toynbee) of a new civilization—that is, of Western civilization.

By combining his gentilician *corso* with the Augustinian sacred history, Vico has doubly burdened his construction with the Roman model. The *recursus* of his *corso* is modeled on the coincidence of the Roman pragmatic course with the phase of spiritual history that culminates in Christianity, and through the adoption of sacred history he has burdened the *ricorso* with the mood of a historical *Götterdämmerung,* which stems from the Augustinian experience of the sack of Rome by the Visigoths. These shortcomings, however, should not induce a rash condemnation of Vico's work. Its qualities have to be appraised in comparison with the principal alternative constructions: the medieval, Joachitic contraction of the meaning of history into the movement of the spirit, the Spenglerian abolition of the spiritual history of mankind, the secularist hubris of interpreting history as a process of human self-salvation, the Gnostic "internal" construction of history as a process in which the Logos comes to its self-reflective fulfillment in a present without a future. Placed in this company the genius of Vico impresses us because of his mastery of the empirical dimensions of the problem, from the transcendental irruptions of the spirit that determine the meaning of history for the *genus humanum,* through the life of the spirit in a civilizational *corso,* to the dynamics of pragmatic history that carry the spirit on the stream of *usus* and *necessitas.* He impresses us, moreover, by the spiritual instinct and intellectual caution that prevent him from pressing into dubious consequences a theory that is still too heavily burdened with the inevitable imperfections that stem from the state of science in his time. This last point merits our particular attention because, in spite of our greatly enlarged historical horizon, we cannot boast of having substantially penetrated the theoretical problems of history and politics much further than Vico. If our critical analysis of Vico's theory has shown anything, we hope it has shown the formidable complexities of the problem. In view of these complexities it would seem foolish to indulge in predictions concerning the future course of history at large, or concerning the future course of Western civilization and its present crisis, on the basis of even the most carefully considered philosophy of history.

§9. The *Storia Eterna Ideale*

The theory of the gentilician *corsi* is embedded in the Augustinian philosophy of sacred history. The integral system of Vico's thought therefore continues the problem of a universal history of the *genus humanum*. Nevertheless, the theory of the *corsi* is the centerpiece of the system, and the novelty of the *Scienza nuova* lies in the evocation of the *storia eterna ideale*, of the typical course to which the histories of all nations conform. The *corso* itself is the principal subject matter of the New Science, and in our analysis of Vico's meditation we have reached the point where, after decades of tentative treatment of the problem, the principles of the new historical science themselves come into view. However, even in this last phase, that is, in the period of the First, Second, and Third *Scienza nuova*, the meditative character of Vico's speculation makes itself felt in the formulation of its principles. Even now we do not find a system that would be rationally closed. Rather, Vico's formulations have the character of aphoristic outbursts in which the principles disengage themselves abruptly from the matrix of historical materials. As a consequence, the system itself remains an entelechy that makes the formulations converge toward an ultimate form, rather than actually attain the form itself. As a further consequence, the interpreter has to treat the formulations with some caution in order not to deflect them too far from their point of convergence.

a. Formulation of the Principle

The uncertainties hovering around the ultimate systematic meaning make themselves felt particularly in Vico's formulation of the cardinal principle of his New Science. It is contained in the previously quoted passage: "That this world of history is most certainly made by man, and hence we can find, we must find, its principles in the modifications of our own human mind."[23] We have discussed already the Neoplatonic implications of the principle. Vico transfers the *formula naturae* to the *mondo civile*. The world of history is conceived as an analogue of the world of nature: as God is the maker of nature, so man is the maker of history. Man knows the world of history from "inside," in a way analogous to God's knowledge of

---

23. *Scienza nuova*, no. 331.

nature. The science of history is the only true science because in this realm man is at the same time the maker and the knower. In this extreme formulation the principle would establish history as an intramundane science, and the principle would be incompatible with Vico's recognition of sacred history. Our previous analysis has already clarified this point, and we need elaborate no further warning against pressing the formulation to its ultimate logical consequences.

b. The Historicity of the Mind

The insight that the formulation has to be balanced by other explicit statements of Vico that invalidate its radical consequences does not make more intelligible, however, the mental process in which it was produced. We have to scrutinize the aphoristic texture of Vico's thought itself in order to find at least a clue to the understanding of his radical and mutually incompatible theorems. Such a clue is offered by the very context of the passage in which the formulation of the principle occurs. The principle itself is followed by a reflection on the curious fact that philosophers should have been so persistent in exploring the world of nature, of which only God has true science, while neglecting the world of the nations, which is penetrable by the human mind. Vico goes on to explain the curiosity by a tendency of the human mind to sense bodily things first and only then to proceed to reflective self-understanding because "the mind is immersed and buried in the body."[24]

This explanation adds a historical dimension to the theoretical problem. The new metaphysics of the mind is valid in science at all times, but it can be realized in a philosopher only at certain times in the intellectual history of mankind. Hence the metaphysics of nature and the metaphysics of mind are not simply false and true positions with regard to the problem under discussion. Rather, they are necessary historical phases in its penetration. For the full understanding of Vico's position it is necessary to take into account its character as a step in a historical process. In Vico's thought the historicity of the mind affects the meaning of the propositions advanced by the thinker. And the problem of historicity is taken

---

24. *Scienza nuova*, no. 331. See also "Degnità, no. 63," translated as "Elements, LXIII," *The New Science*, no. 236.

consistently by Vico not only as the problem of placing his own thought in the intellectual history of mankind, but also as the problem of placing every phase of his own thought into his personal meditative process because the personal process of the mind is the source of all transpersonal history. If we use a later biological term we might say that Vico has advanced a phylogenetic law of the mind, namely that the intellectual biography of the thinker is an abbreviation of the intellectual history of man. The passage under discussion itself illustrates the problem. The explanation of the curiosity, offered by Vico, is worded in the same terms as his earlier position with regard to the "moral sciences" in the *Liber metaphysicus:* that the moral sciences are the least certain because the movements of the mind are most deeply buried in matter. In the course of his meditation, Vico himself proceeded from a stage where his mind was buried in matter so deeply that he assigned the superior degrees of *certezza* to mathematics and physics, to a stage of reflective self-understanding in which the *certezza* shifted to the mind. Hence the radicalism of the late formulation does not signify an absolute position on a Cartesian tabula rasa; it is rather the aphoristic reflex of a light that shineth in the darkness.[25] For the meditative moment, the brilliance of the light relegates to obscurity the qualifications that would have to balance the insight in a nonaphoristic, systematic discourse.

This interpretation is borne out by the qualifications contained in the parallel passage in the *Scienza nuova prima.*[26] In this earlier edition the language does not yet have the high-pitched sharpness of the later, and the path that has led to the ultimate insight is still visible. We do not find here the rigid opposition of a *mondo naturale* and a *mondo civile*. Instead we find the more precise language of a *mondo delle gentili naziono* that is created by man. History as a whole is certainly not made by man, but only the world of the gentilician nations, because sacred history is governed by a different principle. Moreover, even for gentilician history the Neoplatonic touch of the later formulation is considerably toned down because the systematic relation of the great principle to other parts of Vico's doctrine is given due consideration. To be sure, we

25. "In tal densa notte di tenebre . . . apparisce questo lume eterno." These are the opening words of *Scienza nuova,* no. 331.
26. *La scienza nuova prima* I.11, in *Opere,* III:29; *Vico: Selected Writings,* 98–99.

still gain the insight that the principles of gentilician history are to be found in the nature of the human mind, but Vico reminds the reader strongly that the human mind is not a closed monad but an open field of operations for divine forces. "The metaphysics of the human mind was formerly a contemplation of the mind of individual man in order to guide it toward God as the eternal Truth (which is the most universal theory of divine philosophy); now it has become the contemplation of the *senso commune del genere umano* as a certain human mind of the nations in order to guide it toward God as eternal Providence (which would be the most universal practice of divine philosophy)."[27] The metaphysics of the mind does not construct an abstract true system but is a process of contemplation that leads toward God. It does not start with the ontology of the individual in order to ascend—like the Augustinian meditation—toward the *anima animi* and to reach out toward God in the *intentio*. Rather, it starts from the *senso commune* and ascends to an insight into the structure of history as a work of Providence operating through the mind of man. The historicity of the mind emerges from this passage more clearly as the providential plan for the unfolding of the potentiality of the mind in the course of a historically existing society. The contemplation of the civilizational course reveals the providential structure, and the contemplator himself is part of the providential course. The human mind in which the principles of history are to be found is not human in the sense of an immanentist philosophy. Rather, it is the medium of Providence in history, and the mind of the thinker can penetrate the structure of history because it contains itself the providential core that guides it toward historical understanding. Hence nothing could be further from a correct interpretation than the suggestion, which in fact has been made, that the achievement of Vico consists in the "psychologization" of history.

c. Providential Contemplation

The New Science "is, under one of its principal aspects, a reasoned civil theology of divine Providence."[28] Such a civil theology has to supplement the former natural theology. Its content is a demonstration of "the historical fact of Providence." Hence it will have

27. *La scienza nuova prima* I.11, in *Opere*, III:29; *Vico: Selected Writings*, 99.
28. *La scienza nuova*, no. 342.

to be a history of the order that Providence (without taking human counsel and quite frequently against the purposes of man) has given to "this great city of mankind." Whereas this world of history is created in time and concretely, the providential order is universal and eternal.[29] The order of the civilizational course, which is the object of the New Science, thus can be found neither as an abstraction from empirical observation nor as an empirical psychology of the individual. It has to be found by means of a "history of human ideas" concerning the necessity and utility of human life. Necessity and utility, as we have seen, are the human instruments through which Providence operates in order to achieve the meaningful course of man in history. On the *occasion* of the necessities of life in society the eternal idea of a just order among men becomes clarified and gradually realized. The human ideas concerning necessity and utility, which are embodied in the social institutions, are not themselves the eternal order, but for the historian they will be the material on the *occasion* of which he can disengage the eternal order that transcends the human ideas at every single point of this course.[30] Divine Providence creates a meaning in history beyond the humanly created ideas. This meaning, which is immanent in the course as a whole but transcends every single phase of it, is re-created by the historian in his contemplation. The meaning of history that emerges from contemplation thus reproduces the providential strand in the human fabric of the course. This providential line is what Vico calls the *storia eterna ideale* "according to which run in time the histories of all the nations in their rise, progress, [maturity], decadence and end."[31] The ideal history is the pattern that the affairs of nations *must* follow in the past, present, and future. The historian "who meditates this science narrates to himself this ideal eternal history insofar as he makes this history when he proves that it *must* take this course in the past, present, and future; and since he, who makes the things, tells them himself, history cannot be more certain." This science proceeds like geometry, which constructs the world of magnitudes out of its own elements, but it contains much more reality than geometry because the order of man is more real than points and

---

29. *La scienza nuova,* no. 342.
30. *La scienza nuova,* no. 347.
31. *La scienza nuova,* no. 349.

lines. The demonstrations of this science are of a divine order, "and they should, therefore, oh reader, give you a divine pleasure for it is only in God that knowing and making are the same thing."[32]

This aphoristic elucidation of the principle reveals that Vico has grappled with the problem of meaning in history more seriously than most other philosophers. The question is, indeed, a formidable one. Intellectual and spiritual meaning, which Vico assumes to exist in history, can appear only as the precipitate of intellectual and spiritual action; it presupposes a creative agent. Can individual man be this agent? Vico's answer is negative. The meaning of a historical course transcends the action of individual man. We have to introduce a nonhuman subject as the creator of meaning. This nonhuman subject Vico calls Providence. If, however, we assume a nonhuman creator of meaning, then the question of intelligibility arises. How can a nonhumanly created meaning be understood by man? As far as the meaning of the whole is concerned, we have discussed the question previously and the answer is clear: it cannot be known. The meaning of history is unknown unless we accept Revelation. This is the methodological superiority of the Christian answer over the secularist constructions: it does not have to cheat on the question of meaning by pretending that man can find an answer empirically. Vico accepts Revelation for the meaning of the whole. This acceptance, however, still leaves him with the finite, transindividual meaning of the historical course. The problem presents itself to him in the following terms. Because, as a matter of fact, a transindividual meaning can be discerned in the *corso*, this raises the question: which metaphysical assumptions do we have to make in order to explain the fact of such meaning as well as the fact of its intelligibility? He solves the problem by introducing a transindividual factor into the structure of the individual mind. The transindividual Providence is present as the guiding principle in man that directs the successive generations along a line of meaning without their intention or knowing. This assumption explains the fact of meaning. The fact of intelligibility has to be solved correspondingly by the assumption of Providence as present in the mind of the philosopher in such a manner that the providential line of meaning itself produces in history a constellation in which the meaning becomes intelligible through human

32. *La scienza nuova*, no. 349.

contemplation. This solution is classical insofar as—in the present state of science—we cannot improve its structure. To be sure, the metaphysical symbolism can be changed. The transindividual element need not be called Providence, and it need not be conceived in the imagery of a transcendental irruption. Schelling, for instance, called it the unconscious and experienced it as a welling up from the ground of existence. And the nineteenth century produced a wealth of biological, organological, sociological, and psychological symbols that all had the function of providing a collective subject for the transindividual meaning unfolding in the history of a group. No choice of symbols, however, can change the structure of the problem, and symbols such as Vico's Providence or Schelling's unconscious ground, in which the individual merges with the substance of the universe, are methodologically preferable to symbols borrowed from the empirical realms of being because they keep alive the awareness of the transempirical character of the problem. Considering Vico's profound insight into this problem, we can well understand the tone of mystical joy in his announcements to the reader and his divine pleasure in tracing, as the tool of Providence, the line of meaning drawn by the finger of God in history.

§10. The *Senso Commune*

From the principle of the *storia eterna ideale* we have to turn, finally, to the conceptual apparatus for its execution. We shall confine our analysis to one or two fundamental concepts because we can refer the reader for the details of Vico's construction to a number of presentations now available in English.[33]

a. Positive Definitions

The key concept for the construction of the ideal history is the *senso commune*. All human groups are divided into those that have

---

33. Voegelin listed Croce's *Philosophy of Giambattista Vico* and the Fisch and Bergin introduction to the *Autobiography*. As indicated in the first note to this chapter, the study of Vico has increased enormously in the past half century. In Italy, Nicola Badaloni's *Introduzione a G. B. Vico* (Milan: Feltrinelli, 1961) has diverted scholarly attention from Vico's ideas to the social and historical context. Croce's influence has continued to be felt in the English-speaking world through first the work of R. G. Collingwood and then that of Isaiah Berlin. In the United States excellent monographic studies by Michael Mooney, Donald Philip Verene, and Mark Lilla have addressed specialized aspects of Vico's work, as have other equally useful studies by Donald R. Kelley, Leon Pompa, Frederick Vaughan, and Gino Bedani.

received special divine assistance on their civilizational course and those that have not. The first, like the Hebrews, are the subject of sacred history; the second, the ordinary fallen men, are the subject of gentilician history. The civilizational history of ordinary fallen man originates in the appearance of the *senso commune,* following a state of savagery after the deluge. The meaning of the *senso commune* is defined in the *Degnità,* the "Elements" of the "Third" *Scienza nuova.* "The *senso commune* is a judgment without reflection, experienced in common by a whole class, by a whole people, by a whole nation, or the whole mankind."[34] The corollary explains: "This *Degnità* [no. XIII] is a great principle that establishes the *senso commune* of mankind as the criterion given by divine Providence to the nations for the purpose of ascertaining the natural law of the *gentes.*"[35]

The "First" *Scienza nuova* amplifies those definitions somewhat. "Divine Providence is the architect *(architetta)* of the world of nations."[36] The divine architect has created the nations equipped with the *senso commune;* the consensus of the *senso commune* of all nations is the wisdom *(sapienza)* of mankind.[37] "The workmaster *(fabbro)* of the world of nations, in obedience to the divine architect, is human free will, otherwise uncertain in the individuals as to its direction, but not determined by the wisdom of mankind, and equipped with the measuring rods of human utility and necessity which are uniformly possessed by all individual men; this human necessity and utility, determined in such manner, are, according to the Roman jurists, the two sources of all the natural law of the *gentes.*"[38]

These passages should be sufficient to clarify the construction of the concept as well as its systematic function. The *senso commune* is the point of origin of a civilizational course. It comprises the primordial religious and legal institutions of a nation, and the unreflected ideas embodied in these institutions are the stock of meaning that is penetrated in the historical course increasingly by reason until, at the *akme* of the course, the moment of perfect

---

34. "Elements, XII," *Scienza nuova,* no. 142.
35. "Elements, XIII," *Scienza nuova,* no. 145.
36. *Scienza nuova prima* II.1.38; *Vico: Selected Writings,* 104.
37. *Scienza nuova prima* II.3.39–40; *Vico: Selected Writings,* 105.
38. *Scienza nuova prima* II.3.39–40; *Vico: Selected Writings,* 105. See also "Elements XI," *Scienza nuova,* no. 141.

balance between substance and reason is achieved. The meaning of the *corso* is the refinement of an initial, dense, unreflected substance to a maximum of rational differentiation. The later, rational phase does not add to the substance. Reason can operate only on the initial stock. In the practice of historical interpretation, this means, for instance, that Roman jurisprudence "is a science of the mental content of the *decemviri* concerning the civil utility in the more severe times of the Roman people."[39] It would be vain to search in Roman jurisprudence for the elaboration of principles that presuppose another, for instance the Christian, initial substance. Under this aspect, the concept of the *senso commune* established the great principle of civilizational interpretation that the history of a civilization is the history of the exhaustion of its initial myth and of such mythical elements as may have entered the course from other sources.

Moreover, we have to note on the occasion of this concept certain methodological refinements that did not appear with equal clearness in the discussion of the general principle of the *storia ideale*. We see now how Vico better distinguished the human sphere proper from the providential factor. The human element, the *arbitrio umano*, is a constant force in history, advancing under the pressure of utility and necessity, which by themselves would lead to no social order at all but are bent to the providential purpose by the light of the *sapienza volgare*. The course of a civilization results only from the cooperation of the two forces, the providential and the human, the *architetta* and the *fabbro*.

b. Critical Clarification

This question will receive further clarification from a survey of the criticisms extended by Vico to several erroneous approaches to the problems of politics and history. The Epicureans and Stoics deviated, each in their own way, from the *sapienza volgare* and became thereby incapable of mastering the problems of man in history. The Epicureans made chance the ruler of human affairs. The pleasures of the senses were supposed to direct the passions, and utility was supposed to be the rule of justice. They neglected

39. *Scienza nuova prima* I.12.30; *Vico: Selected Writings*, 100.

the providential factor. The Stoics, on the other hand, recognized eternal justice, but they destroyed integral humanity when they condemned the passions and made all crimes equal. Moral severity destroys the function of the passions as the instrument of Providence for realizing justice in society. Only Plato gained the proper balance, but even he failed because he fell into the error, "common to the human mind," of measuring the nature of others by his own nature. This error caused him to conceive the origin of justice in the mind of the philosopher instead of in the *sapienza volgare* of the barbarian and crude initiators of gentilician humanity.[40] The moderns do not fare better than the ancients. Grotius was a Socinian and hence assumed the nature of primitive man to be good. He did not need Providence to equip savage, fallen man with a *senso commune*, and his solitary simpletons associate under the direction of utility. And Selden, misguided by his profound Hebrew studies, committed the mistake of using the Hebrew people as the model for his development of natural law, overlooking the fact that the Hebrew development is not typical of gentilician history.[41]

These criticisms are not always justified. Grotius was a bit more than a utilitarian; and the *Laws* bring the return to the Cretan origins of Hellenic civilization because Plato had seen the flaw in the position of the *Republic*. But the justness of the criticisms is not our concern at the moment. In their aggregate, they supply an excellent table of the typical mistakes that a philosopher of history must avoid. He must not base his system on a psychology of passions because in this case the structure of history (the gestalt, to use Koehler's term) will escape him. Nor must he oppose an eternal idea of justice to the concrete motivations of man in political action, because in this case he will miss the problem of the realization of a meaningful order through the instrument of the life of passions. He must not erect the contemplative existence of the philosopher into a model of man because then the actual forces of historical growth, which are not at all contemplative, will be neglected. He must not be a Pelagian, who assumes the essential goodness of man, because he will fail to grasp the tension of political existence between the evil of force and the realization of an idea. And finally, he must not

---

40. *Scienza nuova prima* I.3.12; *Vico: Selected Writings*, 84–85.
41. *Scienza nuova prima* I.5.14–17; *Vico: Selected Writings*, 86–89.

mistake the problems of spiritual history for problems of pragmatic history.

c. History and Philosophy of Humanity

His own counterposition, which avoids these mistakes, Vico has formulated most concisely in his demand for a science "which shall be, at the same time, history and philosophy of humanity."[42] The philosophers have hitherto meditated on a human nature that is already civilized by religions and laws, but the religious and legal institutions are precisely the medium within which the function of philosophy grows as a rational penetration of the initial mythical substance. The philosophers have not meditated on the human nature that produces religions and laws that in their turn produce the philosophers.[43] Philosophical speculation has no creative function. Within the civilizational medium it has no authority of its own, but such authority as it has is derived from the civilizational substance on which it reflects. The authors of books follow the authors of nations at a distance of more than a millennium.[44] If the philosopher does not realize his position within the civilizational medium, his speculation will move between the poles of a naive erection of his civilizational values into an absolute system and a loss of his civilizational tradition resulting in idiosyncratic aberrations. Only when philosophy is at the same time history, that is, when the philosopher understands his own historicity, can he bring the mythical substance of his civilization within his grasp and orient himself critically within the wisdom of the *senso commune.* He cannot transcend the wisdom of the myth through personal creation, but he can transcend it speculatively by exploring the origin and the course of the myth and by accepting the myth consciously as the transpersonal substance by which his personal meditation lives.

This train of thought obviously leads us back to Vico's personal position. The civilizational substance in which he lives consists not only of the gentilician myth of the Roman *corso* but also of the Christianity of the *ricorso.* Here we touch on the ultimate speculative reason Vico could neither continue the Augustinian sacred history without modification nor become a philosopher of

---

42. *Scienza nuova prima* I.6.18; *Vico: Selected Writings,* 89–91.
43. *Scienza nuova prima* I.6.18; *Vico: Selected Writings,* 89–91.
44. *Scienza nuova,* "Elements, XII," no. 143.

profane history to the exclusion of sacred history. Both Rome and Christianity were for the Italian thinker eminently the component parts of his civilizational substance, and in his speculation he had to bring both within his grasp. And we touch here also on the source of the oscillation and the disquietude in Vico's thought. In spite of the elaborate framework of sacred history into which he places his *corsi*, there can be no doubt that his sympathies are with gentilician history. In the meditation on the *storia eterna ideale* the philosopher experiences the divine pleasure of being maker and knower at the same time. This pleasure is denied to him in sacred history where the *verbum genitum* speaks itself. The philosopher can transcend gentilician civilization, but he cannot transcend Christianity in his speculation. The balance of sentiments in Vico's personality is inclined toward the ecstasies of the philosophizing intellect. The fervor flags when he approaches the sphere where the substance is not amenable to active penetration by the philosopher, but rather where the substance penetrates the man in the passion of faith.

§11. The Political Structure of the *Corso*

A philosophy that is at the same time history has to penetrate beyond the content of civilization to its origins. At the beginning of a civilizational course stand as its originators the *autori delle nazioni*, that is, the men in whom the *senso commune* awakens and who, by virtue of this providential awakening, become the founders of a civilizational community. The course itself consists of the phases by which the original foundation is developed, transformed, and dissolved. We have to survey briefly the origin and the phases of the *corso*.

The *corso* is divided by Vico into two main phases: the phase of creative action, called the poetic age, and the age of reflection, called the human age. The poetic age is subdivided into the divine age and the heroic age, and the divine age is preceded by a primitive phase, following the Fall and the Deluge, called the *stato ferino*. For an authority of his division within the *senso commune*, Vico refers to an Egyptian division of history into the three ages of the gods, the heroes, and men.[45]

---

45. The reference to the Egyptian classification is to be found in "Elements, XXVIII," *Scienza nuova*, no. 173. Vico gives no source; it probably is Herodotus, *Histories* bk. II.

a. Stato Ferino *and Divine Age*

The *stato ferino* is a prehistoric state, characterized by nomadism, promiscuity, and the solitary existence of individuals in anarchy. It serves only as the negative background for the beginning of the historical process itself. Man is incapable of transcending this bestial state by his own efforts. Divine Providence awakens in him the impulse to social order through the phenomenon of lightning, which breaks into the savage time after the deluge. The lightning in the sky arouses in the savage the feeling of his creaturely weakness and of the existence of a superhuman divine power. He reacts to this awakening of religious awe by creating the "false religion" of the pagan divinities as the guarantors of order among men. Vico interprets the pagan gods as poetic, phantastic images, personifying principles of social order, of marriage, of family, of *patria potestas*, of agriculture, and so forth.

The myth of the first age is created not by all men who are living in the *stato ferino* but only by select individuals. Vico assumes a primary distinction between men insofar as some are more capable than others of responding to the call of Providence. "There is a natural difference between human natures." The one nature "is noble because it is intelligent"; the other nature "is vile because it is stupid."[46] The men of the noble, intelligent nature become the creators of social order as the first *patres familias*. The others, the less strong and less intelligent ones, will approach the heads of the families, the primitive monarchs, and beg for reception into the order of the family. They want to exchange insecurity and misery for the status of protected servants, of *clientes* or *famuli*. This original differentiation of men into the heads of social units and the associated agricultural slaves is the origin of the political structure proper of the civilizational societies. We can trace this order of the primary *clientes* through the stages of (1) the associates of the founding heroes, (2) the plebeians of the heroic republic, and (3) the provinces of the imperial people.[47] In this differentiation originates the *materia della scienza politica*, "which is nothing else but the science of command and obedience in a republic."[48]

---

46. *Scienza nuova prima* II.16.78.
47. "Elements, LXXIX," *Scienza nuova*, no. 259.
48. *Scienza nuova*, no. 629.

b. The Heroic Age

The republic itself emerges from the state of the monarchical family through the dire necessity in which the heroic *patres familias* find themselves when the clientele becomes rebellious. The answer to the threat is the association of the independent *patres* into an aristocratic estate, under a king, who exerts a common rule over the *famuli*, who in this new order have become the plebeians. The aristocratic republic has been born with its two estates of the patricians and plebeians. The estates are differentiated socially insofar as the patricians are still the owners of the myth and are consequently the bearers of social order while the plebeians are the men without gods, without auspices, sacred marriage, law, or independent property.

The aristocratic republic does not last. Since the lot of the plebeians is not the best, they begin to resist maltreatment, and in order to offer effective resistance they have to create a sacramental union among themselves. The history of the second age witnesses, therefore, the *contese eroiche,* the wars between the estates, in which the plebeians create their own myth and, in a complicated process, compel the patricians to extend their privileges to them. The dynamics of this period are formulated by Vico in "Elements XCII": "The weak want rights; the powerful deny them; the ambitious, in order to gain a followership, advocate them; and the princes, in order to equalize the weak and the powerful, protect them."[49]

c. The Human Age

Once the equality of mythical order has resulted from the *contese eroiche,* the third age, the human one, begins. In the political sphere it is characterized by the appearance of the popular free republic. In the realm of ideas the phase has been reached where the power of mythical creation declines and reflective philosophy begins the elaboration of reasoned systems of political ethics. Virtuous action is no longer the outgrowth of religious sentiment but recommends itself through the understanding of the idea of virtue. There appears the consciousness of natural equality between men. The order of sacred, and therefore secret, law that characterized the heroic age

---

49. "Elements XCII," *Scienza nuova,* no. 283.

gives way to rational, codified law. The end of the mythical order also changes the dynamics of political history. The dynamics of the aristocratic republic depended on the previously characterized *contese eroiche*. Now that men have become equal, they are differentiated only by their power interests. Hence the struggle between the estates is followed by the struggle between the parties. If this struggle reaches the point where it endangers the existence of the community, the strong monarch of the Augustan type appears and compels submission of the warring parties. This is the final phase of the *corso*. If the Caesaristic experiment fails, the republic will either be conquered by stronger and healthier neighbors, or it will disintegrate internally and sink into a new barbarism of private existence, that is, into the barbarism of reflection. Only divine Providence can then relieve the horror by awakening again the mythical powers in man, thus opening a new *corso*.

d. Summarizing Characterization of the Corso

Vico summarizes the political phases of the *corso* by tracing the fate of the plebeians and patricians from the origins to the end. "Element XCV" concerns the fate of the plebeians: "At first men love to emerge from subjection and they desire equality: this is the plebs in the aristocratic republics, which finally change into popular republics. Then they endeavor to elevate themselves over their equals: this is the plebs in the popular republics when they decay into republics of the powerful. Finally they want to put themselves under the laws: this is the anarchical or unbridled popular republic; there is no worse tyranny than this, because there are as many tyrants in the republic as there are audacious and dissolute men. Then the plebs becomes wise through misery and in order to save itself it submits to the monarchy; this is the natural *lex regia* by which Tacitus legitimates the Roman monarchy under Augustus."[50] "Element XCVI" concerns the patricians: "When the first republics were formed from the families, the nobles who emerged from primordial, prelegal freedom were recalcitrant to restraints and burdens: these were the nobles as lords in the aristocratic republics. Then the plebeians grew in numbers and military valor, and the nobles were induced to suffer laws and burdens equal

---

50. "Elements XCV," *Scienza nuova*, no. 292.

with their plebeians: these were the nobles in the popular republics. Finally they were bent to save the *vita comoda* and were naturally inclined to submit to a single ruler: these were the nobles under the monarchy."[51]

On the general level of human quality, the *corso* runs through a sequence which Vico formulates in "Element LXVI": "Men first sense the necessary, then they notice the useful, afterward they become aware of the comfortable, still later on they take delight in the pleasurable, then they become dissolute in luxury, and finally they fall into the madness of wasting the substance."[52]

e. The Mente Eroica

Since the political theory of Vico has been greatly misused by Sorel and by the Fascist movement, a few warnings against facile misunderstandings may be in order. Vico's distinction of two human natures and the theory of the *sutori delle nazioni* do not imply a praise of elitarian government. They do not imply anything at all with regard to the desirability of one or the other form of government. The unit of theoretical discussion in political theory is not a form of government but the *corso*. None of the phases of the *corso* is preferable to the others; all are equally inevitable stages in the course of a civilization. In the description of the course we are in the field not of ethics but of ideal necessity. No sympathies for aristocratic government will restore to power an aristocracy once the time for the popular republic has come. No sympathy for the democratic republic can prevent the transition to Caesarism. No Fascist or National Socialist enterprise can create a new aristocracy. The government resulting from such attempts will inevitably be the rule of the *ambiziosi* and *dissoluti*.[53] The distinction of the two human natures is not a return to the Aristotelian distinction of natural free men and natural slaves; it does not touch the Christian idea of the substantial equality of men, but is no more than the empirical observation that some men are more sensitive, intelligent, and energetic than others.

51. "Elements XCVI," *Scienza nuova*, no. 293.
52. "Elements LXVI," *Scienza nuova*, no. 241.
53. On the irreversibility of the course, and in particular on the impossibility of a return to the aristocratic republic, see *Scienza nuova prima* II.7.57; *Vico: Selected Writings*, 119–20.

These warnings are necessary not only as a safeguard against mis-understandings of a political nature. They are necessary above all in order to prevent a theoretical misinterpretation. We have hitherto considered the *corso* with regard to the phases from foundation to dissolution. These phases are not a sequence of disconnected political forms; they derive their character as phases from their character as transformations of a political substance that remains identical throughout the civilizational course of a nation. This political substance is called by Vico the *mente eroica.*

The *mente eroica* is the consciousness of the *autori delle nazioni* that through the possession of their *senso commune* they have grown to human stature beyond savagery, that they are set off as superior to those who do not participate in this possession. It is, furthermore, the will to preserve the *senso commune* in historical existence. The consciousness of the initial myth, the love for the religious and ethical values that it contains, the pride in their common possession, and the will to defend them are the component elements of the *mente eroica.* As long as the heroic spirit lives in the members of a civilizational community with such strength that it supports the authority of effective governmental institutions, the community will preserve its political identity and existence in history. With regard to this substance, the successive political forms of *corso* are the history of the wandering of the *mente eroica* from the patricians to the plebeians, and from the plebeians to the monarch.

Vico deals with this problem in a chapter that bears the title "Discovery of the eternal principle by which all republics are born, rule, and conserve themselves."[54] What is this principle? It is "the desire of the multitude to be governed with justice equal for all, in conformance to the equality of human nature." The awakening of the *senso commune* means the growth of man to his spiritual stature. The idea of human nature, equal in all men, is at first realized only through the poetical imagery of the myth, and it is realized only in the "heroes," that is, in the creators of the myth. Nevertheless, it is the principle of all civil society from its beginning, and the position of the heroes as rulers derives its authority from what we might call a virtual representation of the

54. *Scienza nuova prima* II.37.105.

idea. Furthermore, while it may not live actively in the subjects, it is sensed by them diffusely with such strength that rulership cannot be maintained without revolt when the idea is grossly and persistently violated. Hence the *eroismo* can last with the estate of the patricians only as long as they keep the multitude satisfied on this point. The crisis of aristocratic rule arrives when the heroes are falling "from chastity to dissolution, from vigor to laziness, from justice to avarice, from magnanimity to cruelty, and thus have become so many petty tyrants." When this stage has been reached they are ripe for a political fall that successively takes the form of their degradation in the free republic and the monarchy.

The disappearance of the heroes as the ruling class does not entail the disappearance of the *mente eroica* of which they had been the bearers in their proper time. The former heroes are disassociated in the people of the free republic, but "the heroism of the city has concentrated itself in the assemblies." The *mente eroica* has become, in this transformation, "a mind free of affects, as Aristotle divinely defined the good law." It has become the spirit of the laws, and liberty "will always be preserved among those who legislate in this spirit." With the rise of Caesarism, the patricians are reduced by the monarch who undertakes to protect the multitude. The *mente eroica* is now concentrated in the monarch because he alone is of a nature superior to that of his subjects and consequently is himself not subject to anybody but to God. The monarchs preserve this heroism "insofar as they grant to their subjects the equal enjoyment of the laws."

The idea of the wandering *mente eroica* is the key concept in the political theory of the *corso*. Without it the theory of the civilizational course would only be a theory of culture and the political phases of the course would fall apart into a series of forms of government, connected with each other causally through a psychology of the degeneration of a ruling class. The category of the *mente eroica* injects the identity of political existence into the course. The idea of justice, in order to become the organizing principle of a society, has to be realized in human beings. The successive governmental forms of the republic are the modes of its human realization. In the patricians it is realized personally. Every paterfamilias is originally the king-priest of his family group, the living law, acting in mythical immediacy, in a primordial harmony of passion and idea. In the plebeian republic this mythical immediacy begins to dissociate into the passions of the individual members and the objectivity of the laws produced in their assembly. In the monarchy, finally, the primordial harmony has fallen apart into the savior-kingship of the *princeps* and a multitude of private persons who can still accept the protectorate of the ruler but who can no longer rule actively themselves. With this concentration of the *mente eroica* in a single human being, the political existence of the republic itself has become precarious. When a human being can no longer be found who is able to embody the idea of justice adequately, then the substance created by the *autori delle nazioni* is, indeed, exhausted. The ensuing general disorder (Toynbee's interregnum) will last until a new source of founding creativity springs up somewhere.

§12. Conclusion

The *Scienza nuova* is a general philosophy of culture. Besides a theory of politics, it comprises a theory of language and a theory of art. Nevertheless, in isolating the theory of politics against the theories of the other cultural manifestations, we did not isolate it against the general principles of Vico's system. And our analysis of the general principles has been so broad that not much has to be added now in a summarizing appraisal of Vico's position in Western intellectual history. We can limit ourselves to a brief recapitulation of the main ideas by which Vico fixed the counterposition to his age, and then proceed to an equally brief enumeration of the main ideas by which Vico has become one of the founders of modern political science.

Vico found himself in opposition to the Age of Enlightenment and Reason when it had barely started on its course. This was perhaps an advantage because the causes of an intellectual and spiritual disaster can be discerned more clearly before they are obscured by the rank growth of the effects. The enemy was still clearly recognizable, and Vico's attack has a massive simplicity. In fact, as far as the critique of the age is concerned, we can reduce his ideas to five counterpositions.

(1) The counterposition to natural science. The *Scienza nuova* is a conscious attempt to restore a science of the mind against the exuberant claims that the methods of the science of natural phenomena are the model of all science. The problem had been simmering for more than a century, and Pascal had seen the menace

clearly, but Vico's New Science was the first grandiose act in the movement toward the restoration of a science of substance.

(2) The counterposition to the *Cogito ergo sum*. The restoration of a science of substance requires the restoration of philosophical anthropology. The principal enemy in this respect was the Cartesian meditation that finds the Archimedic point of metaphysics in the *cogitare* of solitary existence. The first axiom of a science of substance is the historicity of existence. Reason is not an independent creative principle; reason can operate only within the field staked out by mythical creativity. The *senso commune* of gentilician history and the great transcendental irruptions in sacred history furnish the substance for rational penetration.

(3) The counterposition to Pelagianism. Concerning this point, the principal enemy is Grotius. Against the assumption that man is fundamentally good and can create a social order out of the resources of his immanent substance, Vico restored the finiteness of fallen man who needs the aid of Providence in order to rise above the anarchy of the *amor sui*. To the idea of a humanly created social order Vico opposed the idea of an order in history and politics that is not explicable in terms of the seventeenth-century psychology of the *amor sui* or the eighteenth-century sensualism and utilitarianism.

(4) The counterposition to the contract theory. This is a corollary to the preceding point. If the social order is inexplicable as a result of immanent human action, every single instance of such explanation has to be discarded. The critique of Vico was directed against the contract theories because they were fashionable; a century later, under the impression of French revolutionary history, Schelling directed the same criticism against the fad of constitution making.

(5) The counterposition to progress. At the time when Vico lived, the theory of progress had not yet fully developed. His counterposition was not directed against the explicit idea but against the sentiments that engender it, that is, against the hubris of self-salvation. While the position itself was not yet completely developed, he still was able to develop fully the counterposition in his theory of the inevitable decadence of the civilizational course. Vico was the first of the great diagnosticians of the Western crisis. And he recognized unerringly as its most revealing symptom the sentiment of optimistic reliance on individual man as the source of order. The privatization of the individual is not the forerunner of a magnificent

order that will arise from the release of individual forces. It is the forerunner of an anarchical struggle for power that will end in the Caesaristic monarchy. The principle is valid, although on the occasion of its discussion Vico committed a serious mistake in historical interpretation when he saw in the national monarchies of his time the analogues of the Augustan monarchy. The cause of this mistake is the previously discussed tendency to generalize incautiously from the model of the Roman course.

Vico's critique of the age did not exhaust itself in negation. The five counterpositions imply a positive system, and there is no dividing line running between this positive content and the content of the ideas to which we are now turning. Nevertheless, the distinction between the counterpositions and the idea of the *corso* has its relevance for the understanding of Vico's thought because it stresses his consciousness of being the founder of a new political science. A new science is set off against an old science, and the counterpositions assist us in defining the "modernity" of Vico's thought. The point is of a certain importance because in an age of crisis the intellectual disorder of the community expresses itself in the comparatively undisturbed coexistence of old and new ideas, of exploded systems and new foundations. The term *modern* has no absolute connotation and has been used consecutively in order to designate various phases of postmedieval Western intellectual history. The counterpositions make clear what Vico understands as "old." "Old" is an aggregate of sentiments and ideas that emerged in the seventeenth century, unfolded in the eighteenth and nineteenth centuries, and is still very much alive in our time. The fact that this aggregate of sentiments and ideas was exploded intellectually and spiritually through the work of Vico in 1725 does not mean that we do not have to suffer to this day from its consequences in Progressivism, Communism, National Socialism, and World Wars. And the rise and unfolding of the "new" science in the course of the last two centuries does not mean that it has found wide acceptance. On the contrary, the label *modern* in popular opinion attaches to the ideas that Vico considered "old" in 1725 rather than to the science that he has founded. We shall deal with this peculiar confusion at greater length in the chapter on Schelling.[55] The present remarks

55. See vol. VII, *The New Order and Last Orientation*, Part Eight, chap. 2.

will be sufficient to draw the reader's attention to the fact that in an age of crisis modernity and social effectiveness are not the same. Modern political science, in the sense of Vico's new science, is a comparatively insignificant island in a sea of "old" ideas.

Again, after our broad analysis, we can be brief in recalling the principal ideas of the new science. The restoration of Augustinian anthropology has for its consequence the insight that the structure of the historical course is an objective, irreducible factor in history. The course as such cannot be explained through a psychology of passions or of utilitarian interests. The life of passion is the occasion upon which the objective meaning of the course is realized; it is not its cause. This principle removes from the field of political science, as we have seen, all attempts to reduce the transindividual meaning of history to the operation of economic, biological, or psychological factors. Moreover, the distinction between gentilician and sacred history removes the whole body of secularist sacred histories—whether of the Comtian or Marxian type. Speculations of this type can be classified by the scientist as variants of sacred history, but they are not science themselves. The concept of the *senso commune*, furthermore, establishes the myth as the origin of the polity and disposes thereby the whole body of rationalist speculation concerning the beginnings of civil society. All these partial ideas, finally, are held together by the great, fundamental principle that the *corso* as a whole, not its single phases, is the unit of scientific investigation. The principle is already contained in substance in the Platonic and Polybian theories of the cycle of governmental forms. It was systematically elaborated by Vico when he introduced the category of the *mente eroica* as the substance that remains identical in the sequence of human realizations in the *corso*. By virtue of this principle Vico disposed of the botanical classification of forms of government as well as of the debates about their merits. While this establishment of the *corso* as the unit of investigation is the master stroke of Vico's political science, as far as the principle is concerned, it is at the same time, inevitably, its weakest point in execution. We have discussed the flaws in Vico's construction, which stem from the generalization of the Roman model, as well as from the uncritical adoption of the problem of spiritual history in the form it has received through Saint Augustine. Here is the wide-open field of the new political science. With the increase of knowledge in empirical history, and with the increasing penetration of the theoretical problems of spiritual, evocative, and pragmatic history, we have to expect a development of the new science far beyond the scope envisaged by Vico, an enlargement for which the studies of Schelling and Bergson, of Spengler and Toynbee, are hardly more than a beginning.

4

The English Quest for the Concrete

In the chapter "The Schismatic Nations" we characterized the structure of political ideas in the age of Revolution under its most general aspect, that is, the breakdown of Western Christianity and the emergence of the national communities as schismatic politico-religious bodies. The development of political ideas after 1700 becomes increasingly parochial in the sense that problems that are specific to the several national communities are misunderstood as problems of universal import, and the ideas advanced for their solution are misunderstood as a political theory of general validity. This characterization, however, which is correct for the general structure of ideas, will obviously not exhaust the problems of the age. As soon as we descend to the more concrete levels of the problems, an infinity of complications arises owing to the survival of the general Western tradition in the particular national histories, as well as to the interaction among ideas that arise within the national regions. The "breakdown" of Western Christianity does not mean that it disappears without a trace. Rather it means the refraction and gradual transformation of the common Christian tradition within the national areas. A substantial common stock of ideas remains preserved in this process, particularly at the beginning. A further common substance of problems and ideas arises from the processes of democratization and industrialization that spread (with considerable time lags in the various countries) over the whole area of Western civilization. The problems of representative government, of the formation of parties, of universal suffrage, of the industrial proletariat, of the petty bourgeoisie, of trade unions, of labor legislation, and so forth, evoke everywhere similar ideas and similar technical solutions.

We are not surprised, therefore, to observe an intense interplay of ideas and influences across national boundaries: the influence of Newton and Locke on Voltaire, of Locke and Sidney on Montesquieu, of Montesquieu on American constitutionalism, of Locke on Condillac and Helvétius, of Helvétius on Bentham, of Hume and Rousseau on Kant, of Benjamin Franklin on Herder, of the American experience on Tocqueville, of Humboldt, Tocqueville, and Comte on John Stuart Mill, of Hegelianism in England, of the French *moralistes* on Nietzsche, and so forth. The network of mutual influences is, indeed, so closely knit that, if the eye is fixed on the detail, the observer may be tempted to assume it outweighs in importance the schismatic trend. This assumption, however, would be erroneous. The isolation of the general, schismatic structure finds its justification in the historical fact that, on the level of pragmatic politics, the schismatic tendency has gained ascendancy over the unifying problems and ideas.

The idea of a Western, if not human, validity for the national schismatic developments then hardened into intransigent national missions with the catastrophic consequence that the attempts to realize the claim of universality through imperial expansion were opposed by the prospective victims in prolonged wars. The French Revolution with its climax in Napoleon's imperialism and the German Revolution with its climax in Hitler's imperialism had to be defeated—with the result that the Anglo-Saxon powers with their claims of universality for the English and American variant of democracy have now to face a non-Western civilization, with a universal claim of its own, across the battlefields of Europe. The pragmatic consequences justify an emphasis on the schismatic problem that even a generation ago would have seemed exaggerated.

§1. The Model Polity

The foundations for the English schismatic development, toward which we now turn, were laid in the first half of the eighteenth century. The period is well known as far as the details of the history of its political ideas are concerned, but it is still rather obscure with regard to its gestalt, that is, with regard to the common denominator of its problems. The reasons for this obscurity are highly complex, and their exposition does not properly belong in a context that is primarily one of political ideas. Nevertheless, we have to be aware of the fact that only since the 1920s has the structure of this period come under serious observation and that the process of reassessment is far from being concluded. Our own attempt at an organization of the problems must, therefore, be considered tentative. Future inquiries may compel far-reaching corrections.

a. A Stagnant Population

The title of this chapter, "The English Quest for the Concrete," is intended to designate the common denominator of the problems. The term *concrete* is taken from Berkeley, whose search for the concrete ranged through the realms of being from matter to God and through the varieties of experience from sense perception to faith. That such a search for the concrete is necessary implies that the concrete has become lost: the search for the concrete is correlative to a state of sentiments and ideas that must be characterized as a loss of contact with the concreteness of existence. The violent disturbance of the Puritan revolution, of the Restoration, and of the Glorious Revolution had left as its heritage a profound exhaustion and disorientation. The dissolution of English society was, indeed, so profound that it not only was manifest in such comparatively innocuous symptoms as a temporary confusion of ideas and morals but touched the very biological substance of the nation. It is not possible to establish the extent of the disaster with exactness because the collection of statistics was still in its infancy, but a few comparative figures for the growth of population in various countries are available. The annual rate of increase was for:

England and	1701–1741	0.013%
Wales	1741–1777	0.456%
France	1701–1770	0.184%
Sweden	1700–1748	0.362%
	1748–1770	0.664%
Austria	1754–1784	0.862%
Prussia	1748–1770	0.844%

The facts in themselves are eloquent. In the first half of the eighteenth century the population of England had practically ceased to grow; the Swedish rate of increase in the comparable time was about twenty-eight times as high; and the English rate of increase after 1741 is about thirty-five times as high as before 1741.[1] This retardation in growth is probably not a result of a low birthrate. The birthrate in England rose steeply in the first three decades of the eighteenth century, just as in other countries. In the same way as in other countries it leveled out toward the middle of the century. The retardation is due to an even steeper rise of the death rate in the same period. The population in other countries increased because at this time the divergence between birthrate and death rate became strongly marked, whereas in England the death rate rose faster than the birthrate and even surpassed it during the decade preceding 1740.[2]

b. Gin

The immediate physiological cause of this abnormal development in England is no mystery; it can be found in the "unexampled orgy of drunkenness" that characterized this period.[3] The English drank a lot before the "unexampled orgy" of the Gin Age: in 1688, when the population was about 5 million, beer was brewed to the amount of 12.4 million barrels; two-and-a-half barrels per capita, including infants, is not bad. The orgy itself, however, begins after 1689 when the importation of distilled spirits was prohibited and the domestic distillery developed. The production figures tell the story:

Year	Gallons
1684	527,000
1714	2,000,000
1727	3,601,000
1735	5,394,000
1737	3,600,000
1742	7,000,000
1751	11,000,000

The temporary slump in 1737 is a result of the enactment of restrictive legislation in 1736, but the clandestine trade was soon organized sufficiently to overcome any legal obstacles.[4] The conse-

---

1. The figures in the text are taken from A. M. Carr-Saunders, *World Population* (Oxford: Oxford University Press, 1936), fig. 3, p. 21; see also the diagram on p. 20.
2. For the comparative movement of birthrates and death rates in this period see ibid., chap. 5, "Natural Increases," and fig. 13, p. 61.
3. Ibid., 76.
4. The figures in the text are taken from W. E. H. Lecky, *A History of England in the Eighteenth Century*, new ed. (New York: Appleton, 1903), 2:101–3.

quences of the orgy for the mores of the age are well known; we need not dwell on the atrocious and juicy details. Let us conclude with the summary that Henry Fielding gave in 1751 in his pamphlet *On the Late Increase of Robbers:* "Should the drinking of this poison be continued at its present height during the next twenty years, there will, by that time, be very few of the common people left to drink it."[5]

c. The Purge of the Church

A state of dissolution that endangers the biological existence of a nation is not an ephemeral disorder that has attacked only a part of the society. It is more profound even than a class tension that might burst forth in political revolution. A suicidal indulgence of this kind indicates what every suicide indicates: that existence has arrived at an impasse, that no longer can a meaningful alternative to suicide be seen. The destruction of meaning is characteristic of the epoch, and the rebuilding of meaning is its problem. The nature and magnitude of this problem are little understood even today because, during this dark period of her history, the power of England remained unimpaired and the shell of political institutions continued to function. The high degree of corruption even within this functioning shell is a matter of common knowledge, and we shall not repeat what the reader can find in any treatise on English history. For a moment, however, we have to reflect on one segment of English society, the functioning of which was of the greatest importance for the preservation of the intellectual and spiritual substance of the nation, that is, the Church of England.

The functioning of the church had been impaired, not by an internal development of ideas, but by a series of incisive operations that removed the most vital members from the ranks of its clergy. The first of these operations was perpetrated by means of the so-called Clarendon Code. The Act of Uniformity of 1662 provided that all clergymen, college fellows, and schoolmasters had to accept the new anti-Puritan revisions to the Book of Common Prayer, that they had to conform to the liturgy as it was now established, and that they had to repudiate the Solemn League and Covenant of 1643 by which the signatories had agreed on religious reform according

5. Quoted in ibid., 2:103.

to the word of God and the example of the best reformed churches. The result of the act was that two thousand clergymen refused acceptance, which meant that one-fifth of the clergy of the Church of England lost their positions. The Nonconformist private religious meetings that sprang up as a consequence were suppressed by the Conventicle Act of 1664, which provided severe punishments for dissenting religious meetings at which more than five persons attended. And last, the Five Mile Act of 1655 forbade the expelled clergymen to come within five miles of any incorporated town or of any place where they had been ministers.

For our problem this last act is the most interesting because of the occasion of its passage as well as because of its consequences. The occasion was the Great Plague of 1665, which reduced the population of London by 20 percent. Along with the more affluent part of the population a good number of clergymen fled London and deserted their flocks. In the care of the sick, in burials, and in services their places were taken by volunteering Nonconformists. This outrage, which illuminated somewhat too glaringly where and where not the common man in distress might find bodily and spiritual help, was answered by the Five Mile Act. While the act was difficult to enforce in every instance, its general purpose was achieved: the Nonconformist clergy were effectively removed from leadership in English society by the simple device of removing them physically from town society, where their influence could have been of social relevance. In particular they were removed from the universities since universities happened to be located in towns. The physical elimination of Puritan culture from English society, which lasted for a generation until the Toleration Act of 1689, dealt it a blow from which it never recovered. It is hardly necessary to elaborate the parallel with more recent technical improvements in the political art of destroying the substance of a people by removing its intellectual and spiritual leadership.

The second operation on the Church of England came with the Glorious Revolution. The Oath of Allegiance of 1689 was refused by more than four hundred clergymen who had their doubts about the legality of the transaction between the Convention Parliament and the new king; in 1690 they were deprived of their livings. This blow against the so-called nonjurors would not be so interesting if it had done no more than remove the Jacobite faction from the church. As a matter of fact, however, a goodly number of political Jacobites remained in the church and took the oath. The removal of the nonjurors was important because among them were the principal representatives of the patristic, sacramental, and old Catholic conception of the church. While the first operation had removed the reforming left wing, the second operation removed the reforming right wing. As a consequence of this double amputation the church was deprived of practically all its living forces. What remained were its worst elements, the mediocrities, the rakes, and the opportunists. The process of castration was completed in 1717 when, on occasion of the Bangorian controversy, the convocation of the Church of England was prorogued by royal writ. No royal license to transact business was issued again before 1861, and not even a consultative assembly was granted before the middle of the nineteenth century. The church had ceased to have independent public visibility and had been reduced to the position of being a department of state.[6]

If we add to these measures the Corporation Act of 1661, the Test Act of 1673 (nullified in practice after 1689, but repealed only in 1828), the Test Act against Scotland of 1681, which caused some eighty bishops to resign, and the Papists' Disabling Act of 1678, which barred Catholics from Parliament (repealed in 1829) we get the impression of a totalitarian revolution, only slightly relieved by the Toleration Act for dissenters of 1689. And something like a totalitarian revolution had indeed occurred, with destructive effects on the substance of the nation similar to the destructions worked by later revolutions of this type. If the English nation could work her way out of this morass, though not unscathed, and regain firm ground after the middle of the eighteenth century, this was mainly the result of two lucky circumstances. The first of these circumstances we have discussed already in the chapter "The Schismatic Nations." It is the fact that the national crisis occurred at a time when enlightenment and progress had not yet corroded the mass of the common people, so that the populist revival of the nation when

6. For the draining of the Church of England of its vital elements and the consequences see J. Wesley Bready, *England: Before and after Wesley* (London: Hodder and Stoughton, 1938), in particular chap. 1, "Triple Tragedies." For the problem of the nonjurors see H. Broxap, "Jacobites and Non-Jurors," in F. J. C. Hearnshaw, ed., *The Social and Political Ideas of Some English Thinkers of the Augustan Age* A.D. *1650–1750* (New York: Barnes and Noble, 1923), 97–111, and the bibliography at the end of this article. For the Bangorian Controversy see in the same volume Norman Sykes, "Benjamin Hoadly, Bishop of Bangor," 112–56.

it came, through John and Charles Wesley, could still be a revival of Christian fellowship—however spiritually and civilizationally thinned out it may have been. The second of these circumstances is the fact that between 1689 and 1721 the English constitution was created as an autonomous political form, independent of dynastic vicissitudes. The new constitutional system, secured by the Bill of Rights, the Habeas Corpus Act (1679), the Trials for Treason Act (1696), the Act of Settlement (1701), and the establishment of cabinet government and the party system with the accession of Walpole to the premiership in 1721, kept the channels open for the influx of new forces that grew in importance after the middle of the century.

d. Warburton's Political Sermons

The peculiar process of a free constitution emerging from the totalitarian devastation of a nation has found its reflection in the political thought of the age. As a representative example of the manner in which a member of the rump church would come to grips with this problem we select the sermons delivered by William Warburton, the later bishop of Gloucester, in Lincoln's Inn, on occasion of the Scotch Rebellion of 1745–1746.[7]

Warburton starts from a preestablished harmony between Christianity and constitutional government: faith prescribes the rules of civil justice, and a free and equal government favors the profession of the truth. This harmony has become actuality in England, because the civil constitution leaves the consciences free and protects their liberty, and the religious constitution has more than once supported the rights of citizens when they were threatened by arbitrary and illegal power. Opposed to this harmony of light is the harmony of the powers of darkness, that is, of Superstition and Despotism. Concretely, the powers of darkness are Popery and the Arbitrary Power of the Stuarts. Popery brings darkness because it effaces all fear of God from the minds of men. The "Anti-christian policy," the "unchristian Church," achieves this purpose by a series of measures: the "idolatrous adoration of dead men" creates a polytheistic

7. *Three Sermons Preached and Published on Occasion of the Late Rebellion, in 1745;* printed as an appendix to the second volume of Warburton's *The Principles of Natural and Revealed Religion Occasionally Opened and Explained in a Course of Sermons Preached before the Honourable Society of Lincoln's Inn* (London: Knapton, 1753–1754).

system in rivalry with the true God; the doctrine of attrition and absolution destroys the fear of God's justice; the government of the church "by a mere man" destroys the fear of God's dominion; and the Inquisition produces hypocrisy and thereby destroys the fear of God's omniscience. Arbitrary Power destroys the honor that is owed to kings. The arbitrary king is a tyrant who treats his subjects as slaves and thereby produces contempt. He favors superstition in support of illegal prerogative and thereby creates detestation. He makes his will and pleasure the rule of his administration and thereby creates servile fear. And he derives his authority not from the people but from heaven, nature, or conquest and thereby creates distrust. Hence the admonition to fear God and to honor the king (1 Peter 2:17) must be interpreted as meaning that we must support "our holy Religion against popish Superstition; and our equable government against Arbitrary power."[8]

The articulation of the world into a focus on the English children of light and the surrounding darkness enables Warburton to assess the role of England in politics and history. In the present emergency of the Rebellion it is the duty of every Christian and Briton to rally to the defense of the country, for this country is "The pride and confidence of our friends! The envy of our neighbours! The terror of our enemies, and the admiration of mankind!" "Happy nation! the nurse of heroes, the school of sages, the seminary of holy martyrs, the distinguished favorite of Heaven!"[9] In relation to other nations this England has now "the distinguished glory of being the Depository, as it were, of civil and religious Freedom, for the rest of mankind. And while we continue faithful to our trust, there are still hopes that the degenerate sons of men may, sometime or other, catch this noble fire from us, and vindicate their ravaged birthright. But, in our destruction, Liberty itself expires; and human nature will despair of evermore regaining its first and original dignity."[10] "The preservation of British liberty" is the preservation "of the liberties of Mankind."[11] The men who attack such light and glory obviously must be unpleasant characters; and, indeed, Warburton's fierce indignation is aroused by the thought "that a mighty Kingdom, a people that still gives laws to the Main, and

8. Warburton, "Sermon I" (November 1745), in ibid., 3–14.
9. "Sermon I," in ibid., 16.
10. "Sermon I," in ibid., 17.
11. "Sermon III," in ibid., 73.

has long held the balance between contending Empires, was suddenly overturned by a rabble of superstitious ruffians, of mountain robbers, of half-armed and half-starved barbarians, with a wild and desperate Adventurer at their head; and reduced, by the madness of these miserable varlets, from the most free and happy people upon earth, to be a Province to France, a Warehouse to Spain, and a patrimony to the pretended successor of St. Peter."[12]

If the forceful and lurid Manichaeism of "Sermon I" exhausted the politics of Warburton, not much importance would attach to his ideas. We could discount them as the rantings of a smug nationalist. Warburton certainly was smug and conceited, but in addition he had a good deal of astuteness. He knew very well what was going on all around him. He was not blind to the fact that English society of his time was abysmally rotten, and he must have been aware that his unqualified praise of English glory would sound funny to an audience of lawyers with some worldly discernment. In his "Sermon II" (December 1745) he repairs the omission of the first sermon and develops a shrewd argument that makes the corruption of a people compatible with its glory. Good Christians might draw, and at the time actually did draw, conclusions with regard to the fate of England through analogy with the fate of Israel. God punished his chosen people for their sins by delivering them into the hands of their enemies. Might he not do the same with England? Warburton denies the validity of this argument. He denies "that, because the *private* vices and impieties of men under that economy have, by the just judgment of God, often brought distress upon the *community*, that they have now the same tendency to provoke his wrath and indignation against ours."[13] The English people are rich in vice, and the state of immorality may lead to disaster, but such disaster will come in the order of natural causation insofar as the dissolution of the individuals may ultimately undermine the social order. It will not come as a judgment of God. The analogy with the fate of Israel is impermissible because under the Christian dispensation God has separated the problems of private and public morality. The state is an independent moral agent and is not responsible for the conduct of individuals. "Society is an *artificial man*, having like the *natural*, all those essential qualities, which constitute a

12. "Sermon I," in ibid., 18.
13. "Sermon II," in ibid., 32 f.

Moral Agent."[14] The state may be punished by God for its own viciousness, but there is no necessity for inflicting on the community punishment for the crimes of individuals. Because of the viciousness of individuals, "the sanctions of our religion are future rewards and punishments."[15] Hence the rottenness of the people, while fraught with natural dangers, is no cause for defeatism with regard to the fate of the nation in international politics. On the world scene only the morality of the state is crucial in the present contingency. With regard to this point we can rest assured, for the state of England is a paragon of public virtue.

The remainder of "Sermon II" is devoted to an elucidation of English virtue in international politics. Warburton's task was not as easy as it might have been because England happened to be involved at the time in the War of the Austrian Succession, and virtue had little to do with that affair. Nevertheless, he arrives at a happy conclusion. The continental wars are inspired by the dark design of unsettling "that established and equitable balance of Power, so necessary for the peace and felicity of Europe." Supporting the balance of power is synonymous with supporting "the liberties of Europe, against the most detestable perfidy, the most unjust usurpations, and the most lawless and destructive ambition." England has a cause in this war "for which it may not only with decency supplicate the protection, but with confidence appeal to the justice of Heaven: a cause founded on the solid basis of self-defense, public faith, and the liberties of mankind."[16]

The speculation with regard to the domestic and international excellence of England is rounded out in "Sermon III" by a piece of philosophical history. History is articulated into antiquity, the middle ages, and the modern period beginning with the Reformation. The oppressive Roman empire had to be torn to pieces by "the fierce and free nations of the North." Within the realms of their conquest they established polities on the principle of the liberty of the people. "And erected on so just a plan, these Gothic governments might have stood till now, had not the rank influence of Papal superstition viciated those generous policies." By the time of the Reformation the Western world was as deeply lost in civil as

14. "Sermon II," in ibid., 38.
15. "Sermon II," in ibid., 32.
16. "Sermon II," in ibid., 42–43.

it was in ecclesiastical slavery. "For the triumphant Hierarchy had amply revenged the fallen Empire on the necks of its destroyers." With the Reformation begins the era of political as well as religious freedom, for "where the Spirit of the Lord is, there is liberty." In this struggle for new freedom, England is "at present most indebted to providence of the whole race of mankind." It even seems possible that "we may be selected by Providence, in these latter ages, to preserve the memory of civil liberty amidst a slavish world, as the house of Israel was formerly, to keep alive true religion amidst apostasy."[17]

The political evocation of Warburton holds a peculiar fascination for us because here we can observe in its origins the state of sentiments that later, after having outgrown the remnants of Christian tradition, develops into the totalitarianism of our time. Warburton's position may be characterized as a totalitarian national constitutionalism. The structure of the constitution has separated from the moral and spiritual substance of the nation. Infidelity and Luxury are "the two capital evils of our infatuated countrymen. The height, to which they are both arrived, cannot be aggravated; and need not be particularly described. The case is notorious, and confessed."[18] The rottenness of society may even engulf the state, because precisely the procedural protections accorded by a free constitution may degenerate in practice into the protection of the criminal against punishment.[19] Nevertheless, the constitution is perfect. It is free even if it suppresses Nonconformists and nonjurors and deprives Catholics of political representation. It is wholesome even if it gives free reign to dissoluteness to the point of criminality. The idolatry of a shell without substance, which in our time has produced the fantastical situation of the overthrow of democracy by the means of democratic procedure, is fully developed.

Moreover, this free constitution is the political form of a nation. We see fully developed the conception of the nation as the chosen people, the Manichaean articulation of the field of politics into the pure nation and the surrounding darkness, the idea of a national mission, the identification of the national civilization with the civilization of mankind, and the identification of the national

17. "Sermon III," in ibid., 65 ff. and 91 ff.
18. "Sermon III," in ibid., 83.
19. "Sermon III," in ibid., 96 ff.

destiny with the destiny of mankind at large. Warburton elaborates a system of national megalomania that, once it is taken over by the other nations, can only result in the war of all against all that we witness in our time. Of specific importance, finally, is the inclusion of the principle of the balance of power into the new dogma. In political practice this principle means that, whenever the balance (which we may assume to be established at a given point of time) is disturbed by such factors as growth of population and technological or economic progress within one nation, the only admissible means for the solution of the problem is a world war that reduces the disproportionately growing power to comparative weakness. Alternative solutions, such as a Western hegemonic confederation under the leadership of the strongest power, or a genuine federation that would dissolve the national ossification and produce new supranational communities, are impermissible because they would conflict with the idolatry of national exclusiveness. Warburton's dogmatism of national exclusiveness and the balance of power is the English equivalent to the French and German imperial expansion. In the disaster that resulted from the clash of these megalomanic nationalisms the Germans have fared worst, while to date the English have managed only to come dangerously close to the point where they have balanced themselves out of power.

e. The Gladstone-Newman Controversy

The totalitarian constitutionalism of Warburton is not a passing mood in English politics. It is a constant that has found its great and representative expression in the nineteenth century in the brilliant debate between Gladstone on the one side and Manning and Newman on the other, which arose on the occasion of the Papal Syllabus of 1864 and the Vatican Council of 1871. Gladstone complained: "All other Christian bodies are content with freedom in their own religious domain. Orientals, Lutherans, Calvinists, Presbyterians, Episcopalians, Non-conformists, one and all, in the present day, contentedly and thankfully accept the benefits of civil order; never pretend that the state is not its own master; make no religious claims to temporal possessions or advantages; and, consequently, never are in perilous collision with the State. Nay, more, even so I believe it is with the mass of Roman Catholics individually. But not so with the leaders of their Church, or with those who take pride in following the leaders." Catholic leaders even pride themselves on their unwillingness to submit to the civil order. Gladstone was particularly aroused by an earlier remark of Manning that there is no other church than the Roman "which does not submit, or obey, or hold its peace when the civil governors of the world command."[20] Again the parochial state, which in the meanwhile has absorbed the heritage of English radicalism and liberalism into its totalitarian dogma, is in conflict with a spiritual substance of universal validity and claim. And still, the remnants of Christian tradition in the parochial substance obscure the danger of the conflict. Today, in retrospect, we may wonder whether Gladstone would be so enthusiastic about submissive churches when the state that they recognize as their master is not the state of England but a National Socialist German or a Communist Russian state, and whether he would be quite so indignant about the insolence of church leaders who pride themselves that they are not unconditionally submissive.[21]

Anyway, Newman's answer is equally succinct: "The rule and measure of duty is not utility, nor expedience, nor the happiness of the greatest number, nor State convenience, nor fitness, order, and the *pulchrum.*" None of these can substitute for conscience as a guide to conduct. "Conscience is the voice of God . . . conscience is not a long-sighted selfishness, nor a desire to be consistent with oneself, but it is a messenger from Him, who, in nature and in grace, speaks to us behind a veil, and teaches and rules us by His representatives. Conscience is the aboriginal Vicar of Christ."[22] In their argument concerning the *Syllabus Errorum,* Newman sharpens the

20. W. E. Gladstone, *The Vatican Decrees in Their Bearing on Civil Allegiance,* in Alexander Campbell, ed., *The Battle of the Giants* (Cincinnati: Vent, 1875), 7. The same volume also contains the Cincinnati debate on Catholicism between Alexander Campbell and John B. Purcell in 1837. To every student of Americana this debate is warmly recommended.

21. The problem of the English attitude was brought home to me in a conversation in 1934 with the master of a college in Oxford, one of the finest contemporary English minds. The conversation turned on National Socialism and the plight of the churches in Germany. My interlocutor took a detached view of the question and opined that the German churches were in a position similar to that of the English and would have to submit to the order of the state like the English. To the consideration that submission to the English civil order was perhaps less of a problem for a Christian church than submission to a National Socialist order, he seemed impermeable. For him, the problem of spiritual substance seemed completely superseded by the dogmatism of the English institutional arrangements.

22. "Dr. Newman's Letter to the Duke of Norfolk, in Reply to Gladstone," in Campbell, ed., *Battle of the Giants,* 74.

issue with regard to the positive content of Gladstone's position when he asks: "Is Benthamism so absolute the Truth, that the Pope is to be denounced because he has not yet become a convert to it?"[23] Gladstone might have answered: Yes—for he was beyond critical doubt and his attitude was inspired by a strong sentiment of its universal validity. With the magnificent pathos of a representative of mankind he clarified the relative positions: It is not anyone who "actually writes from a Papal point of view, that has a right to remonstrate with the world at large; but it is the world at large, on the contrary, that has the fullest right to remonstrate, first with His Holiness, secondly with those who share his proceedings, thirdly even with such as passively allow and accept them. I, therefore, as one of the world at large, propose to expostulate in my turn."[24] The liberal upholders of the autonomous state and its constitution have become the "world at large," the new universal church of which Gladstone is a representative member. The spirit of the schismatic polity develops its universal claim in imitation of imperial Christianity. Across the shambles of the Western-Christian *homonoia*, the infallible Gladstone challenges the infallible pope. It does not need much imagination to extrapolate this trend and to prolong the curve into the contemporary forms of totalitarianism.

§2. The Loss of the Concrete

The suicidal orgy indicates the degree to which English existence had lost its meaning in this period of material prosperity, and the sermons of Warburton are a representative example of the intellectual and moral decline that had followed the great age of Puritanism in the Church of England. The two symptoms characterize the amplitude of the loss of the concrete to which we now turn. The concrete is lost with regard to the fundamental orientation of existence through faith, and it is lost with regard to the system of symbols and concepts by which the orientation of existence is expressed. The two losses are related to each other because the loss of orientation through faith prevents the creation and clarification of symbols, and at the same time the perversion of meaning in the realm of symbols and concepts prevents the return to the orienting

---

23. Ibid., 95.
24. Gladstone, "The Vatican Decrees," in ibid., 6.

experiences. The devastation is far-reaching. The experiences in which meaning originates are smothered, and the symbols by which meaning is expressed are destroyed so thoroughly that it is impossible to give an account of the disorientation in terms of the literary documents of the period. Attempting to present the contents of the works of this period would be an attempt at reproducing a chaos. Hence, in approaching this problem, we must follow the method that contemporary critics, and in particular Berkeley, adopted when they penetrated to the roots of the disorder. There is no sense in repeating the gyrations of thought of men who are in confusion. The critic must diagnose the cause of the confusion and use the pathological cases as typical instances that illustrate the *nosos* in the Platonic sense. Berkeley focused his diagnosis in the symbols of materialism and freethinking, and we shall follow his analysis. We shall accept the two symbols as signifying the principal sources of confusion, and we shall lend them a preliminary precision by defining them as materialization of the external world and psychologization of the self.

a. Materialization of the External World

By materialization of the external world we mean the misapprehension that the structure of the external world as it is constituted in the system of mathematized physics is the ontologically real structure of the world. The tendency of mistaking the laws of mechanics for the structure of the world makes itself felt strongly even by the middle of the seventeenth century under the influence of Galileo's discoveries and even more so under the influence of Cartesian physics. Pascal already has some incisive pages on the subject. The movement gains its full momentum, however, only with the publication of Newton's *Philosophiae naturalis principia mathematica*, of 1687. The impact of this masterful systematization of mechanics on his contemporaries, coming at a time when the sources of an active faith were drying up, must have had a force that is difficult to reproduce imaginatively today. To a spiritually feeble and confused generation, this event transformed the universe into a huge machinery of dead matter, running its course by the inexorable laws of Newton's mechanics. The earth was an insignificant corner in this vast machinery, and the human self was a still more insignificant atom in this corner. We have discussed the

critical early phase of this problem on the occasion of the debate between Kepler and Robert Fludd.[25] The obliteration of the substance
of nature through the propositions of mathematized science that
could still be resisted at the beginning of the seventeenth century
had become an almost accomplished social fact at the beginning
of the eighteenth century. The obliteration had been so thorough
that Western thought has not completely recovered from the blow
even today. The first shock, of course, wore off, and the recovery
of substance became the preoccupation of the foremost Western
thinkers. Nevertheless, from the age of Newton the great cleavage
runs through the Western world between the thinkers who submit
to the "fallacy of misplaced concreteness" (as Whitehead has named
this philosophical mistake) and those who can free themselves of
it. It is not an exaggeration to say that in the history of Western
civilization Newton's *Principia Mathematica* is at least as important as the cause of the great schism in Western thought as it is
important in the advancement of science.[26]

b. Psychologization of the Self

By psychologization of the self we mean the misapprehension that
through reflection on the stream of consciousness, and on the experiences given in it, the nature of man or the substance of the
self can become known. This second misapprehension is closely
related to the first one. When man no longer experiences himself as
embedded substantially in the cosmos, when the unity of creation
that embraces man is torn asunder into a perceived structure of the
world and a perceiving self, problems peculiar to Cartesian and post-
Cartesian metaphysical speculation arise. When the experience of
substantial participation of man in the world is interrupted, doubts
arise about whether the reality as it appears to the perceiving subject

25. See vol. V, *Religion and the Rise of Modernity*, 168, 179.
26. For the further development of this problem the reader should refer to the
chapter on "Phenomenalism" in vol. VII, *The New Order and Last Orientation*. For
an introduction and use of the term "fallacy of misplaced concreteness" see Alfred
N. Whitehead, *Science and the Modern World* (New York: Macmillan, 1925), 72 ff.
The most penetrating analysis of the problem, in particular for the Galilean phase,
is to be found in Edmund Husserl, *Die Krisis der europäischen Wissenschaften und
die transzendentale Phänomenologie*, first published in the international yearbook
Philosophia, ed. Arthur Liebert, vol. I (Belgrade, 1936). English edition: *The Crisis of European Sciences and Transcendental Phenomenology*, trans. David Carr
(Evanston: Northwestern University Press, 1970).

is indeed the reality of the external world, and if the reality of an external world is assumed, intricate problems of the relation between the external world and the self impose themselves. Historically they appear in the speculation of Malebranche and Leibniz under the title of the psychophysical problem. The self has become a consciousness that by sensations and ideas refers to an external world—though it remains enigmatic how the external world can affect consciousness in such a manner that sensations and ideas are produced. It remains equally enigmatic why the reference of these images to an external world should be considered trustworthy.

If the idea of psychologization were carried out consistently in a philosophical system, the result would be a strict solipsism of a stream of consciousness with complete annihilation of all reality outside the stream. This radical possibility, however, need not concern us here because it does not occur in any historically relevant instance. In the historical situation at the beginning of the eighteenth century all instances of psychologization compromise to some degree with reality. The degree of the compromise is a historical problem, and correspondingly so is the degree of destruction of reality. As the minimum of compromise the situational pressure induces the acceptance of the external world, at least so far as it enters into the system of Newtonian physics. The Lockean compromise with its distinction of primary and secondary qualities is typical. Primary qualities are solidity, extension, figure, motion, number, etc.; these qualities are "really" in bodies whether our senses perceive them or not. Secondary qualities such as color, heat, light, etc., do not exist "really" but are sensations in the stream of consciousness.[27]

Beyond this minimum of acceptance the field of variants opens richly. With profound disturbances of the elementary experiences of participation in the cosmos, even the reality of the realm of matter becomes doubtful. Such disturbances cause particularly deep ravages with regard to transcendental reality because the persuasive assurance lent to the reality of the realm of matter by means of the pragmatic tests of experiment and astronomical observation does not exist for transcendental reality. With regard to the radi-

27. John Locke, *As Essay Concerning Human Understanding*, ed. Peter H. Nidditch (Oxford: Clarendon, 1975), bk. II, chap. 7, "Of Simple Ideas of Both Sensation and Reflection," 128 ff.

cal transcendence of the world there is only genuine participation through the trembling experience of faith as substance and proof of things unseen (Hebrews 11:1). Moreover, the symbolism of the dogma has grown historically as the expression of nuances of active faith. When the light of faith is extinguished, the dogmatic symbols lose their luminosity of meaning and become a dead letter, a jungle of logical inconsistencies, and a collection of unverifiable propositions. When the symbols no longer glow with the inner light of faith, the time has come for their examination under the external light of reason.

The symbolization of transcendental reality does not stand up too well under the light of reason. But again: there is no complete annihilation but rather a gamut of compromises. Never was there a greater penumbra of thought than when men were enlightened, because reason itself, by whose light the mysteries of religion were to be examined, was a historically somewhat sputtering notion. The reason that emerges in the philosophy of Locke and of his Deistic followers and successors is not a well-defined function of the human mind but a gradually thinning, secularist derivation of the Christian logos. The antithesis of the light of faith that fills the religious symbols with meaning from within, and of the light of reason by which they are examined from without, must be understood historically as signifying two terms of a series of notions that paper over in spurious continuity the real distance between them. The rationalism of Lockean reason develops gradually out of the suprarationalism of the Christian logos. Specifically, the Lockean idea has developed out of the speculation on the inner light of reason of the Cambridge Platonists.

c. Culverwel's Reason

In our context it is impossible to go through all the steps of this development, but we must characterize at least one or two of the major ones. As characteristic for an early phase of this process we select the speculation of Nathaniel Culverwel (1618–1651). In his *Discourse of the Light of Nature*, this student of Cudworth says: "To blaspheme reason is to reproach heaven itself, and to dishonour the God of Reason, to question the beauty of the image." "What would these railers have? Would they be banished from their own essence? Would they forfeit and renounce their understanding? Or have they any to forfeit or disclaim? Would they put out the candle of the Lord, intellectuals of His own Lighting?"[28] Although the Lockean tone can be heard already in these sentences, Culverwel's reason has not yet become entirely a secular faculty, for this lamp of the Lord shines with a somewhat diminished candlepower because of the Fall. Still, it is reliable enough to serve as a guide in orienting human existence and to be an internal authority that makes man independent of all external authority—be it the classics or the councils. We can sense this Protestant pathos of autonomous reason in this passage: "For this very end God hath set up a distinct lamp in every soul that men might make use of their own light. All the works of men, they should smell of this lamp of the Lord that is to illuminate them all. Men are not to depend wholly upon the courtesy of any fellow-creature; not upon the dictates of men; nay, not upon the votes and determinations of angels: for if an angel from heaven contradict first principles, though I will not say, in the language of the Apostle, 'let him be accursed,' yet this one may safely say, that all the sons of men are bound to disbelieve him."[29]

Nevertheless, it would be a grave misunderstanding to identify this reliable candle of the Lord already with secular reason as the supreme orienting faculty of men. Culverwel's reason is still out-shone by the light of Revelation. "Revealed truths shine with their own beams; they do not borrow their primitive and original lustre from this 'candle of the Lord,' but from the purer light, wherewith God hath clothed and attired them as with a garment."[30] This higher light is not in conflict with the light of reason, and the light of reason alone is sufficient as a guide if faithfully obeyed. But precisely this "if" of faithful obedience seems to be the point at which Culverwel's speculation on reason retains its connection with orthodox Calvinism. Not all men are equal with regard to their obedience, and the ability of obeying is not a matter of human discretion. By the beams of revealed truth we understand that God gave a measure of his unconditional grace to Socrates to improve his "naturals," while he denied this same measure to Aristophanes. The light of reason shines in everybody, but only those who have

---

28. From the introduction to the *Discourse*, quoted in Frederick J. Powicke, *The Cambridge Platonists* (London: Dent, 1926), 134.

29. Culverwel, *Discourse*, 206, quoted in ibid., 136.

30. Culverwel, *Discourse*, 223, in ibid., 138.

been accorded the grace of God will be able to follow it as their guide of conduct. "As take two several lutes. Let them be made both alike for essentials, for matter and form. If now the one be strung better than the other, the thanks is not due to the lute, but to the arbitrary pleasure of him that strung it. Let them both be made alike, and strung alike yet if the one be quickened with a more delicate and graceful touch, the prevailing excellence of the music is not to be ascribed to the nature of the lute, but to the skill and dexterity of him that did move it and prompted it into such elegant sounds."[31]

d. Whichcote's Reason

Let us next consider the meaning of reason in the *Sermons* of Benjamin Whichcote (1609–1683). The strong tension between a light of reason that is common to all men and a receptiveness that is accorded arbitrarily to a few, which characterized the speculation of Culverwel, is reduced to a minimum in Whichcote. The Gospel is accepted as a revelation, superhuman in origin but not in conflict with reason. "The excellency of infinite wisdom, power, and goodness is displayed in it, and God, by it, works powerfully in us, and upon us: and this commanding is in the highest way of reason. No better way of arguing than by strong reason and convincing argument; and no such conviction, no fuller satisfaction, in any undertaking, than in the business of regeneration and conversion."[32] Scripture and reason are in a prestabilized harmony because in the Bible there are these two things: "the consonancy of the things therein contained with the things of natural knowledge, and the report there made of God, agreeable to what reason leads men to think."[33] There is, of course, the problem of interpretation of the sacred text, but this problem will be solved satisfactorily in the direction of reason if we do not insist on putting recondite interpretations on isolated passages. "Scripture as it is a matter of faith, is not a single text, but all the Scripture; and not so much the words as the sense, that sense which is verified by other scriptures." God expects the reader to be "of an ingenuous spirit and use candor, and not lie at the catch: for the Scripture is to be read as a man would

---

31. Culverwel, *Discourse*, 270, in ibid., 140.
32. Whichcote, *Sermons*, 3:86, in ibid., 79 f.
33. *Sermons*, 3:117, in ibid., 78.

read a letter from a friend, in which he doth only look after what was his friend's mind and meaning, not what he can put upon the words."[34]

The audience to whom Whichcote directs these sermons seems to be beset already by problems that inevitably must arise when the traditional expression of faith is swept aside and the content of faith is rebuilt through the interpretation of a document. The danger point is near where reason shades off into the methods of critical philology, and where revelation shades off into a literary text. Whichcote himself is still on the safe side. Reason is for him not yet an autonomous faculty of man that can produce true propositions with regard to transcendental reality and substitute this body of propositions for the dogma of tradition. For him reason is still the result of faith. "The mind diverted from God wanders in darkness and confusion. But being directed to Him, soon finds its way, and doth receive from Him in a way that is abstracted from the noise of the world, and withdrawn from the call of the body; having shut the doors of our senses, to recommend ourselves to the Divine light, which readily enters into the eye of the mind that is prepared to receive it. For there is light enough of God in the world, if the eye of our minds were but fitted to receive it, and let it in."[35] Reason does not orient existence; existence must be oriented through openness to God in order to make reason operative. The interpretation of Scripture will avoid pitfalls only if the reason that interprets it is the Christian logos, that is, reason oriented by faith. Only then will be achieved the harmony of a religion "that is grounded in reason and by divine authority," of a religion "that makes men humble and modest, not proud and conceited; that makes men poor in Spirit, not full of their own mind," of a religion "that makes them loving, and not hard-hearted; that makes men kind, not harsh and cruel." For "an uncharitable Christianity, unmerciful, void of good-nature, is not more religion than a *dark sun* is a sun, or a *cold fire* is a fire. He only can dwell in God who dwells in love. . . . To be out of love and good-will, is to be in the devil's form and spirit."[36] But "the devil's form and spirit" are close

34. *Sermons*, 2:245, in ibid.
35. *Sermons*, 3:102, in ibid., 83.
36. *Sermons*, 3:271–72, 332, in ibid., 80 f.

at hand, and they will take possession of the soul as soon as the tenuous bond of faith is broken and reason is left to shift for itself with nothing to rely on but the historically accidental content of the age.

e. Locke's Reason

The last step is taken by Locke in the *Essay Concerning Human Understanding*. "Reason is natural revelation, whereby the Father of Light and fountain of all knowledge, communicates to mankind that portion of truth which he has laid within the reach of their natural faculties." This part of the passage sounds comparatively harmless, so harmless that in isolation it could perhaps be taken as Thomistic in meaning. The sequel is less harmless: "Revelation is natural reason enlarged by a new set of discoveries communicated by God immediately, which Reason vouches the truth of, by the testimony and proofs it gives that they come from God. So that he that takes away Reason to make a way for Revelation, puts out the light of both, and does much the same as if he would persuade a man to put out his eyes, the better to receive the remote light of an invisible star by a telescope." Now, indeed, Reason is made the judge of the truth of Revelation. "Whatsoever God hath revealed is certainly true. No doubt can be made of it. But whether it be a Divine Revelation or no, Reason must judge, which can never permit the mind to reject a greater evidence for that which is less evident, or prefer less certainty to greater." The bond of faith is broken and the experiences that give meaning to the symbols of myth and religion are lost. Reason has become an autonomous, natural faculty. The formula that it originates in "the Father of Light" is empty because this very symbol is meaningless without the experience from which it springs. This sudden loss of meaning becomes visible in a passage such as the following: "No Proposition can be received for Divine Revelation, or obtain the assent due to all such, if it be contradictory to our clear intuitive knowledge." In this passage the dogmatic symbols have become "propositions," and the faith that creates them has become "our clear intuitive knowledge" (whatever that means) that gives or denies assent after due examination of the "propositions" presented to it. We should also note the change of meaning in the term *Revelation:* from the irruption of transcendental reality in religious experience and its expression in symbols (of which the meaning must be regained through faith concretely by every believer) into a body of propositions of which the meaning is not to be recovered by faith but to be examined critically by Reason. In brief: with this change we are in the jungle of enlightenment jargon in which discussion becomes impossible because the terms are no longer rooted in the concreteness of experience.[37]

f. Locke's Reasonableness of Christianity

The implications of the new meaning of Reason are obvious, and the further course of disintegration that will flow from it is inexorable. The title of Reason from now on covers a highly explosive combination of elements. The principal ones are the following: (1) the historically accidental body of civilizational values that emerges from the century of the Puritan Revolution and Newtonian physics, (2) the apparatus of critical method in philology and history as well as in the experiment and logic of science, and (3) an act of faith that erects these values and methods into absolutes. We are acquainted already with some of the grotesque results of this new creed of reason. We have seen the political constitution without social obligations emerging from reason in Locke's *Second Treatise of Civil Government,* and we have seen how Warburton's God willed the Bill of Rights, the civilizational mission of England, and the holy war for the balance of power. In the present context, however, we have to concentrate on the systematic main line that leads from Reason in the Lockean sense into the problems of materialism and freethinking.

This line can be traced by the use that Locke makes of Reason in his *Reasonableness of Christianity* of 1695. The contents of the work in detail are of no interest to us. What is relevant for our purpose is the destruction that Reason works when it is put to the interpretation of Christianity as the historical religion of Western civilization, and of equal importance will be the patterns of thought that emerge from this work of destruction. We shall properly begin with the external aspect of the destruction.

37. Locke, *An Essay,* bk. IV, chap. 18, sec. 5, 10, "Of Faith and Reason, and Their distinct Provinces," 691–96; bk. IV, chap. 19, sec. 4, "Of Enthusiasm," 698.

When Locke approaches Christianity he makes a tabula rasa of Western history. In the *Essay Concerning Human Understanding* he had swept aside all earlier metaphysical efforts and started philosophizing from scratch. In the present study he makes a similar sweep of all Christian tradition, including the patres and scholastics, and starts on an analysis of the New Testament as if it were a book that had been published yesterday. The mind of the *Essay* is a blank paper ready to receive the impression of the Gospel. Such open-mindedness leads to an interesting discovery, which Sir Leslie Stephen has summarized nicely in the following passage: "Christ and his apostles, on admitting converts to the Church, did not exact from them a profession of belief in the Athanasian Creed, the Thirty-nine Articles, or the Westminster Confession, but were satisfied with the acknowledgment that Christ was the Messiah."[38] We might have guessed it; and Locke probably guessed it, too, before he indulged in his lengthy and painstaking analysis that rendered this meager result. He did not want to prove the obvious. His ponderous exposition of the trite gains its weight through the implication that the later development of Christianity is an illegitimate excrescence. Only under the assumption that his labors restore the true core of Christianity do they make sense. This true core is small. It contains no more than the acceptance of Christ as the Messiah, the belief in the one God, and genuine repentance and submission to the law of Christ. These articles of faith are exhaustive. They are a plain and simple religion, intelligible to "laboring and illiterate men," free of the theological apparatus that creates the impression that the way to the church leads through "academy or lyceum."

Let us consider what Locke is actually doing in this attempt to restore the legitimate nucleus of Christianity. Christian doctrine as it has grown in the tradition of the church is not an arbitrary addition to the Gospel. It is the labor of generations in the attempt to find an adequate expression to the substance of faith in the historically changing economic, political, moral, and intellectual environment of Mediterranean and Western civilization. The Christological struggles of the early centuries absorbed into this expression the Hellenistic intellectual culture, and the

38. Stephen, *History of English Thought in the Eighteenth Century,* 1:80.

Scholasticism of the high Middle Ages absorbed into it the *corpus Aristotelicum*. In general, the history of Christian doctrine is the process by which the substance of faith is built into the civilization of man. It is a process that started in the immediate environment of Christ, and it is still going on. The precipitation of the process in the New Testament represents, for all that we know, a phase that has already advanced materially beyond the generation of Jesus' immediate followers. Locke ignores this problem of the historicity of the Christian spirit. But beyond this statement it is not easy to formulate with precision what he has actually done.

At first sight one might say that, through his return to the New Testament phase of the process, he has deliberately thrown out the intellectual civilization that has been built into the expression of the relation of man to the divine ground in his soul. That is quite true. And the ease with which Locke gets rid at one fell swoop of the whole patristic and scholastic intellectual culture has remained paradigmatic for the wholesale civilizational destruction in which the politically predominant movements of our time engage. Nevertheless, the situation is much too complicated to be covered by the brief formula of throwing out a body of tradition. Above all, this formula ignores the problem of the historical process. A tradition is not a block that can be thrown out. One can throw out a tradition only by throwing oneself out of it. This feat, however, is not so simple as it looks to the naive minds who believe they can return to a "primitive" Christianity without returning to the civilizational state of "primitive" Christians. This feat, if realized socially, would imply the complete destruction of contemporary civilization, not only under its intellectual aspects, but also economically and technologically. This is not Locke's intention. Locke and those who follow him in his course go on to live and to participate in a civilizational environment that has been formed into the remotest wrinkles of its intellectual language by the very tradition they try to remove. Hence, the attempt to return to the earlier phase will result not in a genuine removal of tradition (which would imply the rebuilding of a civilization on a new basis) but in a far-reaching devastation of the intellectual form of contemporary civilization. Since this devastation is accomplished by means of a return to a more primitive civilizational phase, we may call it "primitivization." Under this aspect, Locke's philosophy of Reason is a phase of the anticivilizational revolt that we have described in the chapter "The People of God."[39]

Before we pursue this topic further, let us include in the discussion another problem that Locke raises in his treatise. Locke discovers that Christianity is reasonable. Its chief claim to our respect originates in the fact that we do not find anything in it that man would not find without it. The "rationale and thinking part of mankind" could discover the one, supreme, and invisible God, and the philosophers could discover the law of nature, without Christian guidance—though the body of the law has never been set forth by any philosopher as a clear deductive system. Hence, the question arises for Locke of why his elimination of Christianity should stop short of the New Testament. Why not eliminate Christianity altogether and be reasonable without it? Locke advances several reasons for his preferred option, but the decisive one seems to be the argument of utility. Christ is useful because he lends the authority of a divine command to propositions that can be discovered by reason. The "rational and thinking part of mankind" unfortunately is somewhat small: "you may as soon expect to have all the day-labourers and tradesmen, the spinsters and dairymaids, perfect mathematicians, as to have them perfect in ethics in this way." Christianity, thus, becomes a codification and sanction by divine authority of a body of precepts that can be found by the reason of philosophers, but it will not find social acceptance if it is promulgated by unauthorized thinkers only.

As far as this argument interprets Christianity, it only confirms and clarifies the "primitivization" that Locke achieves through his philosophy of Reason. When Christianity is reduced to a reasonable moral code that after all may be found also in non-Christian civilizations, the realm of spirit is annihilated. With this reduction, Locke has eliminated the Christian drama of Fall and Redemption, that is, the understanding of the spiritual problems of the soul by which Christianity has advanced beyond the Myth of Nature of antiquity. Locke can dispense with the intellectual culture of the patres and scholastics because he has abandoned the culture of the spirit that it serves. The psychologization of the self begins

39. See *The Collected Works of Eric Voegelin*, vol. 22, *History of Political Ideas*, vol. IV, *Renaissance and Reformation*, ed. David L. Morse and William M. Thompson (Columbia: University of Missouri Press, 1998), Part Four, chap. 3.

to reveal its ontological motivation. The psyche of the psychology that begins with Locke is no longer the scene of a spiritual process, that is, of a process in which the human soul orients itself toward transcendental reality. It has become a stream of experiences that refer only to intramundane reality.

In his utilitarian argument, however, Locke is more than an interpreter of Christianity. In this argument he speaks as an ecclesiastical statesman. We must not overlook this issue and its subtle ramifications. What Locke wants is a Christianity that will be comprehensible for "laboring and illiterate men." His attack is directed against the scandal of churches and sects that pester good, plain people with niceties of theological distinction, that instigate them to participate in theological argument with insufficient educational means, that encourage them to have a mind of their own in the interpretation of Scripture, and that make the scrupulous acceptance of this or that complicated codification of the creed a condition of church membership and salvation. Insofar as Locke intends to protect the faith of the people against the dubious theological quarrels of the age, we are happy for once to be in full sympathy with him. For this, he certainly was a better Christian than the quarreling demagogues.

This sympathy will diminish, however, when we reflect on Locke's solution of the problem. The problem itself is as old as the church. It is sociological in nature, and can hardly be solved otherwise than along the lines laid down by Saint Paul and developed by the church: recognize the differentiation of charismata in the mystical body; let the teachers, bishops, and trained theologians conduct the struggle for right doctrine; develop a constitutional procedure for the struggle; let the participants come to a settlement in the forms of the procedure; and have faith that the Spirit of Christ will have guided the constitutional settlement. The solution, as we said, is narrowly determined by the nature of the problem, but obviously such wisdom cannot be of much help to Locke. The breakdown of the institutions that secured the unity of doctrine for Christianity is an accomplished fact. Locke is in search of an authority for what he considers the doctrine of Christianity, precisely because the institutional organization of this authority is gone. We must recognize the full seriousness of the problem: Locke was justified in his intention even when he erred in the solution. When the institutions of spiritual authority have broken down, and when the members of the schismatic rival organizations are diligently engaged in cutting each others' throats for the advancement of the realm of Christ, certainly those who are appalled by the insanity of the procedure have reason to be concerned about the restoration of authority. Nevertheless, while we must recognize Locke's right to be concerned, we must also recognize that the spiritual breakdown of a civilization is not among the problems that can be solved by a piece of philosophical speculation. A man who undertakes such a task in full seriousness is guilty of the very insanity that aroused his concern. He will not solve the problem that he set himself to solve. Instead he runs the risk of setting a pattern of conduct that will create even worse disorder than the disorder he wishes to heal. And that is what happened to Locke. In his role as an ecclesiastical statesman, he decides that Christianity is identical with what he personally thinks and can understand. Christianity has nothing to say but what he, the man of reason (for he does not reckon himself among the dairymaids and spinsters), knows for truth by his own intuitive knowledge. What he is lacking is not insight but authority. The solution for the spiritual breakdown of Western civilization is found: the church must back with the authority of Christ the reason of Locke. The reader should not be shocked too much by the apparent megalomania of the conception. He should rather be touched by its engaging modesty, because Locke at least claims only insight and not yet authority. Less modest men will come after him; they will add authority to their insight and become the founders of the totalitarian state churches. The bonds of sentiment are still strong enough to hold Locke with the shadow of tradition, and only the shadow of the future falls on his solution.

We may resume now the problem of "primitivization." Locke's civilizational destruction is not idiosyncratic or arbitrary. It is not incidental to his ecclesiastical politics but an instrumental part in his program of restoring spiritual authority. The question now arises as to whether the spiritual authority of Christianity can be restored by the Lockean method. And if, as we think, the means is not adequate for reaching the end, what is the end that actually will be reached if this means is brought into play? In reflecting on these questions we must, first of all, be clear that the authority of the spirit does not disappear from the world if its institutionalization in a historical society breaks down. The spirit bloweth where it listeth, and if it does not blow through the soul of men in community it may still blow through the soul in solitude. The solution to the problem of spiritual authority in social crisis is the way of the mystic. It is a problem that arises whenever society is in crisis. We had occasion to discuss it in all detail when it appeared in Hellenic society. For the systematic discussion of its principles the reader should refer back to the analysis of Plato's ideas, in particular to the analysis of the *Gorgias*.[40] But Locke is no Plato. The Socratic "transfer of authority" was not within the range of his personality. A *renovatio Evangelica* is a return into the soul and cannot, therefore, be the external return to a historical state of doctrine. Locke missed the return into the soul—it was reserved to Berkeley to find this way into the depth of the soul and, because of his age, into social oblivion as well.

Locke's missing of the way leads on to the further question: where did the way lead that he actually went? The very fact that Locke returns to the New Testament, as to a literary document, in search of articles of faith is the proof that his profounder motivation is not quite Evangelical, and it also gives us a clue to its true nature. Locke's return is to the text of the New Testament and is an event in the history of English Protestantism, but it also belongs to the generic class of returns to primitive phases of civilization that are characteristic of the age of Western revolution and crisis. Let us remember Warburton's philosophical history, which we have related but not yet commented on. When Warburton makes his plea for England he reminds us of "the fierce and free nations of the North" who broke the Roman empire, who erected their "Gothic Governments" on the principles of liberty, and who might have lived happily ever after had they not fallen under the thralldom of the new Roman superstition. Here we have another instance of the pattern of return, the pattern that we shall find again in the more famous cases of Montesquieu's Germans who were free in their forests, as well as of the natural men of Rousseau who were free before they fell under the oppression of civilization. Moreover, from Locke's own *Treatise of Civil Government* we may remember the nostalgia of primitivism in the cry: "In the beginning all the world was America."

40. Voegelin's reference is to a section of chapter 4 of the original plan of *History of Political Ideas*. It was first published as "The Philosophy of Existence: Plato's *Gorgias*," *Review of Politics* 11 (1949): 477–98, and reproduced with small changes as chapter 2, "The *Gorgias*," in *Order and History*, vol. III, *Plato and Aristotle* (Baton Rouge: Louisiana State University Press, 1957), 24–45.

In the light of such comparisons, Locke's return to the New Testament looks very much like a beginning of historical Romanticism, like an early case of the return to a historical "myth" for the purpose of assuaging the disorder of the age. The common characteristic of such returns is the open or implied critique of civilization, the assumption that the substance has seeped out of its institutional and intellectual forms, the suspicion that perhaps these very forms have killed the substance, and the growing conviction that the meaning of existence can be recovered only by the destruction of the incubus. In particular Warburton's oratory is suggestive of things to come: when we read his plaints about the "fierce and free nations of the North," about the sad fate of the "Gothic Governments" and the horror of "Papal Superstition," we are reminded of nothing so much as of Alfred Rosenberg's *Mythus des 20. Jahrhunderts* with its invectives against the Roman haruspices who have poisoned the blood and spirit of the noble Nordics. If we consider this aspect of Locke's return (and I think we must consider it), the subterranean connections between Reason and Romanticism become clearer. There is a Romantic touch to Locke's Reason insofar as it reflects the mood of civilizational critique and despair, and insofar as the autonomous Reason emerges as the Lucifer of the community. There is a hesitancy in completing the step because Locke still employs Christ for lending authority to his own light in order to make it socially effective. This hesitancy, however, will appear as such only if we look toward the past. If we look toward the future, Locke's use of the Gospel as a "myth" marks the beginning of a line (though it be a long one) at the end of which we find the fancies of the *Uralinda Chronik* and the Wotanism of the Ludendorffs.

g. *Toland's* Christianity Not Mysterious

In our analysis of Locke's *Reasonableness of Christianity* we have concentrated on what we consider to be its historically and philosophically effective nucleus. This nucleus does not exhaust Locke's attitude toward Christianity. A study of Locke as a thinker would have to explore the vast shadowy field of half thought that surrounds the rather small nucleus that in itself is not too clear. His mode of philosophizing was characterized by a good deal of whim. Spurts of irritation by contemporary evils would push his thought in a direction he would not have moved, could he have seen the end of the road. And he could follow the road with complacency because the energy of the push gave out long before the end came into view. It is an interesting mental constitution. The men who have the happy gift can indulge in irresponsible *boutades* of thought, can produce considerable havoc and misery, and can nevertheless sincerely protest that their intentions have been misunderstood when the mischievousness of their indulgence is held up to them. Speaking less metaphorically: Locke's spiritual gifts and intellectual abilities were no match for the problems he tried to solve, and his ethos as a thinker was deplorably weak.

With regard to the questions under discussion, he did not follow this thought to its conclusions, but let the path conveniently end in an underbrush of sentiments to which historians usually refer as his reverence and his devout Christianity. Locke was aware, of course, that the symbolism of Christianity, even if reduced to the formulations of the New Testament, would not altogether enter into propositions that by any stretch of imagination could be called reasonable. In the *Essay* he distinguishes between religious truths above reason, contrary to reason, and according to reason.[41] He does not, however deny the truth of those that are not according to reason. He recognizes the mysteries of religion as part of Revelation. He gets around the problem of the mysteries by extending reverence to them and putting them beyond a debate that would only sully them. He had neither the strength of the mystic who would make the mysteries luminous by reenacting the religious experiences they symbolize, nor the courage of the philosopher who would let himself be carried wherever his thought led. Nor did he have the plain honesty of giving up a train of thought that led him to results that his sentiments told him were false.

The inevitable happened. A more adventurous and less reverential mind drove the thought of Locke to the point where the consequences became plain. A year after Locke's treatise, that is in 1696, appeared John Toland's *Christianity Not Mysterious.* Toland professed to be Locke's disciple, and Locke was not amused. Again, the details of Toland's work are not our concern. We have to indicate only the principal points where the author went beyond

---

41. Locke, *An Essay*, bk. IV, chap. 17, sec. 23, "Of Reason," 687.

Locke. As a matter of fact, the title of the book summarizes the issue. While Locke was satisfied to find reason in Christianity and let the unreasonable part pass into the shadow of a reverential underemphasis, Toland insisted that there were no mysteries in Christianity—a position that could be maintained only under the assumption that the mysteries were non-Christian. On this issue, however, Toland hedged. He did not state it in so many words, and the second volume of his work, in which he promised further elucidation, was never published. His restraint was probably caused by justified fears of the consequences of publication. Nevertheless, he pressed the argument far enough to make the conclusions clear beyond doubt.

Toland's decisive step is the assumption that the methods employed in the sciences of the external world have an absolute validity for the cognition of all realms of being, as well as the corollary that nothing can be knowledge that has not been found by these methods. On principle, Toland is already an adherent of the scientistic creed. A fact is what can be observed by the senses or what is attested by a trustworthy observer. Knowledge results from the comparison of ideas. In order to be comparable, ideas must be clear. A process of demonstration must be free of contradictions. As long as a proposition is not sufficiently supported by observation and noncontradictory reasoning, our judgment has to remain in suspense. The climax is the introduction of the Newtonian *hypotheses non fingo:* "I banish all hypotheses from my philosophy."[42]

Once this type of epistemology is adopted as a standard, the mystery in the true sense, that is, the paradox in religious experience, must dissolve. Toland defines mystery as a proposition that is known to us through revelation alone. That is to say, as long as it is not revealed to us we do not know it. Once it is revealed it must be rationally intelligible just as any other proposition that we have found without revelation. A revealed truth must show the characteristics of divine wisdom and sound reason. Propositions about something that is inconceivable are not a religious truth but nonsense. Toland concentrated this position in the algebraic sentence: "Could that person justly value himself upon his knowledge who, having infallible assurance that something called a Blictri had

---

42. For the content of Toland's work I am following the account in Stephen, *History of English Thought in the Eighteenth Century,* 1:85–100.

a being in nature, in the meantime knew not what this Blictri was?" This is as far as Toland dares to go. He leaves it to the discretion of the reader to make his substitutions for "Blictri."

Beyond this point the position of Toland cannot be discerned clearly: did he conceal his thought or did he believe, like Locke, that his thesis was compatible with orthodox Christianity? Was he a sincerely troubled soul, or an ambitious one who wanted to ride to fame on Locke's coattails? We do not know. One thing is certain: he took a decisive step, one that was immanent in the logic of Locke's position, namely the step of erecting a consciousness that is turned in cognitive acts toward the external world into the model of the self. Whatever opportunistic or truly reverential lip service may be paid to the dogma, the *cognitio fidei* is annihilated and the symbols that express this realm of experience are discarded as unreasonable. With this step, we may say, freethinking proper begins. The literature of this class is not worth any detailed attention in our context. Let us only indicate the main lines of thought. With regard to the Christian dogma freethought evolves from a reverential Trinitarianism through Unitarianism and Deism to Atheism. With regard to ethics it evolves from a reverential acceptance of traditional standards through the psychology of pleasure and pain into the variants of hedonism and utilitarianism. With regard to psychology it evolves from the reverential acceptance of the stream of consciousness as the residue of the Christian soul to a straight materialism that explains psychic phenomena as epiphenomena of matter. With regard to the external world it develops from the reverential acceptance of creation, through the "fallacy of misplaced concreteness," into the conception of the world as a mechanism of matter that runs its course according to Newton's laws.

Let us conclude this account with the judgment that Swift rendered in his *Argument against Abolishing Christianity in England:* "Who would ever have suspected Asgil for a wit, or Toland for a philosopher, if the inexhaustible stock of Christianity had not been at hand, to provide them with materials? What other subject, through all art or nature, could have produced Tindal for a profound author, or furnished him with readers? It is the wise choice of the subject, that alone adorns and distinguishes the writer. For, had a hundred such pens as these been employed on the side of religion, they would have immediately sunk into silence and oblivion."

§3. Absolute Space and Relativity

The loss of the concrete, thus, is substantially a spiritual disease. With the thinning out of faith into a reverential attitude toward symbols, the meaning of the symbols themselves is thinned out to propositions the truth of which has to be demonstrated by reason. As a residuum of reality there remains only the structure and content of consciousness, that is, of a self no longer open toward transcendental reality. This general pneumato-pathological state, which in itself may occur and has occurred in other periods of history, receives its specific coloration as a result of the coincident rise of mathematical physics. A new world-filling reality, emerging from Galilean and Cartesian physics and systematized in Newtonian mechanics, is ready to substitute for God and his creation. The new science, on principle, is a science only of phenomenal nature; that the edifice of science could assume ontological functions is a result of the "fallacy of misplaced concreteness." This fallacy becomes the vehicle of the trend toward materialism in the sense of a worldview wherein all realms of being are reduced to the one and true reality of matter. The pathos of this view, insofar as it is carried by the new science itself, is expressed in the anecdote of Napoleon and Laplace: when questioned by Napoleon whether, indeed, he had not mentioned God in his *Mécanique céleste*, Laplace answered proudly, "I have no use for this hypothesis!" The mechanism of matter extends infinitely, and God has been squeezed out of his world.

When the issue is stated in such bald language, it seems almost unbelievable that the movement of enlightened scientism could have the strength and duration that it actually had and still has, and that it should have taken the work of generations of thinkers to dissolve such crude mistakes of thought. We do not intend to diminish this impression. Reading the literature of this movement is an ordeal to the infidel and causes him the same exasperation as the reading of Marxist or National Socialist literature. It would be a mistake, however, to conclude that the authors are particularly deficient in intellectual capacity. Their inability to handle elementary speculative problems rather illustrates that there is no limit to intellectual disorder once the *nosos* of the spirit has corroded the personality of the thinker. Nevertheless, the situation is not quite as bad as it looks at first sight. There is one real and very serious theoretical problem involved in the position of enlightened scientism. Even though this problem was too peripheral to be of great concern to spiritualist thinkers, as long as it remained unsolved it greatly strengthened the position of those who for other reasons were inclined toward adopting the scientistic creed. We are speaking of the problem of absolute space that was built into the foundations of modern science through Newton's *Principia* and that has found its full and satisfactory solution only through Einstein's theory of relativity.

We must discuss this problem for two reasons. In the first place, it was Berkeley's starting point for his recovery of the concrete. Beyond this restricted importance in the English quest for the concrete, however, it has an importance for understanding the impact of enlightened scientism on the Western scene that can hardly be exaggerated. The Newtonian theory of absolute space lent a semblance of justification to the "fallacy of misplaced concreteness." Without this piece of Newtonian doctrine scientistic materialism, with its ramifications in the Encyclopedist movement, in utilitarianism and positivism, in the sociology of Comte and Mill, in Marxism, and so forth, would have had little ground to stand on. The belief that science is the key to the understanding of nature in an ontological sense has entered as a decisive ingredient into every one of our political mass movements—liberalism, progressivism, Darwinism, Communism, and National Socialism. The historical root of this belief is the Newtonian theory of space.

a. Relativity from Copernicus to Leibniz

The problem of absolute and relative space does not begin with Newton. It begins with Copernicus and his assumption that the sun is at the center of our planetary system. In the theory of Copernicus we could discern a tendency toward making the sun the ontologically real center of the system, but the predominant motivation was still the simplification of the mathematical description of planetary movements. The problems of scientific description and of ontology were clearly distinguished. We have seen in an earlier part of this study that the issue was well understood in the sixteenth century and that it was carried to its systematic solution before the century's end.[43] Copernicus justified the revolutionary shift of his system of coordinates from the earth to the sun by explaining the relativity of movement. He made it clear that the "real" movement of two bodies that are moved relative to each other is in no way affected by the assumption that one or the other is the origin of the coordinates that are used for the description of the movement. Bodin, in his late work, saw the point with equal clearness and drew the conclusion that one might as well shift the coordinates back to the earth. Astronomers might prefer the sun as a center because the assumption allowed for a simpler mathematical description. He, as a philosopher of politics and nature, preferred the earth as a center for reasons of his own.

Relativity must be taken seriously. If the theory of space as an absolute extension around the earth is a fallacy, the theory of space as an absolute extension around the sun is no less a fallacy. Giordano Bruno had given the systematic elaboration of the problem. Space is phenomenally infinite because this infinity is a projection of the form of the human mind. Ontologically, in the mind of God, the universe is One and the celestial worlds are embraced by this Oneness. The celestial worlds are not embraced as by a space, but they in their turn embrace this Oneness as every part of the soul embraces the soul. The empirical analysis of space, as well as the transcendental analysis in the Kantian sense, touches only certain aspects of the total problem. Cosmological speculation is the theoretical instrument for its complete formulation. This solution of Bruno needs elaboration and reformulation, but in principle it can hardly be improved. On the level of empirical science it has been carried out and confirmed by the theory of relativity through the assumption of an unbounded, curved space that runs back into itself.[44] As far as the Copernican problem is concerned, Bruno drew the conclusion that an infinitely closed space has no absolute center. Its center is everywhere and

43. See vol. V, *Religion and the Rise of Modernity*, chap. 5.
44. See Albert Einstein, *Ueber die spezielle und allgemeine Relativitätstheorie*, 3d enl. ed. (Braunschweig: Vieweg, 1918), §§ 30–32. English edition: *Relativity: The Special and General Theory*, trans. Robert W. Lawson (New York: Holt, 1920).

nowhere, and the choice of the place for the origin of coordinates is arbitrary.

The correctness of the relativistic formulation impressed itself on the contemporaries of Newton. Leibniz developed the problem perhaps furthest in the course of his phoronomic studies. Geometry as the logic of mathematics should be supplemented by phoronomy, a general theory of motion, as the logic of physics. The first principle of motion, however, is that the movement of a body can be observed only in relation to another body, which is assumed to be resting. Movement is a mutual and inevitable shift of position of material parts. In any system of bodies in relative movement with respect to each other we can chose one of the bodies as being at rest and refer the movement of the other to the coordinates originating in the "resting" body. Such choice of a resting body for the purpose of description Leibniz calls a "hypothesis." One of these hypotheses may render a simpler description than the other, but its simplicity does not make the hypothesis "truer." On principle, all such hypotheses are "equivalent." The "general law of equivalence" is Leibniz's formulation of the problem of relativity.[45] The meaning Leibniz attached to this principle may be gathered from the fact that he wrote a memorandum on this question with the intention of inducing the Curia to admit the Copernican system. He argued that from the point of view of logic there is no opposition between the Copernican and the Ptolemaic systems. The choice of heliocentric or geocentric coordinates is equivalent, and the greater descriptive simplicity of the Copernican system does not imply the proposition that the movements as described by it are real in an ontological sense.[46]

b. Galileo's Conflict with the Inquisition

At the time the trend toward a theory of relativity, however, could not fully unfold because the various aspects of the problem were not

45. See Leibniz's letter to Huyghens of June 12/22 1694, in G. W. Leibniz, *Hauptschriften zur Grundlegung der Philosophie*, ed. Ernst Cassirer, 3 vols. (Leipzig: Meiner, 1903–1915), 1:243 ff. See, in the same volume, Cassirer's introduction to the correspondence between Leibniz and Clarke, 108 ff.

46. For Leibniz's intention in writing the memorandum see his letter to Huyghens of September 4/14, 1696, in ibid., 244 f. The memorandum itself is published in *Leibnizens mathematische Schriften*, ed. C. L. Gerhardt, 7 vols. (Berlin: Asher, 1848–1863), 6:144 ff. For comment on the question see Cassirer's previously quoted introduction to the Leibniz-Clarke controversy in *Haupschriften*, 109.

yet sufficiently clarified by philosophical analysis. These various aspects are (1) the objectivity of science, its "truth" that is rooted in its method; (2) the empirical view of the world that results from the application of the method to the partial phenomena of the external world; and (3) the speculative interpretation of the cosmos that expresses the relation of man to the totality of his world experience. In the physics of the seventeenth century these elements still formed an undifferentiated compound. The speculative element was not yet completely eliminated from the method, and, as a consequence, the empirical results carried implications that properly belonged to the speculative sphere.

This historically inevitable, but nevertheless unfortunate, transitional state of the problem led to the much misunderstood conflict of Galileo with the Inquisition. The crucial question concerned the kind of "truth" that should be attributed to the Copernican system. Cardinal Bellarmine suggested a solution to Galileo that substantially was the solution that Leibniz advanced in the previously mentioned memorandum. Galileo admitted that it was not the same thing to show that with the Copernican hypothesis phenomenal problems could be solved, and to prove that the hypothesis was true in nature. Nevertheless, he continues, a system is false if it does not account for all the phenomena, and a system is true if it accounts for them in the most satisfactory manner. "For one cannot and must not search for a higher truth in a proposition of science than that it accounts for all the particular phenomena."[47]

---

47. " 'È vero che non è istesso il nostrare che con la mobilità della terra e stabilità del sole si salvano l'apparenze, e il dimostrare che tali ipotesi in natura sien realmente vere, ma è ben altrotanto e più vero, che se con l'altro sistema communemente ricevuto non si può rendere ragione di tali apparenze quello è indubitamente falso, siccome è chiaro che questo che si accommoda benissimo può esser vero, nè altra maggior verità si può e si deve ricercar in una posizione che il risponder a tutte le particolari apparenze" (It is true that it is not the same to demonstrate that with the earth's mobility and sun's stability appearances can be saved, and to demonstrate that such hypotheses are really true in nature; however, it is even truer, that since it is impossible to explain such appearances with [the aid of] the commonly received system, that system is unquestionably false; since it is clear that, because this one which accommodates itself very well [to appearances] may be true, no other major truth can and must be sought in a position that can respond to all the particular appearances). Galileo's letter in Berti, *Capernico e le vicende del sistema copernicano in Italia* (Rome, 1876), 130; quoted in Ernst Cassirer, *Das Erkenntnisproblem in der Philosophie und Wissenschaft der neueren Zeit*, 3d ed., 3 vols. (Berlin: B. Cassirer, 1922), 1:410. With regard to the historical materials I am following Cassirer in this question; I cannot agree with him, however, with regard to their interpretation.

The situation is both fascinating and revealing: the representative of the Inquisition is willing to settle for relativity, but the physicist has absolutist hesitations. The reasons of Galileo's hesitation are clear. They are contained in his formulation that one must not look for a higher truth in a proposition than its adequacy for the interpretation of phenomena. He has understood that the truth of science rests in the objectivity of its method. The Copernican interpretation is, therefore, "true" because it accounts for the phenomena in the most satisfactory manner. Moreover, he is quite right in his enunciation that one must not look for a higher truth in a scientific proposition. The adequacy of interpretation is all the truth there is in science, and hence the Copernican theory is true, while the Ptolemaic is false. What he is apparently not able to grasp (and in this respect he is the forerunner of generations of physicists) is the possibility that the interpretation of nature cannot be exhausted by a science of phenomena. While, indeed, there is no more truth in science than he can find in it, there is plenty of truth beyond the science of phenomena. The view of nature that emerges from the application of scientific methods to phenomena certainly is true, but it is the correlate of the methods that have been applied and no more than that. The problem of the absoluteness of space is not a problem in empirical science, so that the methical and empirical truth of the Copernican system does not so much as touch it.

Hence the curious distribution of roles in the conflict. Cardinal Bellarmine apparently understood that the absoluteness that was his concern had nothing to do with empirical science; any theory in science was bearable as long as it did not raise claims that would pull the earth from under the feet of man who, indeed, is the center of the world of the religious and metaphysical symbols that he creates. The interest the church had in the Ptolomaic system did not fundamentally concern its validity as a scientific theory of the planetary world. The religious interest touched the validity of a symbolism that originates in the experience of the human soul and its spiritual destiny as the center of the cosmic drama. Since souls are embodied and the bodies are located on the earth, the cosmos has its symbolic center in the scene of its climactic drama. The shift of the spatial center becomes an attack on the experience of the spiritual drama if the shift is construed as the displacement of the "real" center in the symbolic sense. While

Bellarmine's instinct in these matters was sure, his analysis of the problem did not go far enough to convince Galileo. His suggestion of a settlement in terms of two hypotheses neither of which would have a bearing on reality reduces the problems of speculation and of science to the same level. It does not differentiate between the realms of religious symbolization and metaphysical speculation on the one side, and the realm of empirical science on the other side. That the beautiful Copernican theory should be no more than a "hypothesis" could hardly be made palatable to an enthusiastic scientist unless it could be made clear to him at the same time that the function of science for the interpretation of the world is in principle limited. Galileo in his turn did not differentiate the components of the problem any better than Bellarmine, and, moreover, he was at a disadvantage because he did not even have the cardinal's instinct for the problem. His enthusiasm for the new science, which unfolded its potentialities under his hands and those of his contemporaries, sustained his indulgence in the belief that now a "true" system of the world had been found, and it was destined to supersede the old one. In this respect again, Galileo is the forerunner of generations of physicists who indulged in the fallacy that the advancement of science could affect the truth of metaphysics and religious symbolization. The error of Galileo, which stands at the beginning of the scientistic movement, is the same error that lies at the bottom of the evolutionist creed movement in the wake of Darwin.

c. Newton's Assumption of Absolute Space

On occasion of Galileo's conflict with the Inquisition the issue of absolutism versus relativity became clear as far as the general problems of the truth of science and of the truth of speculation and religious symbolization are concerned. These general problems were formidable. Nevertheless, they might have been cleared up quickly, and they were cleared up in principle by Leibniz. The obstacle to a rapid advancement toward a theory of relativity in physics arose from the internal problems of the new science. This obstacle was present already in Galileo's theory of motion, but it became fully visible only with Newton's formulation of the general law of gravitation and the consequent elaboration of a general theory of physics in the *Principia Mathematica*.[48] Newton found it necessary to assume the existence of absolute space and of absolute motion. In the Scholium to Definition VIII he defines: "Absolute space, in its own nature, without relation to anything external, remains always similar and immovable. Relative space is some movable dimension or measure of the absolute spaces; which our senses determine by its position to bodies; and which is commonly taken for immovable space." A bit further on in the Scholium he explains the reason for his assumption: "Because the parts of space cannot be seen, or distinguished from one another by our senses, therefore in their stead we use sensible measures of them. For from the positions and distances of things from any body considered as immovable, we define all places; and then with respect to such places, we estimate all motions, considering bodies as transferred from some of those places into others. And so, instead of absolute places and motions, we use relative ones; and that without any inconvenience in common affairs; but in philosophical disquisitions, we ought to abstract from our senses, and consider things themselves, distinct from what are only sensible measures of them. For it may be that there is no body really at rest, to which the places and motions of others may be referred." Newton envisages absolute space as an absolute order of "places"; this order of places is a "primary" system to which motion ultimately can be referred. Only "translations out of those places" are truly absolute motions. Since, however, these absolute places cannot be observed by the senses, the question arises as to what purpose we should assume their existence? This delicate question Newton covers by his vague reference to the "philosophical disquisitions" that make such deeds necessary.

Embarking on such philosophical disquisition, Newton finds that rest and motion, absolute and relative, can be distinguished by their properties, causes, and effects. "It is a property of rest, that bodies really at rest do rest in respect to one another." This definition of rest holds good in spite of the fact that such absolutely resting bodies, if they exist at all, may be found only in the region of the fixed stars, or even beyond that region, whereas absolute rest cannot be determined "from the positions of bodies in our region."

48. The following quotations from Sir Isaac Newton's *Principia* are taken from Florian Cajori's English edition, *Mathematical Principles of Natural Philosophy* (Berkeley: University of California Press, 1946), 6 ff.

While empirical observation does not show any bodies at absolute rest, Newton nevertheless introduces this concept. Here we have tracked down the first serious reason that would induce a physicist to make the assumption of absolute space: he needs the assumption for the purpose of defining rest. And he needs this concept in order to maintain the first law of motion that "Every body continues in its state of rest, or of uniform motion in a right line, unless it is compelled to change that state by forces impressed upon it." Without the assumption of absolute space no meaning can be given to the notion of absolute rest, and absolute rest seemed to Newton, as it did to Galileo, a fundamental experience that could not be dispensed with in the formulation of the first law of motion.

The second reason for Newton's assumption of absolute places was his belief that he could observe cases of motion without change of place. Absolute motion in this sense had to be distinguished from relative motion. The criterion for this distinction is given through observations with regard to centrifugal forces. "The effects which distinguish absolute from relative motion are, the forces receding from the axis of circular motion. For there are no such forces in a circular motion purely relative, but in a true and absolute circular motion, they are greater or less, according to the quantity of the motion." An important instance of such effects is the polar flattening of the earth due to centrifugal forces.

d. The Influence of Henry More

In the face of such difficulties the theoretically indicated course would have been to revise the fundamental definitions and to drop the concepts of absolute rest and absolute motion. This is the course that was actually followed by Ernst Mach in the second half of the nineteenth century. Newton, however, did not contemplate this possibility. His insistence on absolute space seems to have been fortified by motives that appeared more clearly in the *Scholium Generale*, which he attached to the second edition of the *Principia*, of 1713, as well as in the additions to the second edition of his *Optics*. These additions reveal how strongly Newton's theory of absolute space was influenced by Henry More, the Cambridge Platonist (1614–1687).

More's metaphysics of space arises at the intersection of his Neoplatonic mysticism with his interest in the new Cartesian physics. He was not satisfied with Descartes's identification of extension and matter that would have materialized space; nor was he satisfied with a subjectivist analysis that would have defined space as the concept of a relation between bodies, that is, with the analysis of the Hobbesian type. He recognized that distance is a relation between bodies, but he insisted that this relation has a basis: "The basis of this relation is something real."[49] Spatial extension reaches to infinity, has existed from eternity, and will exist into eternity; and it exists independent of our thought. Since extension is a "real attribute," a subject for this attribute must exist. This subject cannot be found in the corporeal world of our observations, with its limited and discrete extensions. The real subject of absolute space, as well as of absolute time, can only be the divine substance that manifests its own infinity in the double infinity of absolute space and time. More is explicit on the religious motivation of his assumption. He intends to bring God back into the world through the same gate through which Cartesian philosophy tried to shut him out from it.[50]

More's metaphysics of space held a double appeal for Newton. More's mysticism struck a responsive chord in Newton the mystic. His anti-Cartesianism was an important support to Newton the physicist. In the *Optics* Newton gave the most concise formulation of his own position. From the phenomena of nature it follows that "there exists an incorporeal Being, living, intelligent and omnipresent." This Being uses space "as it were as its sensorium"; and by this sensorium it "sees all things intimately in themselves and perceives them throughout, and in its presence embraces all things present in it." The sentient and thinking principle within us, on the other hand, can perceive only the images of things by means of its *sensoriolum*, its little sensorium.[51] The position of the second edition of the *Principia* does not differ from that in the *Optics*. Let us quote only a passage that will communicate the pathos of Newton: "As a blind man has no idea of colors, so have we no idea of the manner by which the all-wise God perceives and understands all things. He is utterly void of all body and bodily figure, and can

49. Henry More, *Enchiridium Metaphysicum sive de Rebus Incorporeis*, pt. I, chap. VIII, sec. 5; quoted in Cassirer, *Erkenntnisproblem*, 2:443.

50. More, *Enchiridium Metaphysicum*, pt. I, chap. VIII, secs. 6–7; quoted in ibid., 2:444.

51. Newton, *Optice*, Latin edition of 1740, Quaestio XVIII; quoted in ibid., 2:447.

therefore neither be seen, nor heard, nor touched; nor ought he to be worshiped under the representation of any corporeal thing. . . . We know him only by his most wise and excellent contrivances of things, and final causes; we admire him for his perfections; but we reverence and adore him on account of his dominion: for we adore him as his servants; and a god without dominion, providence and final causes, is nothing else but Fate and Nature. Blind metaphysical necessity, which is certainly the same always and everywhere, could produce no variety of things. All that diversity of natural things which we find suited to different times and places could arise from nothing but the ideas and will of a Being necessarily existing. . . . And thus much concerning God; to discourse of whom from the appearances of things, does certainly belong to Natural Philosophy."[52]

The passages from More and Newton reveal the connection between the new science and the problems of freethinking. The Cartesian materialization of extension would fill the infinity of space in the universe with matter and its mechanism. There would be no mystery left in the existence of the cosmos. Into its remotest recesses the universe would be known as a configuration of matter, and God, indeed, would be shut out from his creation. If the nature revealed by the new science was the nature of the cosmos, there was, indeed, no use for the "hypothesis" of God. More's device for counteracting this tendency through positing the divine substance as the *fundamentum* of spatial extension was ingenuous but fraught with dangers. For a short while the device could serve as an argument against atheists and materialists in the literature that tried to prove the existence of God. The very science that at first seemed a danger to religion now furnished the most convincing proof of God. The most important treatise that used this argument was written by Newton's friend Samuel Clarke.[53] The joy, as could be expected, did not last long. The attempt to save God by science soon ran into pantheistic difficulties. An omnipresent God who was the spiritual substance underlying phenomenal extension was a bit too present in the world to retain at the same time his "dominion"

---

52. *Principia, Scholium Generale,* in *Mathematical Principles of Natural Philosophy,* ed. Cajori, 545 f.

53. Samuel Clarke, *A Discourse Concerning the Being and Attributes of God* (London: Botham, 1705/6).

as the transcendental Lord of creation. Worse, however, than these difficulties, which dragged on in a long and dreary debate, was the fact that men of a less religious temper simply did not care about the divine substance underlying absolute space. The intellectuals who absorbed the Newtonian system, in particular after its popularization through Voltaire, were satisfied with Newton's recognition of absolute space and could dispense with his religious motivation. The system of the *Principia* was complete with the first edition; the *Scholium Generale* of the second edition added nothing to empirical physics. Here was a system of the world, legitimated by the genius of the man whose name at this time carried more authority in the intellectual world than anybody else's. And this system showed the world as consisting of nothing but matter obeying a uniform law. The theory of absolute space sealed this system ontologically against God, and by virtue of this character, the Newtonian system became socially effective. The well-intentioned theory of absolute space had resulted in precisely the disorder it had intended to avert.

e. Berkeley's Psychological Criticism

The genius of Newton lay in the field of mathematics and physics. When he let his thought wander beyond this province, the results were of doubtful quality. The *Principia* was the great cornerstone for the edifice of science that was to be erected in the following centuries, but the definitions and theoretical excursions in the scholia could only arouse the vehement criticism of philosophers. In particular Newton exposed himself to criticism with his proud declaration of autonomy for the new science. Physics could go its course, as it actually did, without regard for the debates of metaphysicians, conscientiously applying the well-established methods to observed phenomena. The *Scholium Generale* had announced the precept *hypotheses non fingo:* "whatever is not deduced from the phenomena is to be called an hypothesis; and hypotheses, whether metaphysical or physical, whether of occult qualities or mechanical, have no place in experimental philosophy." The assumption of absolute space was a glaring contradiction to this declaration; certainly this fundamental "hypothesis" was not deduced from the phenomena. We shall not be surprised, therefore, when now we turn to Berkeley and his criticism of Newton's theory, to find some pungent remarks concerning the boundaries between physics and metaphysics. In his *De Motu* (1721) Berkeley writes: "For the rest, it would be convenient, setting aside that it is a well established custom, to distinguish between sciences in such a manner that each is well circumscribed by its proper boundaries. The philosopher of nature should remain entirely with his experiments, his laws of motion, his mechanical principles and the conclusions derived therefrom; if he has something to say on other matters, he should relate what is accepted in the respective higher science." The context leaves hardly a doubt that the remarks about the *philosophus naturalis* are meant to put Newton in his place.[54]

Berkeley's criticism of Newton's theory moves on two planes. With regard to the method of physics he returns to the principle of relativity. A body can be recognized as moving only in relation to another body that is relatively at rest. The idea of absolute motion is incompatible with the conditions of experience. Motion can be measured only by things given to the senses. Since absolute space is not given to the senses, it cannot be used for the distinction of different types of motion. The conception of an absolute motion is impossible.[55] Moreover, in empirical science we do not need such a conception. All that we need is a system of reference that permits us to distinguish between bodies that are relatively at rest or in motion. And such a system we have given in the heaven of the fixed stars. We do not need the assumption of an absolute space for the formulation of the laws of motion because they are valid if we use the fixed stars as the system at rest instead of absolute space.[56] The laws of motion are generalizations from observations and no more. We must "distinguish between mathematical hypotheses and the nature of things." Motion belongs to the world of senses, and we must be satisfied with relative measurements.[57]

Berkeley's second approach to the problem lies on the way of a psychological analysis of the illusions that lead to the assumption of absolute space. The idea of a space without a content is empty, it is a *merum nihil.*[58] We are deceived, however, into the assumption

---

54. Berkeley, *De Motu* §42, in A. A. Luce and T. E. Jessop, eds., *The Works of George Berkeley*, 9 vols. (London: Nelson, 1948–1957), 4:42.
55. *De Motu* §63, in ibid., 4:49.
56. *De Motu* §64, in ibid.
57. *De Motu* §66, in ibid., 4:49–50.
58. *De Motu* §§53–54, in ibid., 4:45–46. The argument of these paragraphs is substantially the same as that of Berkeley's *Principles of Human Knowledge* (1710), §§116–17. *Principles* is vol. 2 of ibid.

because in speculating on the problem of space we subtract all bodies but forget to subtract our own. If we imagine space emptied of all content we still have an experience of space because we have the experience of our body and of the movements of its members. The experience in itself is not deceptive, but what we experience is the relative space defined by the parts of our body. The attribution of absoluteness to this space is a fallacy.[59]

The meaning of the somewhat brief passages in *De Motu* becomes clearer through the more discursive analysis in the *Principles of Human Knowledge*. As far as the observation of moving bodies is concerned, says Berkeley in the *Principles*, we never can observe anything but bodies moving relatively to each other. The physicist is such an observer of moving bodies, and hence in physics nothing can be admitted but a concept of relative motion. Nevertheless, we not only observe motion, we can also experience it. "Now, I ask any one whether, in his sense of motion as he walks along the streets, the stones he passes over may be said to *move*, because they change distance with his feet? To me it appears that though motion includes a relation of one thing to another, yet it is not necessary that each term of the relation be denominated from it."[60] Berkeley, thus, recognizes the experience of absolute motion, but he considers it impermissible to inject this experience into mathematical physics. The laws of science can only describe the observed motions, and observed motions are relative.

Knowingly or unknowingly, Berkeley has touched with this argument on one of the actual historical roots of the Newtonian conception of absolute space. In his correspondence with Descartes, Henry More had advanced the experience of absolute rest and motion as an argument against Descartes's radical concept of "reciprocal" movement: "When I am sitting quietly, and another man who moves away, let us say a thousand steps, becomes red in his face and fatigued, while I who am sitting do not become red-faced and fatigued, it certainly is he who has moved, while I have been at rest during the time."[61] More used the experience of absolute motion as an

59. *De Motu* §55, in ibid., 4:46.
60. *Principles* §113.
61. Henry More, "Letter to Descartes," March 5, 1649, in *Oeuvres de Descartes*, ed. Charles Adam and Paul Tannery (Paris: Cerf, 1903), 5:312 f. The argument is directed against Descartes's *Principia Philosophiae*, pt. II, art. 29. For Descartes's answer see his "Letter to More," April 15, 1649, in *Oeuvres de Descartes*, ed. Adam

argument against relativity. This double use to which the argument could be put (for or against relativity) indicates the insufficient differentiation of problems that characterizes the state of theory at this period. It indicates also, however, that the problem of absolute motion has its complexities. Berkeley was of course right when he protested against the injection of experienced absolute motion into the description of observed relative motion. Nevertheless, we are faced with the fact that there are some bodies in the universe, namely human bodies, who *know* when they are in absolute motion and when at absolute rest. One may eject absolute motion from physics, but the problem will reappear on the level of speculation, and with it there will reappear the problem of absolute space. The difficulties that Galileo had with the Inquisition appear now on the level of a conflict between the relative motion of physics and the analysis of the experience of absolute motion. The relativity of motion in science does not abolish the problem of an absolute order of the universe that is revealed and centered in the experience of man.

The complexity of the problem showed itself in the opposite use that Berkeley and More could make of the argument from absolute motion. It shows itself, furthermore, in the opposition of purpose between the two thinkers. More wanted absolute space to serve as the immaterial, divine *fundamentum* of infinite phenomenal space in order to save the existence of God. Berkeley wants to get rid of absolute space for precisely the same purpose. The chief advantage that arises from the elimination of absolute space "is that we are freed from the dangerous dilemma . . . of thinking either that Real Space is God, or else that there is something beside God which is eternal, uncreated, infinite, indivisible, immutable. Both which may justly be thought pernicious and absurd notions."[62] Berkeley has achieved his purpose of saving God by disentangling him from the space of physics—but this saving action does not solve the

---

and Tannery, 5:345 ff. On More's argument against Descartes see Henri Bergson, *Matière et mémoire*, 24th ed. (Paris: Alcan, 1928), 215, and the same author's *Durée et simultanéité: À propos de la théorie d'Einstein*, 2d enl. ed. (Paris: Alcan, 1923), 37. For an elaborate analysis of the relation between the experience of motion (in the sense of More and Berkeley) and the experience of space, as well as of the relation between experienced space and the space of geometry, see Henri Poincaré, *La science et l'hypothèse* (Paris: Flammarion, 1908), pt. II, "L'Espace." English edition: *Science and Hypothesis*, trans. J. Larmor (New York: Dover, 1952).

62. *Principles* §117.

problem of space. His psychological analysis has led us a good step deeper into the problem. It has brought the distinction between generalizations from observed phenomena in physics and the realm of human experience, but it has left the problem of absolute space more or less where it was before.

f. The Deadlock

A psychological analysis of the Berkeleyan type can dispose of the concept of absolute space as a *merum nihil*, it can trace the idea to its origin in the experience of the body, it can show the fallacy of hypostatizing this experience into an objective quality of phenomenal space, and—what is most important for Berkeley—it can by such effective criticism clear the way for the *philosophia prima*. It cannot, however, persuade a physicist to consider his problem solved. When Galileo discovered the law of motion he did not consider a body at rest in relation to the fixed stars. He considered it absolutely at rest. The laws of science are meant to be valid absolutely. As a follower of Newton expressed it: "From the observation of nature we all know that there is motion, that a body in motion perseveres in that state, till by the action or influence of some power it be necessitated to change it, that it is not in relative or apparent motion in which it perseveres in consequence of its inertia, but in real and absolute space."[63] If we assume with Descartes that the place of a body is determined by its relation to the bodies in its neighborhood, the law of motion would have to announce that a body on which no external force is applied cannot change its position with regard to the surrounding bodies. This law is absurd because obviously the relative position can be changed by applying forces to the surrounding bodies. In brief: the criticism of the philosophers, as Berkeley did with Newton, is not constructive. As far as physics is concerned, the only result will be that the physicists will have to put them in their place. And this is what actually happened through Leonhard Euler in his *Réflexions sur l'espace et le temps* (1748). The philosophers were told that the certainty of the laws of mechanics must be the starting

---

63. Colin Maclaurin, *An Account of Sir Isaac Newton's Philosophical Discoveries* (London, 1748), II.1.§9; quoted in Cassirer, *Erkenntnisproblem*, 2:478. Maclaurin's book was printed for the author's children by A. Millar and J. Nourse. A facsimile reprint is available (New York: Johnson Reprints, 1968).

point of the inquiry. Any criticism that is in conflict with those principles must be rejected, however conclusive in itself it may be. The metaphysical principles must be chosen in such a manner that they will be compatible with physics.

The physicists and their philosophical critics had come to a deadlock. It was a deadlock with rather grave consequences. If we take Euler's demand seriously and generalize it, we arrive at the rule that every time an empirical scientist makes a mess of his fundamental concepts—which is a rather ordinary occurrence—the philosophers would be faced by the alternative of either clearing up the mess for him, or of henceforth talking nonsense in epistemology and metaphysics. The demand has a touch of the burlesque. Nevertheless, it could be imposed with a measure of success. The graveness of the situation may be gathered from the fact that even Kant submitted to it, after some vacillation, at least to the extent of recognizing the *Faktum der Wissenschaft* including Newton's absolute space.[64] Before we elaborate, however, on this curiosity of our intellectual civilization, we must briefly outline the further differentiation of the problem of absolute space and the solution toward which it tended.

g. Leibniz

The differentiation of the problem was, on principle, achieved by Leibniz. We have reflected already on his general relativistic position; we have now to add the principal points of his differentiating analysis.

First of all, he located the crucial point of the difficulty by differentiating between geometry and phoronomy on the one side and mechanics on the other. The relativity of position and motion is indisputable as long as we deal with them as "purely mathematical" problems. Nature, however, does not offer the spectacle

---

64. Kant had made a very successful attack on the problem of absolute and relative motion in his early work *M. Immanuel Kants' Neuer Lehrbegriff der Bewegung und Ruhe und der damit verknüpften Folgerungen in den ersten Gründen der Naturwissenschaft* (1758). He attacked the crucial point by eliminating the concept of inertia and reformulating the first law of motion. He surrendered, however, this hopeful start and, in subsequent works, bowed to the authority of Euler. After 1770 the problem lost interest for him because the epistemologically relevant part could be solved through his critical philosophy. On the position of Kant see Ernst Cassirer, *Zur Einstein'schen Relativitätstheories, Erkenntnistheoretische Betrachtungen* (Berlin: B. Cassirer, 1921), chap. V, "Der Raum- und Zeitbegriff der kritischen Idealismus und die Relativitätstheorie."

of abstractly shoving bodies that change their relative positions chaotically. It offers the spectacle of a calculable order in the relative movements. This order in the movements cannot be explained within the realm of geometry. For the purpose of its interpretation we have to go beyond the purely mathematical principles and introduce a "metaphysical" principle. "Whether we call this principle Form, or Entelechy, or Force, is irrelevant as long as we remember that only the notion of forces will express it intelligibly."[65] This step of clarification impressed even the physicists to a certain extent, because Euler adopted the relativistic conception of space and motion at least for the phoronomic part of his last presentation of the Newtonian system, the *Theoria Motus* of 1765, though in the part on dynamics he reverted to the Newtonian position.[66] Moreover, by localizing the difficulty in the theory of dynamics, Leibniz correctly marked the direction in which the solution had to be sought and ultimately was found, that is, the geometrization of physics. That the new physics should be constructed as a science of extension had been the great idea of Descartes. However, it proved impossible to carry out the idea in the system. Descartes's *Principia* show the famous break between the theory of "reciprocal" motion in the geometrical part of the work and the quiet adoption of the law of motion in its conventional form, with its absolute implications, in the part on mechanics. Leibniz arrived at his own theory of forces through the critique of Descartes's *Principia*. His new dynamics is supposed to solve the problem that was left open by the geometrical approach of Descartes. Within empirical physics, the problem of relativity was ultimately solved, indeed, by transforming the crucial problem of "force" into a geometrical problem.[67]

65. Leibniz, *Specimen Dynamicum* (1695), in *Opera Omnia*, ed. L. Dutens, 6 vols. (Geneva: Tournes, 1768), 3:321.

66. See on this episode Cassirer, *Erkenntnisproblem*, 2:482 ff.

67. For the problem that arises in the transition from the mathematical treatment of motion to the physical, see Bergson, *Matière et mémoire*, 214 ff. *Matière et mémoire* was written before Einstein; the state of the problem at that time was still substantially the same as at the time of Leibniz. See for instance Bergson's excellent formulation of the problem on 215: "Descartes traite du mouvement en physicien après l'avoir défini en géomètre. Tout mouvement est relatif pour le géomètre: cela signifie seulement, à notre sens, qu'il n'y a pas de symbole mathématique capable d'exprimer que ce soit le mobile plutôt que les axes ou les points auxquels on le rapporte" (Descartes deals with movement as a physicist after having defined it as a geometer. For the geometer, every movement is relative: in our sense that means only that there is no mathematical symbol capable of expressing what a body in motion is, rather than the axes or the coordinates to which it corresponds). These

The localization of the difficulty is the first step toward a solution, but it is not the solution itself. At first sight, the introduction of the "metaphysical" principle of force seems to inject the absolute problem into theory rather than to eliminate it. Let us be clear, therefore, first about the point that in the language of Leibniz the term *metaphysics* is wider in content than in modern usage. Metaphysics is for him the general science of principles, exclusive of mathematics and geometry only.[68] The principles of physics as a science of phenomena (such as the category of causation) belong to metaphysics in this sense. Hence the introduction of force is immediately followed by the differentiation into *vis primitiva* and *vis derivativa*, that is, into force in the sense of an inherent quality of substance and force in the phenomenal sense. Primitive force (whether active or passive) is substantial force, and its problems belong to metaphysics in the narrower sense. This primitive force belongs among the "general causes" that "are insufficient for the explanation of phenomena." Derivative force arises "as it were through a limitation of primitive force through the interaction *(conflictus)* of bodies in various ways."[69] The differentiation of primitive and derivative force, and in particular the definition of phenomenal force, is the decisive achievement of Leibniz. The problem of absoluteness is eliminated through the definition of phenomenal force as force in relation to other forces. Phenomenal force is relative force by definition; and only this phenomenal force is the object of physics. Force has no meaning beyond the meaning that is contained in the differential equations of physics. The laws

---

pages of Bergson practically adopt the position of Leibniz's *Specimen Dynamicum* as far as the differentiation of the problems is concerned; his solution, however, is not the Leibnizian theory of force but a pragmatic theory of motion on the line of the Berkeleyan analysis. After Einstein, the problem of physics comes into clearer view for Bergson; on the historical line from the attempted geometrical physics of Descartes to the realized geometrical physics of Einstein see his *Durée et simultanéité: À propos de la théorie d'Einstein,* chap. 2, "La relativité complète." On Einstein's own position see his *Relativity.* The geometrization of force in Einstein's theory is succinctly formulated by Sir Arthur S. Eddington in *The Nature of the Physical World,* Gifford Lectures 1927 (Cambridge: Cambridge University Press, 1948), 133: "Einstein's law of gravitation controls a geometrical quantity *curvature* in contrast to Newton's law which controls a mechanical quantity *force.*"

68. See for the definition of terms in this sense §1 of the *Third Letter* of Leibniz to Clarke, *Recueil de lettres entre Leibniz et Clarke,* in *Opera Omnia,* ed. Dutens, 2:120. See also the footnote of Cassirer on this question in Leibniz, *Hauptschriften,* ed. Cassirer, 1:133.

69. *Specimen Dynamicum,* in *Opera omnia,* ed. Dutens, 3:316.

of nature refer to derivative forces and their phenomena only.[70] In order to avoid all misunderstandings Leibniz adds explicitly that the *Entia Mathematica* (that is, the meanings contained in an equation) cannot be found really in nature; "they are only the instruments of abstract and exact calculation."[71]

We have now gained a concept of phenomenal nature as a field of relative forces, the actions of which are described in the differential equations of physics. The ideas of space and time used in science refer to this phenomenal nature. The third step in Leibniz's analysis is the clarification of the ideas of space and time. His most mature formulation of this problem is to be found in the correspondence with Clarke, which was an indirect correspondence with Newton because the latter collaborated with Clarke in the answers. The problem of space runs through the whole correspondence. A first formulation is the following: "I have stressed more than once that I consider space something *purely relative,* just as time; it is an order of coexistences, just as time is an order of successions. For space signifies, in terms of possibility, an order of things that exist at the same time, insofar as they exist together, without determining their particular way of existing."[72] Again: "One says that space does not depend on the position *(situation)* of bodies. I answer: it is quite true that it does not depend on this or that position of bodies; nevertheless, it is the order which makes bodies *positionable (situables)* and by which they have a position among themselves when they exist together; just as time is this order with regard to successive position."[73] And finally: "I have shown that space is nothing but an order of the existence of things, which is to be noted in their simultaneity."[74] Space and time of physics, thus, are not qualities of reality; they are orders that the mind applies to the interpretation of phenomena. The problem of absolute space cannot arise if space is understood as an ideal form that consti-

---

70. Ibid., 3:317.
71. Ibid., 3:318.
72. Leibniz's *Third Letter* §4, in ibid., 2:121.
73. Leibniz's *Fourth Letter* §41, in ibid., 2:132 f.
74. Leibniz's *Fifth Letter* §29, in ibid., 2:148. The position of Leibniz at the time of his correspondence with Clarke does not differ materially from his earlier position. For variant formulations see the *Bemerkungen zum allgemeinen Teil der Kartesischen Prinzipien,* of 1692, in particular the remarks on Descartes's *Principia* II.8–19, *in fine* (Leibniz, *Hauptschriften,* ed. Cassirer, 1:307 f.); and *Gegen Descartes,* of 1702 (ibid., 1:330–33).

tutes the order of phenomena. This solution not only eliminates the Newtonian problem of absolute space critically, it also gives a positive answer to the question of "objectivity" in science. We do not have to search for the "absolute" validity of propositions in an absolute reality because the objectivity of science has its source in the order of the mind.

This is the solution that was further developed by the transcendental critique of Kant into the theory of the noetic function as an autonomous source of knowledge. At the time, however, its significance and finality were hardly understood. To the formulations of Leibniz came the pained answer of Clarke (and behind him of Newton): "I do not understand the meaning of the words: An order, or a position, which makes the bodies positionable. To me this seems to say that the position is the cause of the position."[75] This complaint carries us beyond the theoretical discussion into the human situation. The complaint was sincere: Clarke and Newton did not understand. As far as the physicists are concerned, this was the end of the debate for the next century and a half.

h. The Problem of the Rotating Star

Several aspects of the problem had been differentiated by Leibniz, which led to the insight that the concepts of absolute space and absolute motion were inadmissible in physics. The next task would have been the reformulation of the Newtonian definitions and of the first law of motion in such a manner that they would have become compatible with the logic of science. This reforming work, however, did not get under way for more than a century. The principal cause of the stagnation was the fact that deficiencies in the theoretical structure did not impair the advancement of science. An internal incentive to revise the fundamental concepts of physics arose only in the second half of the nineteenth century with empirical observations such as those of the Michelson-Morley experiment.

Besides indifference, there was positive resistance to a revision. The motive for this resistance was formulated by Clarke in his *Fifth Replie* to Leibniz: "One maintains that motion implies of necessity a relative change of position in one body with regard

75. Clarke, *Fourth Replie* §41, in Leibniz, *Opera omnia*, ed. Dutens, 2:140.

to other bodies, but one does not show how one could avoid the absurd consequence of this assumption: that the movability of a body depends on the existence of other bodies, or that a body which exists alone would be incapable of movement, or that the parts of a rotating body (as for instance the sun) would lose their centrifugal force if all external, surrounding matter were annihilated."[76] We do not know the answer of Leibniz to this argument, for the death of the philosopher brought an end to the correspondence. But, as we shall see presently, we can form a fairly good idea of what it would have been. Anyway, at the time this argument remained unanswered, and it remained one of the great motives of resistance against a revision of the Newtonian theory. The argument still was alive in 1870 in Carl Neumann's treatise on the Newtonian theory.[77] In almost the same words as Clarke, Neumann put the case of the rotating star that had assumed the shape of an ellipsoid. If we imagine all other bodies removed from the universe, then the rotating star would have to be at rest according to the relativistic theory. Its centrifugal forces would disappear and its body would become spherical in shape. "This insufferable contradiction can be avoided only if we drop the definition of motion as relative, and if we conceive the motion of a material point as something absolute."[78] In response to this argument at last came the answer of a physicist, Ernst Mach. There is no profit in making a senseless assumption for the purpose of avoiding a contradiction. Moreover, in a mental experiment only nonessential circumstances may be modified. That the existence of the surrounding material world is without influence, however, must not be assumed a priori. If, therefore, the hypothetical elimination of the material world leads to contradictions, we have to consider this result as proving the importance of the relativity of motion.[79]

The answer is excellent in its firmness and intention but is lacking somewhat in theoretical precision. There is a serious unclearness in Mach's answer insofar as it does not define the criteria for the "essentiality" or "nonessentiality" of circumstances that may

76. Clarke, *Fifth Replie* §§ 26–32, in ibid., 2:174.
77. Carl Neumann, *Über die Principien der Galilei-Newton'schen Theorie* (Leipzig: Teubner, 1870).
78. Ibid., 27 f.
79. Ernst Mach, *Die Mechanik in ihrer Entwicklung*, 4th rev. and enl. ed. (Leipzig: Teubner, 1901), 290 f.

or may not be modified in a mental experiment. But we can repair the lack of precision of 1901 by a return to the theoretical culture of 1715. The correspondence with Clarke was ended, as we have said, through the death of Leibniz, but we can construct the answer that Leibniz could have given to Clarke's argument. For Leibniz the relativity in physics is not a relativity of space and time only. Relativity extends also to the *vis derivative*, that is, to phenomenal force. Force is not exempted from phenomenality and relativity. Hence, the physical phenomenon as a whole, in all of its aspects, must be conceived as part of a field of phenomenal relations. Relativity is not an appurtenance of objects that exist in themselves but is part of the logical structure of a science of phenomena. Hence it is impermissible to isolate a phenomenon and ask what properties, for instance, a rotating star would have "in itself" after the relational field in which it is a phenomenon is abolished. An experiment can and must abstract from concrete, physical circumstances in order to isolate that part of the total phenomenon that can be mathematized and expressed in a law of science. It cannot, however, abstract from the logic of science and still remain scientific. The argument from the body that rotates in absolute motion makes precisely this epistemological mistake. With the clarification of the mistake the problem of absolute motion disappears.[80]

i. Science, Power, and Magic

The further development of the problem of relativity from Mach to Einstein belongs in the history of science; it is not our concern in a history of political ideas. We can proceed now to an appraisal of the results of our analysis, and we shall begin this appraisal with a few reflections on the relation between power and the advancement of science. These general reflections will then be followed by a description of the pattern of ideas that emerges from our analysis.

The advancement of the science for which Newton is the great, representative genius has profoundly affected the political and economic structure of the Western world. Let us list the principal

---

80. In this construction of Leibniz's answer I am reproducing substantially Cassirer's construction in his n. 158 to the Leibniz-Clarke correspondence; see Leibniz, *Hauptschriften*, ed. Cassirer, 1:219–21. I have toned down only the neo-Kantian terminology of Cassirer, which somewhat veils the original strength of Leibniz's position.

features of this change: the ramification of science into technology; the industrialization of production; the increase of population; the higher population capacity of an industrialized economy; the transformation of an agricultural into an urban society; the rise of new social groups, that is, of the industrial proletariat, white-collar employees, and an intellectual proletariat; the concentration of wealth and the rise of the managerial class; the ever increasing numbers of men who depend for their economic existence on decisions beyond their influence; the dependence of national power on a highly developed industrial apparatus; the dependence of the industrial apparatus on the political accessibility of markets and raw materials; the power premium on industrialization; the political decline of nations that do not possess the raw materials, or the population figure, or the territorial expansion that is necessary for the effective utilization of industrial technology; the corresponding political ascendancy of nations who possess these factors; the helplessness of agricultural, in particular of Oriental, civilizations against the economic and political penetration by industrialized civilizations; the rise in the standard of living as a result of industrialization; the political tensions in the Western world as a consequence of differences in the degree of industrialization possible in the various national states; the further increase in the standard of living in some of the industrialized societies because of a ruthless exploitation of the industrial power premium in foreign relations; and so forth. This enumeration is far from exhaustive, but it is sufficiently long to make it clear that the advancement of science after 1700 is the most important single factor in changing the structure of power and wealth on the global scene.

In order to understand the interrelation of power and science fully, we must, furthermore, consider that science is not simply the cause of the enumerated effects. Rather we must speak of an interaction between science and environmental changes. The "usefulness" of science for the increase of power and wealth was quickly seen and has become a strong incentive for putting the means of power and wealth at the disposition of scientists for their further pursuit of knowledge. More subtly, the advancement of science itself is today unthinkable without the laboratory equipment that presupposes a technology of production that, in its turn, is unthinkable without previous advancements in science. This interrelation between science and power has become so decisive in international politics that, in the wake of modern wars, the conqueror resorts to such measures as prohibition of research, destruction of laboratory equipment, wholesale abduction of scientists into a more or less gilded slavery, and deindustrialization of the conquered nation. The strict rationality of the procedure, without regard to human or civilizational values, resembles closely the procedure of the most rational of conquerors, Genghis Khan. When the Mongols conquered a country they took the skilled craftsmen and the shapely women for their personal use and let the rest of the people perish. The advancement of science and the rationality of politics have become interwoven in a social process that, in the retrospect of a more distant future, will probably appear as the greatest power orgy in the history of mankind.

We must recognize the atmosphere of power in which the advancement of science moves, because there are certain peculiarities incidental to the process that otherwise would appear as sheer lunacy. The source of these apparent lunacies is the utilitarian rationality of science. The idea of power through science has a rational core. If we have knowledge of causal relations we can form means-end relations, and if we have the means we can achieve the end. Hence, knowledge in this sense is eminently useful. This rational, utilitarian core in itself is of necessity to be found in all human existence, both personal and social. Utilitarian rationality determines a segment of life in primitive as well as in high civilizations, and in itself it is not the specific determinant of any particular society. Under the impact of the modern advancement of science, however, this core has acquired the characteristics of a cancerous growth. The rational-utilitarian segment is expanding in our civilization so strongly that the social realization of other values is noticeably weakened. This expansion is carried by the mass creed that the utilitarian dominion over nature through science should and will become the exclusive preoccupation of man as well as the exclusive determinant for the structure of society. In the nineteenth century this idea of utilitarian exclusiveness crystallized in the belief that the domination of man over man would ultimately be replaced by the dominion of man over nature, and that the government of men will be replaced by the administration of things. At this point we have to beware of the error into which critics of the totalitarian movements have fallen so frequently: the error that an idea is politically unimportant because philosophically it is stark nonsense. The idea that structure and problems of human existence can be superseded in historical society by the utilitarian segment of existence is certainly and plainly a piece of nonsense. It is equivalent to the idea that the nature of man can be abolished without abolishing man, or that spiritual order can be removed from existence without disordering existence. Any attempt at its realization can lead nowhere but to the self-destruction of a society. Nevertheless, the fact that the idea is nonsensical has not in the least prevented its becoming the inspiration of the strongest political movement of our age. Here we can see in the raw the fascination of power that exudes from the new science: it is so overwhelming that it eclipses an awareness of the elementary problems of human existence. Science becomes an idol that will magically cure the evils of existence and transform the nature of man.

This humanly destructive obsession is to be found not only in the totalitarian movements in the narrower sense. We find it in the same manner in the so-called liberal or progressive movements. Here it assumes the form of the belief that the rather obvious calamities that accompany the age of science must be cured by more science. We have gained dominion over nature through science. In order to avoid the misuse of this power (runs the argument) we must now gain control over our social environment through a corresponding advancement of social science. Scientists of more social prestige than human wisdom stand before large audiences and tell them in full seriousness that social scientists will have to come around and, in emulation of the natural scientists, will have to do their share so that the perfect society can be realized. No suspicion seems ever to have stirred in such brains that the effects of natural science, both beneficial and destructive, are a result not of the genius of scientists but of the objective structure of the realm of phenomena, which permits the introduction of human action into the chain of cause and effect once the law of the chain has been discovered. There is no suspicion that this objective structure does not prevail in the realm of substance, that no wisdom of a Plato could prevent the suicide of Athens and no climactic synthesis of a Saint Thomas could forestall the end of imperial Christianity. The knowledge of phenomena certainly is the key to their utilitarian mastery, but the understanding of human substance is not the key to the mastery of society and history.

The expansion of the will to power from the realm of phenomena to that of substance, or the attempt to operate in the realm of substance pragmatically as if it were the realm of phenomena—that is the definition of magic. The interrelation of science and power, and the consequent cancerous growth of the utilitarian segment of existence, has injected a strong element of magic culture into modern civilization. The tendency to narrow the field of human experience to the area of reason, science, and pragmatic action, the tendency to overvalue this area in relation to the *bios theoretikos* and the life of the spirit, the tendency to make it the exclusive preoccupation of man, the tendency to make it socially preponderant through economic pressure in the so-called free societies and through violence in totalitarian communities—all these tendencies are part of a cultural process that is dominated by a flight of magic imagination, that is, by the idea of operating on the substance of man through the instrument of a pragmatically planning will. We have ventured the suggestion that in retrospect the age of science will appear as the greatest power orgy in the history of mankind. We are now venturing the suggestion that at the bottom of this orgy the historian will find a gigantic outburst of magic imagination after the breakdown of the intellectual and spiritual form of medieval high civilization. The climax of this outburst is the magic dream of creating the Superman, the man-made Being that will succeed the sorry creature of God's making. This is the great dream that appears first imaginatively in the works of Condorcet, Comte, Marx, and Nietzsche, and later pragmatically in the Communist and National Socialist movements.

For the historically and theoretically detailed exposition of this problem the reader should refer to Part Nine of this study, "The Crisis."[81] In the present context we had to give a preliminary sketch of its nature in order to sharpen our awareness of the political importance of the patterns of thought that were forming at the opening of the eighteenth century.

j. The Pathos of Science and the Spiritual Eunuchs

We have spoken metaphorically of the cancerous growth of the rational-utilitarian segment in modern civilization. We now must

---

81. See vol. VIII, *Crisis and the Apocalypse of Man.*

go beyond the metaphor and indicate the concrete sentiments and ideas that determine this growth in its formative stage.

The sudden and disproportionate expansion of one single element in a total structure at the expense of other elements presupposes a serious disturbance of a previously existing balance. We have amply discussed the nature of the disturbance already under such titles as the disorientation of existence through weakening or loss of faith, and we have seen the disturbance expressing itself in such symptoms as Locke's "primitivization" of intellectual culture. The sentiments and attitudes that appeared on the occasion of the discussion of the problem of absolute space are further specific symptoms of primitivization in the wake of a general existential disorientation. The absolutism of a Galileo or a Newton cannot be labeled and shelved as a theoretical mistake to be corrected in the future. The attribution of "absoluteness" to the new science expresses the will of finding an absolute orientation of human existence through intramundane experience, and the correlate to this new will is the unwillingness to orient existence through openness toward transcendental reality. The new science assumes the function of a new order of existence. In his "Ode to Newton" (printed in the first edition of the *Principia*) Edmund Halley celebrated the achievement of his hero by placing it higher than the civilizing work of the sages and founders of antiquity: what is an ancient lawgiver (presumably a Moses or Lycurgus) who orders nothing more important than human society beside the man who discovers the order of the heavenly polity? Even if we make due allowance for conventions and clichés, and discount the generally hyperbolic tone of the ode, there will still remain the sentiment that a discovery concerning the order of phenomena is an event of the same rank, if not of a higher one, than a new spiritual insight.

Intimately related to the sentiment of absoluteness is the pathos of autonomy and self-reliance that animates the advancement of science. Exactness of mathematical form and verification through experiment become self-sufficient standards of truth. A scientist need not look left or right in his pursuit of knowledge as long as he abides by his standards, and no extraneous speculation can affect the truth of a proposition in science. The Newtonian *hypotheses non fingo* has become the proud expression of this pathos. At this point we touch on one of the most important sources of the modern existential disorder. If this pathos expressed nothing but the peculiar methodological situation of the exact sciences, it would be perfectly legitimate. Unfortunately, however, it has come to express a good deal more. The expansion of meaning is achieved through a process that we may call the transfer of pathos from a special pursuit to the existence of man. Science as an evolving system of knowledge is the result of an occupation of human beings. If the pathos of science is transferred from the occupation to the existence of the man who is engaged in it, such transfer may result in a serious warping of the individual personality, and if this transfer of pathos from science to the scientist becomes a model that is imitated on a socially relevant scale, it will result in far-reaching civilizational destruction. As a matter of fact, this transfer and its social imitation have occurred on such a scale in our civilization that the destructive effects defy repair in any visible future. Let us briefly characterize the attitudes and ideas through which this work of destruction is effected:

(1) The transfer of pathos from science to existence expresses itself concretely in the growth of the belief that human existence can be oriented in an absolute sense through the truth of science. If this belief is justified, then it becomes unnecessary to cultivate knowledge beyond science. As a consequence of this belief, the pre-occupation with science and the possession of scientific knowledge has come to legitimate ignorance with regard to all problems that lie beyond a science of phenomena. The spreading of the belief has had the result that the magnificent advancement of science in Western civilization is paralleled by an unspeakable advancement of mass ignorance with regard to the problems that are existentially the important ones.

(2) Such mass ignorance would be bad enough in itself. Even so, mere ignorance could be repaired by learning. Scientistic ignorance becomes a civilizational disaster because the substantial ordering of existence cannot be achieved through the acquisition of knowledge in the phenomenal sense. It requires the formation of personality in an educational process, and this process requires institutions. Once the scientistic pathos has penetrated into the educational institu-tions of a society, it has become a social force that cannot easily be broken, if it can be broken at all. The problem, therefore, is no longer one of mere ignorance. If belief in the self-sufficient ordering of existence through science is socially entrenched, it becomes a force that actively prevents the cultivation of human substance

and corrodes the surviving elements of the cultural tradition still further. The spiritual desire, in the Platonic sense, must be very strong in a young man of our time in order to overcome the obstacles that social pressure puts in the way of its cultivation.

Moreover, with regard to the cultivation of substance men are gifted differently (gifted in the Pauline sense of endowment with spiritual charismata). The active carriers of the scientistic pathos will be the men who are deficient in such gifts, and the penetration of society with the scientistic pathos creates an environment that favors the social success of the deficient human types. Hence, the advancement of science and the growth of the rational-utilitarian factor are accompanied by a restratification of society that hitherto seems to have escaped attention because it cannot be expressed in terms of social classes. Restratification through the social prestige and success of the deficient types must be expressed in terms of human substance. We shall use the term *spiritual eunuchism* for the designation of personality traits that make a man a likely victim of scientistic pathos, as well as for the designation of the traits that a society acquires when this human type gains social ascendancy. For the further elaboration of this problem the reader should refer to the analysis of the great prototype of the spiritual eunuch, Auguste Comte, in Part Nine of this study.[82] In the chapter on Comte the reader will also find a closer analysis of the relation between spiritual eunuchism and the utilitarian will to power. For the present let us say only that the nineteenth century has hardly a parallel in the history of mankind as a period of rapid transformation of a civilization through the eunuch type, preparing for the spiritual anarchy of the twentieth century.

(3) A further trait connected with the transfer of pathos is the rise of aggressive dilettantism in philosophical matters. Again, this is not a question of simple ignorance or dilettantism that may occur at any time. The new and dangerous element is the readiness of the dilettante to impose his ignorance as a standard on others. Clarke's "I do not understand" in answer to Leibniz's exposition of the problems of time and space is the ominous symptom of the new attitude. He really does not understand—and that settles the argument in his favor. What the scientistic dilettante cannot

82. See ibid., chap. 3.

understand must not be proposed in discussion of a problem. Comte has made this postulate one of the formal dogmas of the scientistic creed. The *Letters* of Clarke, in his correspondence with Leibniz, are in general a document of first importance for understanding the new atmosphere. There are sections in Clarke's *Letters* that move on a technical level of philosophizing that would have made a student in the Academy raise his eyebrows with amused contempt.[83] And again, even aggressive dilettantism would be comparatively harmless unless it were at the same time socially successful. Newton's theory of absolute space would be a weakness not worth our attention if it had not, through the social prestige of Newton the scientist, become determinative in the development of materialistic psychology, philosophical anthropology, and political ideas. The theoretical dilettantism of the great scientist is socially effective; the argument of the great philosopher is socially ineffective. What Leibniz had to say in his correspondence with Clarke was socially of no visible importance. It did not even noticeably affect the course of theoretical physics. What Newton had to say in his definitions of space affected the formation of political ideas immeasurably. The social success of Newton's theory of absolute space is the first great instance of successful dilettantic theories, advanced either by scientists themselves or (after the transfer of the pathos of science on a relevant scale) by the great spiritual eunuchs of the nineteenth century. Without the prestige effect of scientism, such major intellectual scandals as the social success of Positivism, or Darwinian evolutionism, or Marxism would be unthinkable.

In conclusion, let us mention the pattern of the civilizational schism that begins to emerge on the occasion of the debate on absolute space. The problem of the schism becomes apparent in the situation that we termed the "deadlock." The clarification of the problems of space and motion does not induce the physicists to revise their fundamental theoretical concepts. Science goes on as if nothing had happened, and Euler even demands that the

---

83. In order to measure the technical enormity of the performance, the reader should, for instance, compare Clarke's argument concerning space and time (in *Third Replie* §4) with the corresponding treatment of the problem in Plato's *Timaeus* or Saint Augustine's *Confessions*. Leibniz's answer to this section of Clarke's argument (in *Fourth Letter* §§14–16) is in no way original but simply represents the tradition of philosophical craftsmanship.

philosophers adapt their speculation to the confusion of physics. At the time, such a demand could be only partially successful. The spiritual and philosophical tradition of Western civilization did not break down at the first blast of a physicist in the eighteenth century. Instead, a situation developed in which the later schismatic break was performed because the philosophers continued their speculation and simply circumvented the problem of physics. We have seen that Berkeley analyzed space and motion critically to the point from which he could safely embark on his own *philosophia prima,* and we have seen that Kant accepted the state of physics and then went off in the direction of his transcendental critique. The schism was already a fact in the eighteenth century, but the fact remained more or less below the threshold of consciousness. That a break between the ascendant scientistic and utilitarian segment of civilization and the spiritual and intellectual tradition had actually occurred became fully conscious only with Schelling, and by that time, the spiritualist was already on the defensive.[84] In the course of the half century after Schelling the conflict was decided in favor of scientism, and the spiritual eunuchs became the socially effective formers of ideas for the masses. With the politically effective organization of these masses in the totalitarian movements, the schism assumed the external forms of social suppression and physical extermination of the continuators of the tradition.

That in the end, through Einstein, the foundations of physics were revised in conformance with the position of Leibniz is an important event in the history of science, but it has, for the moment at least, no visible social or political importance. The damage of scientism is done. As a philosophical friend put it aptly, the insane have succeeded in locking the sane in the asylum.[85] From this asylum no physical escape is possible. As a consequence of the interlocking of science and social power, the political tentacles of scientistic civilization reach into every nook and corner of an industrialized society, and with increasing effectiveness they

84. For Schelling's position with regard to this problem the reader should refer to *The History of Political Ideas,* vol. VII, Part Eight, chap. 2.

85. The scientist-utilitarian dream of transforming society into a prison without possibility of escape begins to take shape after the middle of the eighteenth century. For the beginnings of this dream, the reader should refer to the chapter on Helvétius in vol. VIII, *Crisis and the Apocalypse of Man,* chap. 1.

stretch over the whole globe. There exist only differences, though very important ones, in the various regions of the global asylum with regard to the possibility of personal escape into the freedom of the spirit. What is left is hope—but hope should not obscure the realistic insight that we who are living today shall never experience freedom of the spirit in society.

Index

Absolute space and motion, 189–91,
  193–99, 199n, 202–3, 205, 210,
  213–15
Act of Settlement of 1701, 156
Act of Uniformity of 1662, 153
Adams, H. P., 92n
Adolescentes, 116
Aequum utile, 112
Aeterni veri semina, 108
Africa, 38
Akme, 88, 117, 118, 123, 133–34
Alcohol use in England, 152–53
Ambiziosi, 141
America, discovery of, 38
American Political Science Asso-
  ciation, Research Committee, 2,
  6
Amor sui, 95, 108, 112, 113, 145
Anabaptists, 69n38
Analogia entis, 60
Anglicanism, 52, 75
Anima animi, 61, 129
Anima mundi, 100, 106
Anthropology, 111–13, 147
Aperte cognoscere (to know plainly),
  96, 98
Apostasy: and Bossuet, 34–38;
  continuity of Christian with
  intramundane problems, 44–51;
  introduction to, 9–11, 20–22; and
  "parallel" histories, 7; reconstruction
  of historical meaning, 40–44;
  secularization, 51–57; Vico's reversal
  of, 94–96; and Voltaire, 9, 10, 21,
  38–40, 57–70, 95, 113
Arbitrio umano, 134
Architetta, 134
Argument against Abolishing

Christianity in England (Swift),
  182–83
Arianism, 66
Aristotelianism, 105, 141
Aristotle, 105, 143
Astronomy, 53
Athanasian Creed, 66, 173
Atheism, 8, 49, 57, 71, 75–76, 117, 182,
  193
Augustine, Saint: and *anima animi,* 61,
  129; and Bossuet, 35; on God, 111; on
  history, 20, 40, 116–26, 136, 147; on
  saeculum senescens, 20, 32, 43, 119,
  121, 124; and Vico, 20, 113, 116–25,
  136, 147
—Works: *Civitas Dei,* 35, 110, 111;
  Confessions, 213n
Augustus, 140
Autobiography (Vico), 15, 18, 92n, 93,
  94, 105
Autonomy of the spirit, 113–14
Autori delle nazioni, 137, 142, 144
Averroës, 65
Averroism, 51, 63, 65

Babylon, 122, 123
Bacon, Francis, 18, 93
Badaloni, Nicola, 132n
Bangorian controversy, 155
Bayle, Pierre, 95n7, 112
Bedani, Gino, 15n20, 132n
Bellarmine, Robert, Cardinal, 187, 188
Bentham, Jeremy, 72, 114, 150
Bergin, T. G., 92n, 132n
Bergson, Henri-Louis, 148, 200–201n67
Berkeley, George, Bishop, 20, 21, 151,
  164, 184, 194–98, 214
Berlin, Isaiah, 14nn18–19, 132n
Berry, Thomas, 15n

WITHDRAWN

DEC 2 0 2023

PROPERTY OF
DAVID O. McKAY LIBRARY
BYU-IDAHO
REXBURG ID 83460-0405